AND KNOW THIS PLACE

AND KNOW THIS PLACE
POETRY OF INDIANA

Compiled and Edited by
Jenny Kander and C. E. Greer

Indiana Historical Society Press | Indianapolis 2011

Printed in the United States of America

This book is a publication of the
Indiana Historical Society Press
Eugene and Marilyn Glick Indiana History Center
450 West Ohio Street
Indianapolis, Indiana 46202-3269 USA
www.indianahistory.org
Telephone orders 1-800-447-1830
Fax orders 1-317-234-0562
Online orders @ http://shop.indianahistory.org

The paper in this publication meets the minimum requirements of American National
Standard for Information Sciences—Permanence of Paper for Printed Library Materials,
ANSI Z39. 48–1984

Grateful acknowledgement for support of this book is made to IHS Press
and the following offices of Indiana University, Bloomington:

> Office of the Vice Provost for Research
> Office of the Provost
> College Arts and Humanities Institute

Library of Congress Cataloging-in-Publication Data

And know this place : poetry of Indiana / compiled and edited by Jenny Kander and C. E. Greer.
    p. cm.
ISBN 978-0-87195-292-9 (cloth : alk. paper)
1. American poetry—Indiana. 2. Indiana—Poetry. 3. Indiana—In literature. I. Kander, Jenny, 1933–
II. Greer, C. E. (Charles E.)
PS571.I6A53 2011
811.008'0358772—dc22
                    2011003660

To Tamar, who paved my way to Indiana,
and to all this state's poets—J. K.

To the memory of Helen Sheppard Greer who loved poetry,
and to Ella, Charlie, and Josette that they might—C. E. G.

*The printing of this book was generously
supported by a gift from the Maurer Foundation.*

Contents

Preface

We shall not cease from exploration
And the end of all our exploring
Will be to arrive where we started
And know the place for the first time.
T. S. Eliot—"Little Gidding," *The Four Quartets*

The seed for this book was planted in 2002, in conversations with various editors on the recent popularity of place as a theme in literature, but its lack of representation in a book of poetry. We set out to fill this void with a call for contributions from poets who live or have lived in Indiana long enough to acquire a sense of the place. We initially wanted that sense to be conveyed as integral to the poems submitted, and asked for evocations of life here in its varied settings: wild, rural, and urban, and in all contexts: social, historical, and cultural, imaginary and real. Over time we broadened our criteria, dropped an initial plan to include poets' statements of context for each poem, and added the layered perspective of poets' voices from decades past.

From the wide variety of work thus available to us, we set about choosing those poems we felt would create a vibrant ensemble. Our central criterion for selection was quality of the writing, and we chose those poems that cover the spectrum of experience in both place and time, in settings from city streets to wilderness tracks, covering the state from Goshen in the north to Floyd's Knobs by the Ohio River, and from Gessie on the Illinois line to Cottage Grove 150 miles east. Necessary considerations of book size and cost have forced us to set limits on the numbers of poets and poems we could include, but we have taken care to include representatives of communities from the academic to the artistic and the social encompassed in the state. In a few cases, technical matters such as difficulty in obtaining permission to reprint poems forced adjustments to the collection we would have preferred to put between covers.

As the book took shape, we settled more firmly on the quote from T. S. Eliot's *Four Quartets* as a fitting title and overall theme. The picture emerged of a place very much evolved beyond the home for some two million, mostly rustic, Hoosiers in 1900, and beyond the barely globalized state of a quarter century ago. We are more than six million residents now, overwhelmingly urban by definition of the Census Bureau, but with a fabric unique to our part of the Midwest and few other areas: as the smallest towns have died and farms been abandoned, the hardwood forest has returned to significant portions of the land, while at the same time large and medium-sized cities have appeared with their suburbs and exurbs, and more poets than ever are drawn to explore all the richness this postindustrial landscape has to offer.

We would like to acknowledge these Indiana University librarians who went not just one extra mile to assist our research efforts, but many more: Mary Strow, head of the reference department, David Fraser, Anne Haines, Lou Malcomb, Heiko Muehr, Kelly Polacek, Judy Quance, Emily Schramm, and Gabriel Swift.

Also, for significant help that greatly facilitated our endeavors, our thanks to: Roger Mitchell for invaluable guidance, Sonia Gernes, Donald Platt, Maura Stanton, Anne Roecklein of Indiana University Press Rights and Permissions, and Paula Sunderman.

We consider ourselves most fortunate that Professor Emeritus Roger Mitchell agreed to write the foreword. The breadth of his knowledge and perspective furthers the intent of this book in which poets' voices and styles provide so many ways in which to explore and know the place anew.

Jenny Kander
C. E. Greer

Foreword

An Extraordinary Legacy

Within a week of deciding to move to Indiana in the mid-1970s, I stumbled onto a complete set of the works of James Whitcomb Riley in a used bookstore in Milwaukee and bought it. I knew who he was. I had even read a few of his poems here and there over the years. They had the quality of taking me completely into their world, both real and nostalgic, one in which life was simple, plain, and rarely subject to the twisted emotions characteristic of Edgar Lee Masters's *Spoon River Anthology* or Sherwood Anderson's *Winesburg, Ohio*, books that came from states on either side of Indiana and that had received much greater critical acclaim, but books that did not belong to their states the way Riley's poems did. I knew almost nothing about Indiana in the mid-1970s, except that a well-known poet came from there. To me, an outsider, Indiana was a state, the only one I knew of that when mentioned, immediately called up the name of a poet. What an extraordinary legacy, I thought. Yes, Riley's poetry was of another time, and it was marred by a pleasantness uncharacteristic of life itself, though some would, and have, argued that it was less uncharacteristic of life than it was of literature. I could not read it in terribly large batches, but I could see how his prosodical skill was at least the equal of his contemporaries, William Wadsworth Longfellow, John Greenleaf Whittier, Oliver Wendell Holmes, James Russell Lowell, etc., poets, in truth, who had not fared much better than Riley in the lecture halls and critical journals of the advanced and difficult twentieth century.

Indiana, it turns out, has given the country some of its best writing, though few seem to know it. I certainly did not when I moved here, in part because writerly orthodoxy dictated that if you were to succeed as a writer, you had to get out, certainly to the major cultural centers in the United States—Boston, New York, possibly Philadelphia, Chicago in a pinch—but absolutely to Europe, especially London, Paris, and Rome. William Dean Howells could hardly have become William Dean

Howells had he stayed in Xenia, Ohio. Ezra Pound would have probably become a cattle baron had he stayed where he was born, in Idaho. Of course, if Pound had stayed in Crawfordsville, Indiana, where he taught literature for one semester at Wabash College, we would know him as an Indiana poet (no less) who wrote colorful imitations, plus a few translations, of troubadour poetry and Homeric epic, in a manner that would have barely ruffled a feather in the faculty lounges.

A list of the better-known artists who came from Indiana but who felt they had to leave to succeed is rather impressive. William Vaughn Moody, born in Spencer, left behind one volume of poems that some consider the equal of any poetry written in America in the first decade of the twentieth century, when he died in Colorado Springs, Colorado, at age forty-one. Kenneth Rexroth grew up in Gary and later became a major poet, as well as the central figure of the San Francisco Renaissance. David Wagoner, also from Gary, after getting the first master's degree in creative writing at Indiana University made his way to the Pacific Northwest. Theodore Dreiser left Terre Haute for Chicago, where he wrote his early novels. David Smith, the sculptor, learned welding from his father who worked in a plant in Elkhart, but his home and the repository for his work sits on the side of Prospect Mountain above Lake George, New York. Cole Porter of Peru, whose lyrics have now been collected for the Library of America series, lived on both coasts, to be near the stages where his art was performed. Porter also lived in Paris. Ned Rorem, born in Richmond, left for Paris in his twenties and returned after several years to a life in Manhattan. Hoagy Carmichael, like Porter, had to be where the songs were called for and made. But he was buried where he was born, in Bloomington. Indiana also has the distinction, I believe, of being the only state to have its name assumed by one of its artists. Robert Clark of New Castle changed his name to Robert Indiana, best known for his sculpture, *LOVE*, which was later elevated to a U.S. postage stamp. John Woods of Martinsville spent most of his life teaching at Western Michigan University. Marguerite Young, born and raised in Indianapolis, eventually became a Manhattanite, although she frequently wrote often about Indiana and the Midwest. Jean Garrigue, born Gertrude Louise Garrigus in Evansville, graduated from Shortridge High School in Indianapolis, and, as soon as she could, changed her name and moved to Greenwich Village, the real home of her poetic aspirations. Ruth Stone, though born in Virginia, spent many formative years in Indianapolis before settling in the northeast. Robert Hazel found work finally in Kentucky, as close as he could come to the state of his birth. Clayton Eshleman, born in Indianapolis, has made an international reputation for himself as poet, translator, and magazine editor, living most recently in Ypsilanti, Michigan.

The story is repeated around the country, of course. Amy Clampitt from Iowa lived her adult life in New York City, and Mary Oliver of Ohio in Provincetown, Massachusetts, just to mention two more. This is a particularly prominent feature of the Midwest, which has given the world the likes of Mark Twain, Ernest Hemingway, F. Scott Fitzgerald, Sinclair Lewis, T. S. Eliot, Saul Bellow, Toni Morrison, John Dos Passos, Marianne Moore, Thornton Wilder, Theodore Roethke, and many more, most of whom got out.

Part of Indiana's poetry, then, like all its art, comes from people who started here but either wanted more than Indiana offered or could not find a way to support themselves in the state. However, it is never much of a struggle to find in their work what it was they kept. Garrigue never forgot the love of English literature she learned from her teachers at Shortridge High School, particularly Elizabeth Brayton. She dedicated her first two books to Brayton, who died, like Garrigue, at an early age of cancer. Clayton Eshleman writes amusingly of his efforts to "swing," to become a second Bud Powell, as a kid in Indianapolis. His later work explores pre- and non-European cultures in its search for the foundations of human experience, and I can see how trying to learn jazz piano, an almost purely black idiom in those days, in a city famous for its jazz musicians, may have been a start in that direction. In our time people in general do not sit still. It is not just artists who have to leave town. It is practically everybody. Young implies as much in her wonderful essay, "The Midwest of Everywhere": "The Middle West is probably a fanatic state of mind. It is, as I see it, an unknown geographic terrain, an amorphous substance, the ghostly interplay of time with space, the cosmic, the psychic, as near to the North Pole as to the Gallup Pole." This anthology would be a quarter as large as it is if it did not include the work of people who found their way into Indiana for one reason or another from somewhere else or found their way to someplace else from Indiana, the state of their birth, that, by the way, contained in 1910 the demographic center of the country. As a nation of migrants, we could hardly have fashioned anything, including the nation, in any other way. And so it is we have poets "here" who have a toehold elsewhere. We have them, whether they think that way or not, even after they have left. We sense the inevitable sticky substratum of Indiana down somewhere in the plumbing of their work.

Only one living poet I can think of, who, having been born in Indiana, managed to stay here: Jared Carter. It is not an easy thing to do.

What, then, is an Indiana poet? This anthology, as it should, indicates that the road to it is a broad one. Born there? Not a requirement. Lived or lives there? Well, yes, but I would love to read the anthology of Indiana poems written by poets who never set foot in it. Many are written, I believe, though not by that New Hampshire native, Gary Hoisington, who gave himself the nom de plume Gary Indiana. How long does one have to have lived in Indiana? As long as it takes. Does the Indiana poet write about Indiana? It depends on how wide or deep your definition of Indiana is. But no, he or she does not have to. With such latitude, the editors, Jenny Kander and C. E. Greer, have assembled a quilt of the state's mind as it takes shape today in poetry. Americans are a people that want to come from somewhere, not just from the United States, but from somewhere inside the congeries of disparate places, and they want that to matter. This is a nation of movers, not just a nation of immigrants, but a nomadic people.

Anthologies of Indiana poetry do exist, but they are precious few: *Songs of the Hoosier Singers, with Portraits* (1898), a slim compilation of six utterly forgotten poets, and the 464-page *Poets and Poetry of Indiana, 1800 to 1900* (1900), edited by Benjamin Parker and Enos B. Heiney. Other than Riley and Lew Wallace, the author of *Ben-Hur*, who has two poems included in it, *Poets and Poetry of Indiana* has had little success in passing down to us names that we are apt to recover and revere. More recent and successful attempts to stake out Indiana in writing include A. L. Lazarus's *The Indiana Experience* (1977) and F. Richard Thomas and Michael Wilkerson's *The Landlocked Heart* (1980). Neither of these admirable volumes, though, devotes itself to poetry. I should also mention *Indiana Writes*, the precursor to *Indiana Review*, both of which were brought into being by the efforts of Wilkerson and others and were intended to provide Indiana writers with a homegrown venue. Indiana, by curious circumstance, has not, in living memory, found a way until now to display its poetry, despite being the only state in the Union made famous by a poet. Which is another part of its extraordinary legacy, the part we hope herein to erase or at least smudge—the legacy of departure and silence.

Roger Mitchell

Memo to the 21st Century

It was like this once: sprinklers mixed
our marigolds with someone else's phlox,
and the sidewalks under maple trees
were lacy with August shade,
and whistles called at eight and fathers walked
to work, and when they blew again,
men in tired blue shirts followed
their shadows home to grass.
That is how it was in Indiana.

Towns fingered out to country once,
where brown-eyed daisies waved a fringe on orchards
and cattle munched at clover, and
fishermen sat in rowboats and were silent,
and on gravel roads, boys and girls
stopped their cars and felt the moon and touched,
and the quiet moments ringed and focused
lakes   moon   flowers.
That is how it was
in Indiana.

But we are moving out now,
scraping the world smooth where apples blossomed,
paving it over for cars. In the spring
before the clover goes purple,
we mean to scrape the hayfield, and
next year the hickory woods:
we are pushing on, our giant diesels snarling,
and I think of you, the billions of you, wrapped
in your twenty-first century concrete,
and I want to call to you, to let you know
that if you dig down,
down past wires and pipes
and sewers and subways, you will find
a crumbly stuff called earth. Listen:
in Indiana once, things grew in it.

Train Whistles

They'd howl us out of childhood dreams
like old dogs mad at the moon,
and I'd lie awake in the summer dark,
thinking *the sounds of night*
are messages of death
and feeling the rails that split the state,
projecting visions of New York
Chicago, necessary evils
For the ends of Indiana roads;
In midnight eyelids I could see
the twinkling cars, portable
fairylands, with names
like Golden West and Silver City,
rattling through the corn fields, past
our shadowy elms, and lacy
spindled porches, carrying
tired men home to lonely women
in Fort Wayne, South Bend,
Kendallville.

Out there in the dark Midwest
they're whistling coal and cattle now,
not salesmen in the smoky club cars,
young men off to battle
with the cities.
Are the somber voices of our past
calling now to someone else's future —
a generation on,
will aging children hear again
that long moaning in the dark,
remembering
the messages of night?

How Evolution Came to Indiana

In Indianapolis they drive
five hundred miles and end up
where they started: survival
of the fittest. In the swamps
of Auburn and Elkhart,
in the jungles of South Bend,
one-cylinder chain-driven runabouts fall
to air-cooled V-4's, 2-speed gearboxes,
16-horse flat-twin midships engines—
carcasses left behind
by monobloc motors, electric starters,
3-speed gears, six cylinders, 2-chain drive,
overhead cams, supercharged
to 88 miles an hour in second gear, the age
of Leviathan . . .
>   *There is grandeur in this view of life,*
>   *as endless forms*
>   *most beautiful and wonderful*
>   *are being evolved.*
And then
the drying up, the panic,
the monsters dying: Elcar, Cord,
Auburn, Duesenberg, Stutz—somewhere
out there, the chassis of Studebakers,
Marmons, Lafayettes, Bendixes, all
rusting in high-octane smog,
ashes to ashes, they
end up where they started.

To the Garbage Collectors in Bloomington, Indiana, The First Pickup of the New Year

(the way bed is in winter, like an aproned lap,
like furry mittens,
like childhood crouching under tables)
The Ninth Day of Xmas, in the morning black
outside our window: clattering cans, the whir
of a hopper, shouts, a whistle, *move on* . . .
I see them in my warm imagination
the way I'll see them later in the cold,
heaving the huge cans and running
(running!) to the next house on the street.

My vestiges of muscle stir
uneasily in their percale cocoon:
what moves those men out there, what
drives them running to the next house and the next?
Halfway back to dream, I speculate:
The Social Weal? "Let's make good old
　　Bloomington a cleaner place
　　to live in—right, men? *Hup, tha!*"
Healthy Competition? "Come on, boys,
　　let's burn up that route today and beat those dudes
　　on truck thirteen!"
Enlightened Self-interest? "Another can,
　　another dollar—don't slow down, Mac, I'm puttin'
　　three kids through Princeton."
Or something else?
Terror?

A half hour later, dawn comes edging over
Clark Street: layers of color, laid out like
a flattened rainbow—red, then yellow, green,
and over that the black-and-blue of night
still hanging on. Clark Street maples wave
their silhouettes against the red, and through

the twiggy trees, I see a solid chunk
of garbage truck, and stick-figures of men,
like windup toys, tossing little cans—
and *running*.

All day they'll go like that, till dark again,
and all day, people fussing at their desks,
at hot stoves, at machines, will jettison
tin cans, bare evergreens, damp Kleenex,
all things that are Caesar's.

O garbage men,
the New Year greets you like the Old;
after this first run you too may rest
in beds like great warm aproned laps
and know that people everywhere have faith:
putting from them all things of this world,
they confidently bide your second coming.

Advising

One after another they come
into the office, muscles,
pimples, wanting conclusions.
Who can blame them? I, too,
used to think that days, nights
came to an end. Now the whiskey
blurs into breakfast. So I tell
them what Rilke said: Never write
love poems. Then, by God, my
typewriter knocks, women walk in,
kick off their shoes, Ann,
Becky, my whole unlucky
alphabet. When did you leave?
Friday? September? 600 AD?
I remember the pavement, the tree
trunks wet in the headlights. So
much for advice. Then dig into
the footnotes, foretell the past.
Look at your watch, for Christ's
sake, it's four o'clock in the morning!
I remember we wept in the dark,
watching next week, next year
disappear down the avenue.
I ought to say: Never go home,
there's rain in the streets,
every corner is vacant. So
shake hands with history, kid,
the professor with the cigar,
excavating the future. Study
calculus, keep it abstract. There's
a long time ago still to come.

Jeopardy

Last night on the TV news I watched
a grunt digging himself a foxhole
in the frigging sand, and behind him
a tank with a gun like a phallus
silhouetted against a sunset
scarlet and black as a hemorrhage
from the gut. An F-15 shot past
like shit off a shovel, and a voice-
over said that we (I loved that "we")
were fully prepared, the President
resolute and at peace with himself.
The dog-face looked familiar. Except
for the leopard-suit and the Wehrmacht-
type helmet, he was Willie or Joe
all over again, under mortars
and 88's, Kasserine, Anzio,
Normandy, tired, patient, and scared, but,
no doubt, resolved, at peace with himself.
The wife and I, sipping decaf, sat
quietly waiting for *Jeopardy*.
A blonde appeared, wrapped in erotic
colors, writhing to sell us a car,
gyrating around a Chevrolet
to explosions of funky jazz-rock
like a gut-shot kid in a burning
B-17 with a wing blown off,
clearly resolved, at peace with herself.
The wife did the usual *tsk tsk*
with her tongue and denture, but I felt
a prickle down deep in the belly,
eyed, for the split second they allowed,
the tight skirt hugging the twisty butt,
and closed my eyes hard, remembering
how I screwed Smitty's girl in Bury
St. Edmunds the night after Smitty
blew up over downtown Regensburg,
wreckage and smoke skidding past our wing,

Smitty writhing and squealing, maybe,
like his girl on that chilly mattress,
surely resolved, at peace with himself.
When I looked up, the news was back on.
Some general with a saddle soap jaw,
strictly thick chicken shit from the start,
wearing a leopard-suit (pressed) to show
he was just another GI, said
our best and brightest were shoveling
sand out in the desert together,
straight poop from the group, that, in a graves-
registration voice selling a war.
When a newswoman asked him whether
the troops were fully prepared, his eyes
went hard-candy balls of homicide
I hadn't seen since the major's sad
bombardier froze up on the flight line,
hugging his parachute like a girl—
I did fourteen, he kept whimpering,
the sun like phosphorus through the fog,
while the major cursed and glared murder,
he like the general no sweet TV
bimbo pumping her pelvis but stiff
as a bomb, freezing my living room
almost fifty years after the fact—
and resolute, at peace with himself.
Then the anchor-woman came on, teeth
like a beltful of fifties, hair mussed
just enough, a back-lighted halo,
lips kissing the words, *casualties, oil,*
that sly voice between Shirley Temple
and Tokyo Rose, the virgin whore
they all try to be, and I was back
in Dakar that time, the wild whorehouse
that Harry found, *l'exhibition,*
three thousand francs apiece for the crew,
amazing us all, even Harry,

women doing those things to themselves
and each other, enjoying it, too.
Whores and professional murderers,
Harry said to me later, that's what
we all of us are, kid. I never
forgot that. Or Harry. He'd have been
over eighty, now. I believe him.
And there on the screen this one sold what
she had, stuck out her knockers, and signed
off, resolute, at peace with herself.
She faded before you could salvo
a load in her face, and the general
was back, with those grab-a-medal eyes
and mouth like a club, and he faded,
and there, still set against bleeding sun-
set and desert, while an orchestra
and kids' choir God-blessed America,
and a dim flag flapped itself dizzy
behind him, and the blonde tooled a red
Chevy from zig to zag all the way
across the screen, on an interstate
back in Utah to judge by the rocks,
there was Willie, with gas-mask and spade,
shoveling sand, slow but sure, digging
a foxhole to China, still patient
and tired and scared shitless no doubt, but
resolute, and at peace with himself.
For a second the boob-tube went black.
Thank goodness that's over, my wife said.
Then big lights and theme music came on,
she was grinning at Alex Trebek,
and I poured more decaf and sugar.
So we sat there, myself and the wife,
pilot, co-pilot, old armchair crew,
watching *Jeopardy,* fully prepared,
deep in our foxholes, deep in our sand,
resolute, and at peace with ourselves.

No

Now he would give anything, give everything,
if he could pick her up and set her on her feet,
dust her off, straighten her skirt, apologize,
tell her it was a mistake anybody might make,
and she would forgive him, use comb and lipstick,
ask for her coat and purse, and they would walk
       together
to the depot the way they used to years ago,
and he would put her on the bus and watch it
       pull away,
and he would walk down Main to Elm and up Elm
to Pleasant, and so home to their impregnable house,
and she would be not here, not here, but on her way
to Boston for one of those old weekends
       with her mother,
and he would drink cold Bud and watch the Red Sox
       lose
another on TV and order a pizza and watch
Saturday Night Live, and with her away the dog
would sleep curled lovingly against him on the bed,
and sometime during the thick darkness of the night
his watch would stop and the clock in the living
       room
stop chiming, and all over town the clocks
       would stop
and the alarms fail and everybody would stay asleep,
and it would always be two-thirty in the morning

Twelve Hawks

From the burning highway where I drove
with my small daughter, I saw their shapes,
blurred through the pane of August,
black lumps sticking to the bones of oak,
and my gorge filled with ancient sickness
and my daughter with strange fire.

When we had climbed the wire to invade
their wild land, and bleached in its blue shroud
the bone-bare tree grew taller,
hooked heads swiveled to our captured eyes,
and the song I had thought was silence
became a dirge of locusts.

A hot wind rustled in the grasses
where the small prey crouched. Close to the creek
a cardinal flashed and whistled.
And she, thigh-deep in briars, hands bright
with goldenrod, laid bare with wary foot
the tiny, broken skull.

Then the heavy, deliberate wings
shrugged loose, broke black against bright air,
exploding out of the bone,
a slow storm of brutal, beautiful
hawks, climbing the wind with heavy grace
and sun-raking symmetry,

Aliki in the Woods

We invented a book, you and I
in luminous woods. The tulip trees
were starfish on fire, and black oaks
your blue alarm clock that sang in wonder
as we fought like drowning cats about
the good sun. We walked at rainy dawn
and you told me how you cared for mice
and icky frogs. Then the dawn got mad.
I took you to our barn. With a pen
you drew a bed of luminous trees.

I Knew a Woman with One Breast

I knew a woman with one breast and we
spent a fresh night together in a tent
at a summer Blue Grass festival. She
invited me in. Bean Blossom. We went
dancing into darkness on the hard grass.
I balanced on her chest, tilting into
our mystery. She was milk. Full breast and ass
on the damp delirious ground. A few
seconds of joy and earth till the dawn air
when we took down the tent and she went back
up north. She was a botanical artist
for text books, sent me letters and a sack
of dry lilies. She lost her other breast.
Her last letter to me held her last hair.

This Evening after I was Asked to Leave

This evening after I was asked to leave
    Tina's Take-Out where I often eat

(it was 8, closing time) I rolled down my sleeve
    to read a minute more in the light

leaking out the November door. Then walked
    toward my car and there, right

under my feet, three pennies, supernovas filled
    with copper souls, showed me

I had friends in the cosmos and I was thrilled.

With My Redneck Sons in Southern Indiana

The pampas of America begin
north of our barn. Glaciers smoothed down the earth
for buffalo and corn, but I live in
the poor south hills where farmland isn't worth
the taxes, and the KKK comes out
of the wet Gothic woods. Our humpbacked barn
is rusty in the patient twilight. Scout-
ing the Blue River bendable as yarn
or glowworms, I am not quite Baptist red-
neck like my sons who often paddle through
the bluffs. But in a barn I placed a bed
and desk and dreamt the world. Gone from the coast,
I camp on hills of vanished Indians a few
calm nights and hear trees talk. I'm still a ghost.

Corn/Sorghum/Sumac

When I think of Indiana it is
cornfields in long light,
and every acre or so
the pituitary surprise
of a single tall sorghum head
nodding.
Or the trash tree sumac,
growing in ditches and auto junkyards,
dull as summer dust until October
when it raises perfect hands in
velvet gloves—color of rusted wheels—
in self applause.

At Horticulture Park

They make a great noise in the leaves,
trying to be quiet, these
ROTC boys, to be stealth
as the bomber eaten
by fog. Their faces
smudged black, their slow
passage under maples, under
the huge oaks. It's fall,
its wild ravishments. Everything's
past camouflage into almost
freeze and rest
and the last thought. They do not
look at my son and me, where
we might walk, or where
we've been in these woods.
And their emptiness, which is
a kind of focus, they practice it
like prayer, like the sad violinist, fierce
and without any hope
of song, climbing his C minor scale
for the twentieth time. Afternoon nearly
lost to twilight. They look—where else?—
perfectly ahead. A line
is a line. And their rifles, even
the smallest—I watch him—holds his
not gently, hard against him.
Oh, to be
a threat, to swallow
anything. *Dear boy, go home.*
Go home, where you left your longing.

Car Covered with Snow

Before I clear the windows, I sometimes
sit inside. And the stillness is such
that I lose how the day works.
It soaks up
all the steely details: March
ripped out of February, a raw thing.
Sometimes my son has patience.
And we sit a few minutes like this
in the weird half-light. He says: *we're
in a closed fist, Mama.*
Or, *it's like the car's eye is closed.*
We're deep in the brain then,
seeing as the blind see, all
listening. Outside, the cardinal
tinks tinks his alarm call,
his scared call. I hear it: the snow
so terribly white.
And he is brilliant,
conspicuous.

The Going Out of Business Greenhouse

The old lady pauses above the register.
I think it's
forgetfulness or grief.
It's stuck, says the other right behind her.
They pitch forward
to see better—diggers
at some neolithic site.

Such a place, out on a dirt road. Chicory
floods the whole way there. This old thing, says one.
And they look at me
and my potting soil. The money feels
stupid in my hand.

They can't get it open. Well, says the other,
and sits down. The light
everywhere is green and broken. She begins
folding up a garden magazine to make
a fan. I think of those orphans out back: coreopsis
and balloon flower and the sullen somber rose.
We've killed off
most all the plants, the first woman tells me,
rather triumphant. The other is
nodding. She fans herself
wildly with the colorful bent page.

I see you're closing, I say lamely,
by way of sympathy, some start
to it. Oh that, says the standing one.
It's just our habit, says the other,
the fan still blurring.
We're good at it, adds the first.
Good at what? Closing? Doing in the stock?
I wait for their laughter
to tell me. But we're done.

Hoes and rakes and trellises . . .
It's private as dust
in there.

Wind Storm, Late March

Poor bees, the tree down in such winds,
the gleaming criss-cross combs
in the split hollow.
              Cold that morning,
the bees clustering for warmth,
stingless in the shock of it, a few
aimlessly rising, the tree splintered—
limbs and trunk in pieces
all over the street.
             Pearl Street,
and the bees in its round yellow light
wanting only the old
darkness of the hollow, the heat
of the bark, rotting wood close enough
to bury the long flights
though, of course,
             they do not dream.
We pretend they do, pretend they sleep
hanging there, all wings
and the hard black thousands of bodies
but that time, they were just
stunned, meaning
what now? meaning *summer, and what
use is it?*
          The men were coming, their
trucks and loud indifferent saws,
bits of honey and wax
to flying air. The bees—not even
angry, soothed almost
by such confusion,
            hovering there,
hovering. What do we know of anything?
The roar of the men, the same
storm all night . . .

Broke Song

Give me a field of lucky pennies,
poppy-colored, that I can roll in, pretend
you're mine for keeps. Narcotized. Oh poppy!

Give me a mattress full of dimes—
I'll hug your pillow. Wake to us growing silver
together. Broke in pieces,

please don't laugh as my spare parts
attack and chase each other. Spare me
some change? Can we

change? Broke in,
like a favorite pair of jeans. His pair,
I used to wear. Broken like a hammer-

smashed phonograph: my autograph,
some fractured graph. Crazed they call
these lines. Smitten kitten.

All I've got left in my piggy bank
are these corny rhymes. In my state
of poverty, serve me up

some aloe tea: make it organic, please.
You can watch me for free, glue myself
together, a mosaic counterfeit

masterpiece. Broke artichoke, without the sweet heart
in the center. That I used to save for you to dip
in fancy French butter. Without

a center centipede. Though I hear bugs
are chic. My tears run down the street
without a spoon, because there's no soup to eat.

I'll dive across the sky's table, the moon
a crumb the lightning bug and I fight over.
Broke up. That's what you did me

yesterday. Stole our account and restated it
all by yourself. Tore me up, that did,
turned my mass into archipelago

Jell-O. Though my friend Genine says
that's the best place to be. Or did she say
too much reflection causes blindness?

Ah well—Richie Rich—give this lady some lemonade.
Give me a field of green. Pretend you're paying
some attention to me.

Broke Song (Later)

You move through the world broken. Navigating
by the stars encoded on your heart's axis. July
grasses. Rain. How the world breaks us.
Midnight scatters across what's left
from an evening prayer. The broken
song of the warbler at dawn
on the last day of winter: You move
through the world gathered
together in a pulse. Running your fingers
up and down what is odd and so familiar.
How dazzling the fit. To be remade
by the glue of your oaths and kisses.

From: 1000 Lines

10 x 12: one hundred twenty full moons
beneath the double-wedding-ring pattern,
designed from remnants of our childhood clothes.
Saloma Byler, an Amish quilter,
wrote us—I still have the note she sent—*Dear
friends, your quilt is ready.* We munched low-fat
Chubby Hubby, watched Baby Bang Your Box,
Ugly George, screwball comedies, and ten-
second TV replays of the police
striking a man fifty times with batons.

Ten years: our bed: a desk, a couch, a horn—
mechanical bird—mortar and grinder—
a spoon for winnowing grains, a lemon
and palm branch in a bundle depicted,
cloud chamber, buoyant in its heaviness,
a modern impression of ancient scales,
a boat without oars, where we heaved and hoed,
made mirth, shook in terror, sighed in relief,
vowed to love God and walk in his footsteps—
the cords thereof—goose-down-libation—fucked

ten different ways. We made our bed into
a marked playing card. Under the covers
of our salted diamond mine, the Pope:
a woman, Elvis alive, Big Foot and
Yeti materialized. Complete with
certificates and old wax seals we built
a forgery of Jonah's whale, that each
night we crawled in and then cut our way out.
Our bed: a blind horse that we bought. Our bed,
a wolf that we thought made a good watchdog.

No Sorry

Do you have any scissors I could borrow? *No, I'm sorry I don't.* What about a knife? You got any knives? A good paring knife would do or a simple butcher knife or maybe a cleaver? *No, sorry all I have is this old bread knife my grandfather used to butter his bread with every morning.* Well then, how about a hand drill or hammer, a bike chain, or some barbed wire? You got any rusty razor-edged barbed wire? You got a chain saw? *No, sorry I don't.* Well then maybe you might have some sticks? *I'm sorry, I don't have any sticks.* How about some stones? *No, I don't have any sticks or stones.* Well how about a stone tied to a stick? *You mean a club?* Yeah, a club. You got a club? *No, sorry, I don't have any clubs.* What about some fighting picks, war axes, military forks, or tomahawks? *No, sorry, I don't have any kind of war fork, axe, or tomahawk.* What about a morning star? *A morning star?* Yeah, you know, those spiked ball and chains they sell for riot control. *No, nothing like that. Sorry.* Now, I know you said you don't have a knife except for that dull old thing your grandfather used to butter his bread with every morning and he passed down to you but I thought maybe you just might have an Australian dagger with a quartz blade and a wood handle, or a bone dagger, or a Bowie, you know it doesn't hurt to ask? Or perhaps one of those lethal multipurpose stilettos? *No, sorry.* Or maybe you have a simple blow pipe? Or a complex airgun? *No, I don't have a simple blow pipe or a complex airgun.* Well then maybe you have a jungle carbine, a Colt, a revolver, a Ruger, an axis bolt-action repeating rifle with telescopic sight for sniping, a sawed-off shotgun? Or better yet, a gas-operated self-loading fully automatic assault weapon? *No, sorry I don't.* How about a hand grenade? *No.* How about a tank? *No.* Shrapnel? *No.* Napalm? *No.* Napalm 2. *No, sorry I don't.* Let me ask you this. Do you have any intercontinental ballistic missiles? Or submarine-launched cruise missiles? Or multiple independently targeted reentry missiles? Or terminally guided anti-tank shells or projectiles? Let me ask you this. Do you have any fission bombs or hydrogen bombs? Do you have any thermonuclear warheads? Got any electronic measures or electronic counter-measures or electronic counter-counter-measures? Got any biological weapons or germ warfare, preferably in aerosol form? Got any enhanced tactical neutron lasers emitting massive doses of whole-body gamma radiation? Wait a minute. Got any plutonium? Got any chemical agents, nerve agents, blister agents, you know, like mustard gas, any choking agents or incapacitating agents or toxin agents? *Well I'm not sure. What do they look like?* Liquid vapor powder colorless gas. Invisible. *I'm not sure. What do they smell like?* They smell like fruit, garlic, fish or soap, new-mown hay, apple blossoms, or like those little green peppers that your grandfather probably would tend to in his garden every morning after he buttered his bread with that old bread knife that he passed down to you.

The Colonists

I have seen the Amish driving front-end loaders
down at the local wood yard,
scooping up bucketfuls of log tops
and gnarled unsplittable rounds,
dumping them into the cavernous beds
of two new Fords.

Papa stands atop the free, U-pick wood pile,
tall and proud beneath a black hat
as though God Hisself selected this age,
this place, this one patient pilgrim
for to impart His vast message.
Papa is working and waiting for the Word,
waiting and working for it.

Sitting in the front seat of one truck,
neatly obscured by her bonnet,
the daughter discovers us, slowly
loading our truck by hand.
My mate and I are wearing flannel shirts;
I'm under a longshoreman's cap,
she in muddy gloves, both of us
wrapped in denim and with long,
decadent ponytails down our backs.
The daughter whispers,
"Papa, she's wearing overalls."

I have seen the Amish restore a sundered barn
with only mallets and glue,
and whip the horse for failing to lift a beam.
I have felt the roar of their heavy machinery
resonating up from wood yard mud,
through scrap logs and work boots and gloves,
as the bucket slams into the pile
then raises unto heaven another load.
Some Amish families allow convenience
for the betterment of the community—

electricity, telephones, chainsaws, bush hogs.
I have seen Amish bush hogs
pulled by Amish tractors refueled
by Amish pickups rumbling across
wide, quiet Amish fields.

O the furniture they must make
to atone for the forgone scythe.
The tremendous thread count
of their quilts is a sermon,
the smoothness of their sanctified
butter and cheese a prayer.

I have seen the Amish shopping at Wal-Mart,
where the little girls eye more than jeans and bras.
One day that daughter will have the Choice:
as a teenager let loose upon the world,
she may stay among the English
if she can't go home again.

But she will come home, this one,
and many after her, to colonies
at the end of dark gravel lanes,
after provocative ideas planted
by temptation, by this modern ashtray Earth
have been expressed away come rumpspringa,
the wild time when the bonnet is lifted from her eyes
and she will find no peace at all
nor fully know it ever again.

At the Indiana Transportation Museum

It's a junkyard arranged in columns,
This grandly named end of the old Monon Line,
Its repainted depot house a cabin in an Alps of blind
      locomotives, funky sleepers, wooden reefers and boxcars
      like derelict barns,
All rusting and splintering into geologic time.
A senior fellow, a volunteer, wearing a train of German syllables
      on his shining nameplate, white mall-walking sneakers,
      operates the trolley for Mary, Patrick, Erin and me.
He explains how the salvaged piece of 1920s Chicago El
      can be powered and steered from front or back, after
      the motorman has swung the overhead electric line around
      like one-man sailboat rigging;
He jerks the backs of the brown leather seats to show
      they could face either direction;
He remembers for us the six and a half cent tokens, the drivers
      who made change, the interurbans that took you all the way
      from Union Station to Terre Haute.
"You'll know why they call this the rock and roll line,"
      he chuckles as we set off shuddering, a trip of
      a few hundred yards into weedy woods, my daughter giggling
      and kicking on the slick old seat.
And I'm close enough in my own memory that I travel
      back down the line; I walk the stony wood floor and
      perch above the rusted heaters and grimy pedestals
      as a briefcase-carrier on an autumn afternoon in a simpler decade.
Serene and sober
Point to point
Woman to workplace and back to her
Law-abiding
Forward-facing
Straphanging, rock and rolling
Feeling, as do none of my hated and unhurried fellow passengers,
The acid sting of the ancient city sunlight that warms our
      companionable shoulders and rusts and splinters
      all that conveys us into time

The Madhouse

I cannot give you the squeak
Of the blue chalk on the cue tip,
The sound of the break, or the movement
About the table, like a ritual of wine;

Then I was not born. My father,
Who saw it, was still in high school;
And there are others who remember
The poolroom on the avenue.

Here lounged the former heroes
Of the high-school team, who took
The Tri-State Crown in '24, and tied
With Massillon in '25. Catholics all,

A backfield composed of Swede
Svendson at fullback, the Baxter brothers
At either half, and handsome Richard
O'Reilly at the quarter.

They had no peers, then or now.
On Saturdays regularly they stood,
Hats firmly on their heads, watching
The procession of hooded Klansmen

Coming up Anderson Street, heading
Toward the Main intersection. Always
The Klan demanded hats removed
Before the flag they carried,

Always the boys at the Madhouse refused,
And began unscrewing the weighted ends
Of their pool cues. People came to watch;
The police stood apart; the Klan

Never got past the Madhouse. That
Was years ago. They're all dead now,
Swede and the Baxter boys, and
Handsome Richard O'Reilly,

Who married the banker's daughter;
And the Klansmen too. Only the men
Who were boys then can still remember.
They talk about it, even now,

Sitting in Joe's barbershop
Watching cars go by, or sipping a beer
In Condon's tavern. It is a story
I heard when I was a boy. Lately

There's been a doughnut shop
Where the Madhouse used to stand.
Mornings when I stop for coffee
I can almost hear it: the nine ball

Dropping in the corner pocket,
The twelve rolling to within an inch
Of the side; voices in the street
Echoing along the store fronts.

The Gleaning

All day long they have been threshing
and something breaks: the canvas belt
that drives the separator flies off,
parts explode through the swirl
of smoke and chaff, and he is dead
where he stands—drops the pitchfork
as they turn to look at him—and falls.
They carry him to the house and go on
with the work. Five wagons and their teams
stand waiting, it is still daylight,
there will be time enough for grieving.

When the undertaker comes from town
he brings the barber, who must wait
till the women finish washing the body.
Neighbors arrive from the next farm
to take the children. The machines
shut down, one by one, horses
are led away, the air grows still
and empty, then begins to fill up
with the sounds of cicada and mourning dove.
The men stand along the porch, talking
in low voices, smoking their cigarettes;
the undertaker sits in the kitchen
with the family.

In the parlor
the barber throws back the curtains
and talks to this man, whom he has known
all his life, since they were boys
together. As he works up a lather
and brushes it onto his cheeks,
he tells him the latest joke. He strops
the razor, tests it against his thumb,
and scolds him for not being more careful.
Then with darkness coming over the room
he lights a lamp, and begins to scrape
at the curve of the throat, tilting the head
this way and that, stretching the skin,
flinging the soap into a basin, gradually
leaving the face glistening and smooth.

And as though his friend had fallen asleep
and it were time now for him to stand up
and stretch his arms, and look at his face
in the mirror, and feel the closeness
of the shave, and marvel at his dreaming—
the barber trims the lamp, and leans down,
and says, for a last time, his name.

Jared Carter

Picnic in the Basement

For the last time this year I clip
what's left of the stunted elm hedge—
brown gaps in it like rotten teeth.
Then I heave the picnic table
no one's eaten at all summer
onto my shoulders, like Atlas, and stagger
through the garage to the black basement,
stumbling over the broken trellis
that held the climbing rose that died
the month after I moved here.
I reach for the wall to steady myself
and grab a handful of plastic pickets
I bought to fence the vegetable garden
I sowed that first year with lettuce
whose leaves tasted bitter as weeds.
The table slips and luckily falls
away from the wall of flowerpots
filled with geranium skeletons
blighted by frost last September,
and lands in the center of the concrete floor
an inch from my foot. I set it upright,
slide one of its splintery redwood benches
to elbow-resting distance from it,
and, panting, take a seat. I'm finished
with outdoor living for another year.
I've oiled my push mower with the price tag
still attached from ten years ago
when I bought it downtown at the hardware store
converted to a savings bank
when the courthouse turned into a mall.
I've taped the orange power cord
slashed in six or seven places
where the suicidal trimmer trimmed it
almost in half but not quite.
I shudder whenever I touch its coils,
remembering the first time I plugged it in
to a living room socket and dragged it outside.

While I hacked the weedy hedge,
my cats nosed past the screen door
and wandered into the strange yard,
bordering a street of speeding cars,
hundreds of miles from where they were born.
When, finished, I wiped sweat from my eyes,
looked up, and saw the door ajar,
I rushed inside and ransacked rooms,
reached deep into closets and hidey-holes.
Finally, desperate, I ran out again.
Crying their names, I crawled the yard
at cats' eye level until—what joy!
I found them cowering under this table—
new then, half rotten now,
with its redwood paint bleached almost white.
That family picnic was our last.
Since then they've watched from kitchen windows
each spring when I haul the grill outside,
each fall when I haul it in again,
though I haven't cooked meat on it for years.
Now they're waiting for me upstairs.
I hear their claws click overhead
as they pace the kitchen, hungry, impatient.
Why not invite them to scamper down
the cellar stairs and join me here,
each with her plastic dish of Friskies
while I gnaw my bone of nostalgia?
I feel my way upstairs and fling
the cellar door open. Suspiciously,
they sniff their way down every stair,
while I slide the other bench
up to paw-resting distance
and set the largest pot of geraniums
over the table's umbrella hole.
It's safe here, sweeties, out of the glare
of the murderous outside world that's dying
for the eleventh time in eleven years.

Richard Cecil

Nothing's scary here but corpses
dragged in from the lawn and garden—
steel cutting edges eaten by weeds,
charcoal long ago flamed to ash,
and our ghostly centerpiece—
branching in your eyes of phosphorous—
flowers of death that bloom in the dark.

Fiftieth Birthday

The towering forked maple down the street
screens nothing ugly out. I almost hear
the shacky house behind it cry for paint,
and through its wiry crown I see lead sky.
Each of its boughs and twigs runs crookedly
as an arthritic finger—useless lumber
if the coming spring wind blows it down,
or city tree men with a cherry picker
forestall its crash by chain-sawing it
to firewood logs from top to stump. No loss.

But when I squint, I make out fuzziness
that blurs the bony outlines of its branches—
buds! So it's not dead, just old and gnarled.
It's planning its next hundred thousand leaves
to paper over views of blight behind it
and to hide its twistedness beneath—
green lies, fluttering in June breeze;
stiff red and gold ornate ones in October.
Today, though, March 14, the naked tree's
forced to work with the truth. Against gray sky
its branches, slicked with drizzle, weave black lace
that decorates the gloom it can't conceal.

Ubi Sunt?

How I miss the senile widow
shouting "Who are you?" each spring
when I washed my storm windows,

and the deaf diva down the street,
who yelled into her phone in German
like Brunhilde in *Die Walküre*.

Renters live in her house now.
They've swept the carved cows from her mantle,
making room for their beer bottles.

Where's my neighbor's redbud tree
whose heart-shaped leaves once masked green siding
which now fills my study window?

Where's the maple which once screened
the intersection's four-way stop sign
until the city chopped it down,

but which also blocked my view
of the abandoned, paintless house
which stares at me when I look up?

Where's the mortgage, now paid off,
that once drove me to take bad jobs
in distant cities to make money

instead of watch decay at home
and groan for everything that's gone
like some bourgeois Francois Villon?

But whining over lost good neighbors,
blighted houses, cut-down trees,
distracts my thoughts from the decline

that stares me in the face each time
I step out of my steaming shower
and wipe mist from my shaving mirror.

Who's that spectre slapping lather
on my cheeks with bony fingers?
He's the Ghost of Present Tense,

although he haunts the past and future.
When he brandishes his razor,
I grin and offer him my throat.

Fetching the Moon in Indiana

1.
Coming home, my flight is delayed two hours, and when I finally
  arrive at the farmhouse on Papermill Road the first thing I set eyes on
in the dim light is a note taped to the mailbox: *Could you please*
  put mail in the box bellow until the birds are done?
For minutes I try to recall what a box bellow might be—
  another miscellaneous crib, speckled with dried kernels of corn,
something my grandmother has upended and dusted. Then
  I notice envelopes jutting from a cardboard box on the ground *below*

until the birds are done. I creak wide the mailbox door to find
a swirl of grasses and twigs, ragweed root and a tatter of blue ribbon.

2.
My Great-Grandma Olive boiled half a dozen eggs for my mother
  to take on the plane to California, where she would meet
my father's family and show them the white gold ring he bought
  by preaching a whole summer of Sundays for the Baptists.
Grandma Olive had never been on a plane. In fact, she had not
  been out of Indiana since '79, when a horse show across the river
drew her into Kentucky for the first time in a decade. Even then
  she would not let go her bulky, quilted purse, its pockets hiding pieces

of taffy wrapped in wax paper, a family joke almost as old as she,
born two weeks before the grand and tidy burst of 1900.

3.
The Chardells tell it that Great-Aunt Gwen was betrothed
  before she knew what her father had done, 17 and reading things
a woman usually didn't: Emerson, for one. So when she went in a calico dress
  to Seth Ferguson and begged he take back the tobacco fields from her daddy
and forget the whole thing, that she was in love with Jesse Chardell till she died,
  she didn't know such a kindred thing as love had taken hold, too, of Seth,
that he'd cry that day, wiping his big hands on his britches, and declare
  he loved her so deep and hard he would pay for her and Jesse's wedding,

if that would truly make her happy. This is what they tell you, the britches,
  the calico dress, never mentioning if happiness is what she got, and each year
the pink blooms on the tobacco plants curl up just before July
  and the whippoorwill scoops up fat yellow worms from the leaves.

4.

I was seven years old when they told me my mother was killed.
   It took another seven for Grandma to tell me how it happened,
the sharp discs of the combine and Mom and Daddy up top, hauling out
   errant stalks of corn long as their legs. They'd guess she got dizzy
or maybe was looking off to the pasture, or even, though this is my
   rendition entirely, had craned her neck to make out the pale half-egg
of harvest moon, turning too quick to direct my father's gaze
   in the afternoon sky, and she fell in. For years they've told Jimmy

it wasn't his fault, that first summer he managed the wheel, though these days
   it's only whiskey Jimmy listens to and the prickly sweat of memory,
knowing my father will no longer come for him in the cool haze of the bar,
   shoulder him up, lay him down in the bed of the Ford to sleep it off.

5.

The Dupont Hornets are raising money for the school library,
   and when I settle on the carrot cake muffins instead of Pamela's
mince meat pie, it hurts her feelings. *Nice of you to come back*,
   she says, palming my quarters. *Nice to be back*, I say, the muffins
wobbling on the paper plate. *There's some people*, she says, *who know
   how a fancy thing goes sour.* Yes, I say slowly, unsure if she's insinuating
my schooling or my marriage. *Yes*, she says back, *Some people think this place
   is all crops and hogs and crossroads.* I stare at a daub of icing on my thumb,

but it's chicory I taste at the back of my mouth. Then she seems sorry.
Your daddy was a fine preacher, she says, *Help yourself to some lemonade.*

6.

The year they drew my mother's body from under the combine,
   I watched my father tear down the wall between kitchen and dining room.
In the rubble he found a newspaper from 1884, a matchstick airplane with only one
   wing, and a handful of buffalo nickels. He stared at the newspaper a long time, as
if he remembered its stories, and finally he stuck it in the back of his Bible
   with the leather cover worn smooth as a horse's neck, his name in the corner
so faded you could make out only the consonants of *Lamar David March*.
   He and Jimmy worked to rebuild the rooms that summer,

Jimmy never speaking of the sister he thought he destroyed, Dad unable
to stop speaking of her, of the moon, of Isaiah, chapters 40 and 41.

7.

If I have learned to take a place seriously, it is Muskatatuck Park,
  just north of the Ohio, cuddled in the outskirts of Jennings County.
No one had to tell me its mute, sacred places under pine and willow,
  the old stories of Susquehanna and Cherokee, even older stories, glaciers
that rippled Southern Indiana like a woman shaking out a tablecloth.
  Here I met shy Eddie Chardell, who came to Muskatatuck in the evenings
to look for the coming winter, striped caterpillars and roots of wild chives
  touched with orange. He never asked why I came, and if he had,

I wouldn't have known what to tell him, something of my mother, perhaps,
  or Great-Grandma Olive, both of whom I was having trouble remembering.
The second time we met, Eddie brought Longfellow, butternut squash,
  and my very first beer. His voice dipped low and he foretold an unkind winter.

8.

Of all the storytellers and wagglers in the county, my Grandma
  is the most reticent. She is the kind of woman who wrote me
a letter each month I was away, relaying things like, *My green beans
  are about this long* ——————— and *You ought to see the forsythia today,
it would stop your breath up short.* In the twenty-two years
  between my mother's and father's death, I never saw her cry,
though she's had this little tremor in her bottom lip as long as I can recall
  and what looks like petals under her eyes, so violet I'd always wanted

to reach up and touch them and ask her things I shouldn't: why water
  arches from the hose like a rope, why the eggs are flecked with dried blood
when I find them, if it hurts to get old, or alone. She's told me enough, though,
  the way *telling*, fashioned like a nest, is not the sound of a thing but its hearth.

9.

Aphids gather on Grandma's porch today, the hard rain calling them up
  from the ground. I try to sketch the fence twined with honeysuckle,
the Heifer from memory, blank-eyed and sweet-milked, but I am tired
  of flowers and roots, weed and fern, the bovine. Today I want the angry
call of a jaybird, a cup to fall and break, the rain and its stink of woodsmoke.
  I drop to my knees and frown at the aphids, their gridded anteriors
nimbly making a path along the steps. I am fetched today: a dweller
  in the bewildering land of the mind, not unlike Indiana, its cavities

and its coils of light, its stones and minnow, its hovering moon
a promise of God's, something like nectar, something like thirst.

Short Visit Home

1.
I let myself in through the back door,
the key still under the oval rock,
and sit at the kitchen table. Sunlight
lands on the table top like a feather on water,
    lands like a green-feathered duck on water,
     a green-feathered duck dipping its head
beneath water.

2.
I want to write *black branches snag the cloudless sky*
a glittering, nameless city pauses
relatives are rubbed stones in my pockets
the scent of hyacinth, heavy and sweet fills the night
smoke-stunned bees, honey in the comb
red scarf in the breeze or small bird falling

3.
Grain trucks fill and drive away,
    return empty, fill and drive away.
I taste gritty dust and breathe it into my lungs,
imagine dust layering there, year after year.

I hear the snap of wings.
Green-feathered ducks rise in unison, their necks
stretch and curve. Their webbed feet
run on water. A *V* in the sky casts a long shadow,
flying to heaven or Siberia.

4.
The plane casts a growing shadow that slips
    over trees and houses, a golf course, a football field.
I watch it skim a lake. New England waits
outside my window. The shadow rushes the runway.

Paradise Postcards

Lone Postcard

I miss you so! My legs have gotten
better but you're my main concern.
I'll call when I can. Tonight, on
this dusty dune, I thought of our night together
in the elaborate hotel. You were wearing
an Egyptian cat mask and I was holding
a scepter that we all know stands for something.

Writer Postcard

I don't mean to rush you regarding
the previously mailed manuscript,
but my mother has been in a coma for years
and I fear I'm losing sight of the eternity
waiting beyond this life . . . in the neighborhood
streets, children on skateboards push each other
down driveways lined with rose bushes and
exotic plants that don't have names.

Little Things That Are True

There is no dirt track in Indiana that hasn't been ridden by my brother.

There is no GE plant in Indiana that my father hasn't worked in.

There is no pond in Indiana that is not the pond of Jason Mattihas.

I have heard of other dirt tracks and GE plants and ponds.

I know of other things that are happening in the world and yet I can't seem to place them.

There was no book, but the book in Indiana. The book in Indiana was a hundred books. Or, the book in Indiana was the book in Indiana.

After all, I'm not Wallace Stevens.

I have other ideas but, the thing that gets me is closer to home.

I can feel the wings growing from my back.

Status Symbol

        i
Have Arrived
        i
    am the
New Negro
        i
am the result of
President Lincoln
World War I
and Paris
the
Red Ball Express
white drinking fountains
sitdowns and
sit-ins
Federal Troops
Marches on Washington
And
prayer meetings
today
They hired me

it
is a status
job . . .

along
with my papers
They
gave me my
Status Symbol

the
key
to the
White . . . Locked . . .
John

Ladies Waiting in the Mall

They refuse to know the name
these parchment ladies
no longer striding in some
social arrogance secure
in gown and guarded graciousness
    They refuse to know the name
    or recognize those faces
    once so grandly patronized
These powdered cafe au lait ladies
quiet now and shrinking.
from the sear of public scrutiny
of Time revealed in pore and line and pouch
in the relentless obscene now
of thinning wave and nylon curl
    Preferring not to know a name
    these once tall ladies.
    groomed and slightly fragrant
        slightly frayed
    wait in the glitz, the aimlessness
    of chic and failing shopping Malls
        for transport
Gone the grandeur once so carefully contrived
the firm if fragile flesh, the haughty stride
the unrelenting judgment, the clear demanding eyes
    All that remains
    a head averted slightly
    and a ragged clutch of pride

Paean for a New Library

. . . It came to pass that
man and wo/man
rose from their crouching
Stood upon their legs and
       walked
In time, styli and brush in hand
They scribed on scroll and on papyri
       a legacy of circumstance
of deeds, of dreams, and dance

And soon the wise ones said we
       need a shelter
where children can come
to bathe in Light
surrounded by wisdom their
       minds challenged
their spirits renewed. . . .
Whereon, the women and the men
created such a haven

And the darkness glowed
For in it they stored sunlight
and water, pastures and plains
snowcrowned mountains raging
storms and circling galaxies
And the people of Alexandria, of Carthage
Then of Rome, of Paris, of New York,
and the Heartland of America each
in their own time, stood around it
       and marveled
For through the luminescence shone the
records of their living, their loving
their anguish, joy, their poetry
their song

We reverence libraries for they hold the past
Contain the blueprints for our future
the impetus toward present possibility. . . .
A beleaguered society, when that society is chaotic
must rush first to defend its children and then
             to secure its libraries

There comes a time when a need is met
a haven prepared, a library built
When the people gather, to reverence and
      re-visit
For libraries are fortress
         and wooded stream
      challenge and surcease. . . .
Repositories of revolution, and of respite
      Staunch
            Enduring
               In them
we find the people's substance, their spirit
      their brilliances and delusions
         their visions
            and their Truths

                  In the end
it is the people, empowered, who prevail
who are their own Enlightenment who
               secure inclusion
Who are their own beneficent result

Learning the Signs

When shall I learn to love
the pure gold of beanfields in October?

When will the sepulchres of corn
perform their miracles?

The carcasses of possum and raccoon
repeat the price of freedom.

Captive in its field, a small pond
teaches living by the rules.

I won't argue that this land's not kind
to those by whom it's used,

but to the stranger it insists on fencing in
and on observing. At a crossroads

one road leads to where I live, and one
leads home. Corn and soybeans lie

in both directions. They won't say
which way I have to go.

Driving in Fog

If I were lost in one of these fields
among the anonymous corn
I wouldn't know which way to turn
home, or toward some nameless town
with its church and peeling feedstore.
The tail of a horse is patient; it sweeps
a window in the fog, while the hooves of a horse
run away across the stubble.
I think this must be what it is like
when the last breath goes, and we wake
in the new dimension. I may be a ghost
like the others, dressed in my tattered clothes,
the crows bits of black cloth
the wind blows past me. And if in the past
I could say, I'm not afraid of anything,
now I am afraid, deeply afraid,
of nothing, and how like smoke the air is
here where it burns.

Refuge
Mount St. Francis, Indiana

You are welcome to walk, but leash
your dog. The heart

can go untethered, nose
to the ground, sniffing

the inevitable perfume of growth
and decay. Practice

brotherly silence
with the trees, or collect

in the cup of your ear the language
of water over

fossil stones. Observe
two barking geese

descend, wing wedded
perfectly to wing.

Call back your heart. Resume
the path. Savor

the deep sweet happiness
of being in this world.

Trilingual Instructions

Ecoutez. Escuche. Don't be shy.
Listen. Fall for the lie that instructions
in Spanish and French are for others. Not us.

Chinese buffet. Mexican workers busing
tables. The owners spear pork with forks.
Mandarin chatter, but me with chopsticks.

Eleven time zones away, in a land
of herdsmen, CNN tells me Knight's fired.
Riots in Bloomington. I email my wife before she wakes.

Euchre at the adult center. What's the world
got to do with us? So far away. Like a dream.
We play without a full deck of cards.

The colorful illusions of autumn trees
are stripped naked by winter's hands.
We see the people then. Reflections of us.

Soy de Indiana. Bonjour, le monde.
Be kind to us, and change us gently
and make the good better.

Trip to Delphi

Lately, I've begun to look
like my father. Dead and gone,
the man has sent his genes ahead
to do his dirty work. Baleful eye
in the bathroom mirror, the curse
of the House. And so I've come
not to the holy city of Byzantium
but to the best I can manage—Delphi,
named for the real thing, Indiana,
home of the Wabash, the professional
choice in swine equipment, Hillinger's
and the IGA. Delphi, where girls
grow up to be auxiliaries
shuffling behind the fire truck
in the parade.
      But I remember
the other Delphi—Omphalos of the World—
how twenty years ago I lay on my back
among cypress, the sky opening above me
consenting to be read at last. All columns
up again reaching to touch it. Funny
how the brain works to put things back.
The rubble around me—cracked slabs
and steps where girls once walked
leading the procession, pieces of
pediment and pedestal, each one
white as a Dover Cliff. Oh peerless
dumping ground to hold such trash!
Hunks of marble big as giants' teeth
and strewn about as if the golden cup of
Zeus itself had fallen off its nightstand,
shattering the ineffable bridge.

But what's the bridge between
all that and this Family Dollar Store
in Delphi, Indiana, where I've ended up?
This temple consecrated to toothpaste,
batteries and bargain underwear. Empty
but for me and the thin-lipped guardian of
the till, priestess on a stool, breathing in
the vapors of advanced righteousness. Oh Harpy
of the tollgate, agent of the family curse,
do not look at me so. In the twin auguries
of your eyes, double and doubly I am
my father's daughter. Each crumbling face
witness to the other, split in half
and shattered by the bifocal line.

Cascade Falls
Lieber State Park, Indiana

Every man I ever wanted
I brought here for a picnic. Walked him out

over these horizontal slabs to
swish our feet in the water. Packed lunch,

my breasts for dessert. I always drove.
It was a surprise, you see. But you

I never brought. Let's face it, you began
as understudy. I had to prompt your lines.

This was big time. Standing Room Only
(those jostling trees). And O, the acting,

the Stanislavsky method working that green O.
The besotted cliffs echoing with praise. Don't

feel bad. By the time you fumbled on the scene
the scene was Greek, and I, burning to bury

not two brothers but a regiment. I was Jocasta
stabbed with dress pins, Medea drenched in blood

not wet enough to wash the anger from my hands,
and Agamemnon's wife, so picnicked out, so wax-

papered in duplicity, I was without shame.
No, I never brought you here, even now,

for what if times's membrane did not hold
and the double axe of Clytemnestra's words

crashed through my teeth, and Jason
snarled again in your voice? What of

Aristotle's unities, not to mention our own,
for how many years of marriage shored up

is dike enough, dead-bolt and chain enough
when such tempting lines are practiced

and cued up on an unsuspecting tongue?

Apollo Comes to Floyds Knobs, Indiana

Only the lover is éntheos, says Plato.
Only the lover is *full of god*.
        —Roberto Calasso

Everywhere is green—forest green,
moss, jungle, viridian. All Indiana
down to the Ohio, pushing against fences,
swelling with juice. A fat lady
taking up two seats on the airplane.

We used to be forest here
before the urge for acreage and the axe,
pickled beets and church on Sunday.
Forest, before there *was* a Sunday.
Even before God took off for Italy
to have His portrait painted.
And this year, despite what you've
read in the Kroger check-out line,
the news for the turn of the millennium
isn't who flicked whom sideways
but that we're being rained on,
flooded, snaked out. Green is in!
When lilacs last in the dooryard bloom'd?
Mister, they're eating up the house.

I tell you, Papa's coming home.
He's fed up writing prescriptions
and orders for the medium indifferent.
He's bought himself a bank of clouds,
some killer luggage, and a watering can.
And no kicking the tires or shivering
prayer in a booth is going to stop him.

Before you know it, Sycamores will be
sawing through your floorboards. A Cedar
big as a myth will rise in your toilet
And more White Pine, Scotch Pine, Loblolly
than you can count will crash out of your
closets, demanding your furniture back.
With no more TV's, PC's, plug-ins for
your little mouse, who knows what else?
You lose your job. Your son becomes
an English major, and your wife
of thirty-two years decides to throw away
all her clothes and frisk in a Laurel tree
naked, insisting she'll not come down
until you learn Greek and climb up,
stripped, hot and hard again with love,
singing *Orea Orea*. Beautiful, beautiful.

You're kidding you say. *My wife,*
Secretary of the Bridge Club, flashing
her puckered thighs and beckoning
like the Lorelei, bewitched in varicose
and droop? Mister, just climb up.
Take your belly and bald head and climb
if only because she *is* ridiculous—
an old hen playing chickie on a balcony,
asking only that you rise like the Cypress
from your knees and clutch her to you
in all her bravery and redeeming foolishness.
Cradle her face the way you would
a crystal cup you could drink from
forever. Then hurl yourself for once
into your heart's voice. The leaves around
your head will whisper what you need to say.

Visitation Rights

I sit by a ravine dumped with November,
every leaf the color of old pennies. Gingko,
oak, maple, hackberry—no difference.
Back to the dirt factory.

Why isn't that comfort comfort enough?
After all, one makes do: a sycamore
preens in a rag of winter sun and
each mica-studded boulder flinging light away
balls up and waits for heat. Still,
April's promise is midget, parsley on a plate,
compared to this:

High noon and no shadow. December's black-
white, bone-bark schematic
that snow, like Noah's sheet, rushes in to cover,
pretending the sinkhole's not there
or the fallen sparrow broken in a ditch. Look.

The sun's out hunting for his children.
A once-a-week father in a blue car.
A regular Mr. Razzledazzle flashing his brights
on every lake, every puddle, every teaspoon of water
searching for the bodies. *Too late too late*
says my cup of tea. *All the honey's gone.*

Chinese Medicine
Indianapolis Museum of Art

This poem will not move.
It is bashful as an overturned
flowerpot that will not show its daisy.
The seven pigeons of the black arts,
the cosmic dancer who pirouettes between
two worlds haven't communicated in weeks.
Now what? Another confession? Two iambs
and an anapest three-legging it around
one more blab of love?

The tiger on the Chinese scroll
rolls his eyes. His tail—a flair, a flip
around the coiffure of the Lady Nong Yu
who stands on his back, balanced as
a bank account. Her eyebrows plucked
for purity. She's composing her poem—
performing her daily surgery on the world
with ink and sharpened brush. The tiger leaps,
catalyst and fire. Her dress white gold.

In the scroll's upper left-hand corner
under a perfection of peach blossoms falling,
the eight immortals of the wine cup
sit in a closed circle pretending to be deaf.
The Lady Yu opens her mouth to speak her lines.
See how the immortals hold their smiles
tight to their faces. See how they grip
their flutes. How white the knuckles.
The Lady concentrates, too busy to care.

I ask for advice. What to do
about this poem stuck in its stanza,
flailing like an anemic fish too tired
to jump the falls. My pen hovers
above my little pad. The guard hisses—
No writing implements allowed. I stuff
my pen in my purse. The Lady Yu brandishes
her inky brush. The immortals freeze
in their endless summer. The tiger explodes.

This Swallows' Empire

Wrought by the odd desire for permanence
I'd hammer down that barn's boards one by one
The ivy's nudged apart and winds have sprung
And icy blows and summer's pounding suns.
Those gaping windows, too, and half-cracked panes,
The door that broke from its hinges leans against
The blackened exit mouth, and all such things
As let the rude rot in and thieving rain
I'd be so prompt to take defense against
And fortify and make so sound
You'd think it'd haunt me on some howling night
When all seems waste unless I could
To all that trouble say: this much will stand,
This swallows' empire for a little while
And bolts of hay in their warm cave
And drifts of straw upon the broad-beamed floor.
Though time must turn all waters for its mill
And nothing is but grist as we well know
What has withstood two hundred years
That rich resistance will do so
If obdurate work allows, for fifty more
For fifty more to house the hay
They cut and piled in striped rows
And will carry in before the sun's flower goes.

As if within this shelter here
For what the toppling wagons bring
From ricks in fields to fill the loft
With rustling fragrance and with warmth
There might be some more delicate thing
Dozing as in some attic in some spring
That shafts in through the windows in a dream
Of meadows in their prime unreaped, uncut,
Unreaped, uncut, and running with the wind—
The golden burn, the darksome gold or green.

Pressed to the rafters all that airy weight
And caught within, now looking out,
Past time's compulsions in the massy dark,
Their golden heads and stalks of light.
I mean those summers of the foursquare fields
That memory by its strange persuasion yields,
And blazoning, from dim abandonment.

The Smoke Shop Owner's Daughter

The illness had wanted to kill her
Although it had not, quite.
It had left her, however, knotted and pale,
Of the size of a twelve-year-old child,
An underground child, mushroom white,
With pitted cheeks and the look
Of the one for whom it is perhaps too late
To grow up, and so who stands
Somewhere off at the start
Of the about to be and the never not.
And always silent. But then—
Speech was a thing far apart.
How could she say. It had been so long
She had been kept inside and away—
Like a child with a pointed head
Kept in bed in the slanting light
In a place cut off where they store old things,
Like a mad prince of the counterpanes—
Except that it was not so rank,
So slanting and dusty in the weak light,
Though with the dog and the cat it was cramped
At the back of the store (with her mother out front)
In the faint greys that had stayed so long
They came as close to her as a friend,
Close as the sickness, and when they went
Took what she had which was them,
Nothing more, and left her to find her way back.

You saw it there in her eyes.
Something sat there like a small thing
That having been taken away so far
Can't hear the echoes from the near
And does not know how to be
With the strange untrue of the real,
There being, neither, no one to say
If it's that or not or to try
However they might to draw her away
From the tense where she lives of the still,
No one to mend her, baffled and cropt.

On the Legends of a Dancer

I was a child in a small midwestern town,
It was a still summer afternoon
Yellow under the great maple trees.
Perfumes of the close-shorn grass and the entranced
Loose-hanging clusters of dark-laced boughs
Sealed me into the heat of a grape-enclosed
Urn of summer's drowse
Under the arbors of vine-weaving ease
When a beautiful woman, my mother's friend,
Famed for her girlhood of violets and beau-taking
Sashes, valances at dances, of supreme
Dew-drenched, liquid-kissing, cyclamen-haunted eyes,
Came to inform us that you were dead.
Into which with the speaking of faraway *death* was mixed
A coquettish condemnation of ardors so fierce
It seemed leopards might spring from the dots and cirques
Of a heat-ringed shade stippled by sun on the wands of the boughs.
And a vast sadness commingled with a vast sense
Of a mystery so obscurely profound
Seemed to wring from the antiphonies
Of an everywhere that the trees described
A music flowing up from their roots
And down through the whole shivering sap of their lives
Whereupon it seemed that I understood
Love, womanhood, and dancing.

Keeping the Hedge

Remnants of original prairie are best
found along old fences and hedge—
rows—the narrow space a plow has
never touched.
             —May Thielgaard Watts

In October she will slip back to the prairie,
measuring light as she might measure
water in a glass. She will follow
the fencerows, the hedges, whispering names
of what has survived: cord grass, fleabane,
turkeyfoot, bluestem, wild rye . . .

Tossing car keys into waist-high grass,
she will run through cattail chimneys
adrift in their own smoky seeds, rock
in the wicker of the willows, recalling the spring
her first bloodroot stained a lap of shade.

She can never explain what men have called
"a distance" in her, what the children
have dug at with little pails and spades.
But the tracks of any tillage proclaim it:
what is once plowed under never comes back.

She thinks how she will wrap in the corduroy
of rubbing grasses, drape gentian rickrack
down her breast like a blouse. She will hold
herself steady under clouds of tenting nimbus.
She will keep her own hedge under sky like a sail.

Dust

The sky was a plate of curds
the autumn Uncle Reuben came, three days late,
in the afternoon mail. His mortal whey
gone to thin smoke above a southern town,
he came north stamped, insured,
delivered RFD to the roadside box
where my mother waited. Nothing
inside but a plastic bag, she said,
and closed it. Kept him
in the cool front room
till prairie skies glazed blue,
a plate washed clean and empty,
and the priest could come.

My parents refused
to distribute the ash—
they will nothing to scatter—
the posthole digger drew a tidy plug,
a sweet core of grassland,
and they dropped him in.

Augering into another autumn,
I remember his smile, his scars from the fire
at the dry cleaning plant. I put down
tulips between the hard frosts,
crocus bulbs with absurd little navels . . .

And so the story ends: no flesh to decay,
no bones to toss up centuries later—
only a woman with a trowel in hand,
only this wind
across the edge of Indiana, this swift
and gritty eddy of leaves,
a scent, perhaps, of something relinquished,
sand in the mouth,
a speck in the eye.

Auction

They are selling my afternoons
stacked up like saucers on the lawn,
my doilies, sewing chest, my coffee pot.

"A fine antique," proclaims the man
with the megaphone face, and the bed
my babes were born in-is gone-

is gone. The heat seams me indoors.
They sell my quilts, what pieces
of flesh and dark I can still recall.

They sell the walnut chest of drawers.
I did not tell them: the mottled mirror
is where the woman lives. I saw her

one twilight, dressed in my wedding face,
with a single jewel I never owned.
Certain nights I rose and could not sleep:

she was Spanish, a duchess, a mermaid,
eyes stippled like a trout stream,
pupils chipped from water and time.

I dared not tell how I floated to join her,
my joints liquid as lamp oil, in a country
far as childhood, a fragrance light as tulle.

Now they check for dovetailed corners,
pry at my life for loose veneer.
When the money is counted, they will

load the old lumber of my bones
in a wheelchair, store me in a sterile
lumber room. She will not store so easily.

Once only she spoke, like water
sucking down a stone. "Hush," she said.
"It has been decided. I will not go

when they take you. They will sell
what is solid. I am breath, darkness,
the essence of rain. I am what stays,

do you hear me? I am what remains."

Plainsong for an Ordinary Night

The Amish sit down on nights of usual weather,
when nothing is wrong in northern Indiana
and nothing particularly right; when September
settles like a brooding hen, they sit and make
their plain and weekly letters for the Budget news:
In Salem, jars and cans are nearly filled with summer,

but the martins left, those busy days, before they knew.
Seed land has opened itself to winter wheat and weather,
and that stray rooster, pecking out the kernel of September
afternoons, will soon end up in the frying pan. Summer
was unkind to muskrats dead upon the road, and Indiana
wants slow-moving signs attached to every buggy made.

Nothing is particularly wrong in northern Indiana,
though Mary Luthy's finger sliced her summer
shorter, and Verna Kropf's grape jars exploded into news.
Mrs. Gabb's son went to drink and never got her coffin made.
but melons are rounding out the air of late September
the way marigolds flare up and fuel the dying weather's

fumes. Gardens are at the stalling point when summer
goes, but underneath the ground, parsnips swell and new
potatoes are fleshier than one expects in Indiana.
Lately, frosts have made a chaste, austere September,
but tonight, a bright moon shines. Youngfolks make
the most of days that linger. Courting buggies weather

ruts that drive older wheels to the shop. That new
horse of Fisher's spooked and skipped the bridge this summer;
the new wife had his ankle to soak and cows to milk whether
she liked it or not. The Alymer depot burned September
first; a load of hymnbooks and harness leather made
an unreined fire. And so things go in northern Indiana:

Mose F. Miller, 91, still steps off early September
walks as though morning itself might be something new.
Alma, who would have been 17, died this summer;
a load of bright, sliding hay blotted out the Indiana
sun too long, and her bees, without being told, made
honey dark, but sweet. Crows mourned the cooler weather.

Toward morning, a steady September rain will weather
out the end of summer. Libations of cider will be made.
And the Millers of Goshen, Indiana, will pluck the late beans like news!

Geese Crossing the Road

Winter again,
and the heart chokes down a little,
driving mid-country, the windshield
an esplanade of rain.

Past prairie towns
scattered on the soil like ancient vertebrae,
I slow the car for a farmer's geese,
a haughty promenade, not to be hurried
as they step out their scorn
of rain, each feather in place,
feet glowing like a beacon.

In another town, you are less secure
than they, wearing my troubled love
like an ill-stitched coat
against such rudiments of weather.

Dear heart,
whatever grief I've caused you,
the truth is this: love at midlife
is not flight, not
buoyant migration to another plane,
but small journeys, sudden
new species of touch, a proud arc
in the lifting neck, a stay
against depletion. It is these geese
crossing the road, calling us back
to some primordial attention
we had wandered from, some forgotten state
where we too touched the earth
and stepped out the essence
of whiteness, of sureness, or morning.

Here, on Earth

Imagine the pleasure inside this storm,
the foam rush from rain gutters. Imagine
yourself here, inside a restaurant

in an unlit street. Say it is a bad neighborhood
even after the rain. Take the immigrant face
of our waiter who is also the proprietor. Say:

Peter, it's been weeks. We've come to eat.
We've been hankering for your phô.
We know what we want—

the same meal we always order—
me, the no. 1 appetizer my wife, the no. 3
For our entrees, the no. 38 and the no. 30.

The booths here are lit by bright faces:
Vietnamese, Thai, Chinese, and Filipino.
Hundreds of years on their faces!

School teachers, witnesses of terror, readers
of Chekhov, office clerks with inner lives.
Then the bottle blonde businessman

in a dress shirt with silver cuff links
moseys in to pick-up his take-out order.
He is tall and pockmarked

like my father; he could almost be
my father except for the dyed blonde hair.
Over the no. 1 and no. 3 appetizers,

we are speculating, my wife and I,
where the businessman comes from—
Manila or Saigon?

Oh, but here comes Peter with our orders
of steaming bowls of phô. Our faces
shining like klieg lights.

Inside this booth, my moon face
is a lantern in the mainstream
lengthening, lengthening.

Lullaby for Rabbit
—After Makoto Ozone

The moon is the mind of Buddha.
The rabbit in the moon is a story.
Says so here in my book.

My book is the necessary nothing
celebrating the fortieth anniversary
of a non-event. In the free market
there are maxims to live by:

"The consumer isn't a moron.
She is your wife. A trellis of trees
is a splendid thing. Walk under it, etc."

Who am I to tell you my story when I am no taller than the trees, or hills, or other humans? That I am as tenuous as an aging rabbit sleeping away his days on earth, that I and he are but frail leaves floating along the same river of time. Forty years ago, in the middle of June, a flood of white light bathed an airport runway. Forty years ago, the moon still awaited its birth. Someone was writing in his journal. When the Buddha was hungry, the rabbit offered itself as sacrifice by jumping into the fire. Fugitive night, distant city, our plane landed and then the taxi driver dropped our luggage on the curb. And here, now in Indiana, I can only imagine the figures huddled in the fog, their slight and foreign bodies.

New Harmony
"The shadows of history are long here, and dark." —John Hawkes

A distant sadness:
A smudge of light against the Golden Rain trees
And then shadows spreading through the streets,
To the fields and the river.
The golden hair
On an arm trembles in a breeze
Like a breath. Utopia lost,
Twice here in this town mapped in a dream.
Clouds build above distant church bells.
The sun dials darken.
Someone turns to leave
And all that was ever meant to be
And could not happen, flickers
As the first sweep of rain across the screened porch
Disturbs the shadows, neither new nor old,
 Of this fragile harmony.

Post Cards from Southern Indiana

I. Lyles Station, Indiana

We take some pictures and look around.
A few trailers, a church, an abandoned school—
All that's left of this freed slave community.
It is very still
And for a moment
Time becomes a wheel turning above us.
Its shadow brushes the lilacs
Outside the school's open door
And it enters with us,
Touches the blackboard listing the names
Of the men serving in Korea, and settles
On the rows of stacked wooden desks.
Our photos won't show the ceiling fan's dusty flutter,
The children seriously reading their donated
Healthy Home and Community books,
Or their young teacher, the light striking
His gold spectacles
As he looks up just now,
Toward some distraction in the doorway.

II. French Lick, Indiana

How many hand stenciled railroad carriages
Stopped before this cracked concrete platform.
How many small, silk stockinged feet
Stepped down in summer light.
How many tennis rackets.
How many hat boxes.
The ruined arch of the hotel entrance
Rises in the streaked sky
And casts its shade
Over the future across the tracks.

Oh tanning salon, oh video store,
Oh brave used car lot.

III. Petersburg, Indiana

Relax. It's only the wind

That moves the window pane,
That waters your eyes,
That makes the dust devils dance in the road.
It's only the wind
That takes your hat,
And the elementary school,
And half the houses
And all the trees on Sycamore.

Relax. We have no secrets anymore.
They've all been blown across the fields
Like flocks of dead birds.
The cow jumped over the moon.
The plate ran away with the spoon.

Relax. That's only the CSX train.

And it's only the wind
That rattles the door,
That flickers the light,
And comes up the stairs
And causes the dogs
To sit up and howl.

And causes the dogs to howl.

Limit 55

October light twists greens tawny
yellow. Traveling south down Indiana
150 from Paoli, plots
of knee-high soy burn golden brown,
and dwarf corn's wicked crowns have
not yet been whittled to the ground.
I come this way with windows down,
but I can't say if it's the sound of insects
I want to hear as I roll over
hilly roads: trailers and run-down
gas stations, the goad of an old
tractor driver motioning all
of us forward. While I suppose
it's better than the interstate,
is this a lie we tell to placate
our need for that song we barely
hear? Better to stall the car
next to the concrete deer,
and walk off this asphalt pier; smell
barley and wheat, let nameless
bugs bite crouched next to the stream's bed,
and disappear, disappear. Do
I tell another lie? Listen,
something blazes in the blue,
and the plants we cannot name, name us,
calling us the dower of separateness,
displaced stewards of some drowning grace.

Chime
From: Door to Door 6

Resting your forehead against just
stacked boxes, something long
forgotten chimes. You have returned
to wrap your parent's things & send
them along. Back after ten years
to East Tenth, its air-conditioned chill
& the smell of your childhood. Now a shell
that hosts your brief return—shelter
from a demanded divorce, from your five
year-old's crying, from the foreclosing
of your four-month bank-teller job.
Then again through the post-work hush
of darkening-day, the bell rings,
its long chime climbing the hall,
decanting memory after memory. Unable
to find the light, you shuffle forward,
feel for & unlatch the front door,
flipping on the outside light. Late
twilight heat & asphalt steam
from the recent rain enwrap you.
Clip-board in hand, a young man
presents his charts & tells his story
about staving off derogation.
          Then you tell yours.

Chris Green

Chances Are, Lafayette, Indiana

You may have visited this strip club
advertised by one high heel, a line
of automatic cursive on the back page
of the college news. I can't remember

if the dancer's stockings show their seams.
We don't see beyond her ankle in the square
white box. What she is and isn't wearing,
how long she can stand, balancing

there. Maybe she's busy filling in the rest
of that sentence: *Chances are, you won't go home
with me. Chances are, I'll get into business school.*
And what business would she start? Don't

say *risky.* You know she's smart, bored, trying
to quit smoking. It isn't sad if we imagine
that she's young—as young as chance,
and as distractible. Chance is an amateur.

Chance hangs out on the back roads.
I had my chance, people say, like they've lost
an umbrella. Chance was just here, but we
keep getting caught in the rain. Chances are

won by some guy in your old neighborhood
at a Dominican store with a Red Sox photo,
a flag in the same frame. Chance is opening
a restaurant near you.

Cause and Effect

Because the girl leaving
Lafayette Beauty Academy
drops one of the blonde
mannequin heads she's carrying
and it bounces, twice,
on the pavement, before she grasps
its plasticity tresses, lifts
it back into her arms, our lady
of the quick save, I am thinking
of La Virgen de Guadalupe
at a shrine in Mexico, in a light
green shawl and a red light dress,
cradling no baby, only her own
prayer-struck hands.

Crux

Every year at the end of winter a moment comes here with chill and clarity all in flux but no sign whether it's more frost or new buds on the way. It's a moment to magnify how every change of weather makes its own little season, sometimes lasting a day or two, sometimes just a few hours.

Late winter, and wild
onions on the forest floor
burst the first brash green.

Once, in the first year we were here, I was walking the bare woods in this breath between winter and spring and caught a glimpse inside the circle of little seasons—what keeps it turning and turning on.

Some bluebird bad luck
by empty oaks has left these
feathers for my hat.

And once heavy rains came just as the ground was beginning to thaw, so it was weeks before the earth was firm again.

Horse prints in spring mud
make little puddles that show
the moon overhead.

We came here from the city like salmon homing on the current of America, when our children were six and nine years old. Now they both have grown and traveled around the world, while my wife and I have stayed, watching after winter for the first white inklings to appear.

Suddenly fresh snow
flowers soften the winter's
wrinkled forest floor.

A shagbush blooming
floats as if the equinox
puffed cloud through the trees.

And So Heavy with Life the Crust of the World Is Still

Sunday after a big rain, the air still heavy,
the creek loaded with silt and fertilizer.
I need to run but my lungs are thick with
too much of some things, not enough of others.
A few mosquitoes, lots of sweat, the calm woods
and if I look close the light from the creek
moving on the undersides of the high leaves.
Why should I care about pronouns and referents
when the purple wildflowers I can't name are
standing tall, when the birds are crooning easy,
when the cricket I saw ten minutes ago
is still crossing the road? I thought
crickets hopped but this one was walking,
hustling but not going fast, a slow foot
onto the blacktop and a long way to go,
some distant kin to the little mammal
like a round tube of hurry that scuffed out
fast onto the highway and met neatly
with my left front tire so that I saw it again,
rolling to a stop in my mirror, a week ago
on the way to Goshen. I said nothing
to my wife and kids, and no one noticed.
It seemed to know what it was doing.
I have had it with road kill poems
larded with large noble animals, with
invisible strangers who leave the terrible
bags of evidence to swell and testify,
and yet I know it is not enough merely
to mourn our own small dead, the ones
we do not know or love until we kill them
helplessly, just going where we need to go.

Hedge Apples

I came out into the streetlight and stars
                      to walk the blocks to my house
and in the intersection, in shadow
            sat clusters hedge apples, though there
was no tree around to bear the street's
                  windfall of ugly fruit

Hiking, our mother used to stop us
             to admire spiked seed pods, waves
of fungus, the intricate hooks of burrs
     and when she found her first hedge apple

she brought home the brainy, bright green fruit
     and slipped it into a crystal pedestal candy dish
It fit perfectly—a strange gem in its setting
             We laughed, and since then

one of us has always stopped along a country roadside
     or hiked miles with a clumsy hedge apple rolling
in our pack to bring one home for her
          So, these lying in the street

look like unexpected gifts
     until I pick some up and realize the January rain
has left them nearly rotten
         I take one home anyway and set it
             in the circle of light on my porch

Frequency

You say its like squeezing the sound   The pedal ups the number of cycles
of the wave oscillation   We're sitting in the grass, the guitar's
thick rhythms rearing up around us   A little girl in a yellow sundress twirls
Last night, when the party next door flooded   into the street and woke us
we were still lying foot in foot   hand in hand   The girl is joined
by more children   and the singer smiles down   surprised at them
the youngest ones in diapers   bending their knees in their first dance
This loud music twists through the city as the sun sets   past the ivies
of the alleyways   past thistles of backyard finches   and I'm left
with a calm so thick   I think I could put it over anything

Brood X
Periodical cicada *(Magicicada septendecim)*

They're here already,
the tiny mounds appearing around trees
at the edges of Dunn's Woods,
hundreds of thousands per acre,
the seventeen-year cicadas.
What kind of life is it,
dark and dormant in dark soil,
weathering seventeen winters
and emerging? I imagine
seventeen years of my own shed
dreams, the crisp brown husk of them,
hard translucent covering over the eyes,
the split down the back where the bug
escapes, fat as a congratulatory cigar,
green-black and shining,
singing, alive in all the trees,
alive enough to balance out, in one
hot summer, that seventeen-year sleep.

Eight-Bar Solo

Ray Brown is God,
my father used to say,
and for proof he'd put on records
of Ella, of Oscar, Ray Brown on bass,
my father's fingers walking the bass lines
in the air with a pop and a thump
and a swing. I learned early how the singer
had to listen to the low notes,
how the bass laid down the rhythm
and the root, how much a man could say
with one blue note.

They're almost all gone now,
all the cats who knew
how to swing so hard even a white boy
from Kansas caught the syncopation,
learned to play. He's gone now, too,
my father, gone eight years. Today
when I heard Ray Brown was gone
I put on "Blue Monk," my fingers
walking the rhythm up and down
in the air, the bass line laying down
everything, the bebop heart of it all.

New Year's Eve in Whiting, Indiana

Year in and year out someone always launched
an aerial bomb too soon. The official Whiting
New Year was announced by the refinery whistle
to start work, on the 12 to 8 shift.
Kids banged spoons on pans out front of their
houses, neighbors with shotguns stepped outside,
loaded up, and blasted the sky. Like every
other night in the history of the world most folks
in Whiting were at a party. A la Fats Waller
they'd be home about eight, just me and my radio.
One hour before midnight whistle they'd hear
Times Square, Ben Grauer calling in the New Year
there. Then it would be 1947 in New York and
1946 in Whiting, for a whole hour we weren't on
The same calendar and 1% of all
New Year's Eves we weren't even in the same
century. There are no corn fields in this poem
but it is as middle western as all get out.
In its arithmetic I mean, in that empty hour
year in and year out, that made a guy wonder,
did God create the world from right to left,
east to west, so that even a New Year is behind
the times by the time it gets to Whiting?

Fire in Whiting, Indiana

My father's last name got him on the front page
once, when we called the Fire Dept. because our kitchen
was burning. HAZARD CAUSES FIRE. He didn't
laugh. In our neighborhood a scary gang of sixth
graders kidnapped dogs and cats. These kids smelled
like big city bus terminals and had names like Russell
and Allen. They took the kidnapped cats and dogs out
to the marshes, tied them to willows and set them
on fire, alive. It was, to them, humorous. I always
despite good advice and threats stole matches
and played with fire. But the Whiting fire worth telling
about was when the Cat-cracker at the Standard (we
made gasoline for a living in our town) blew up.
The whole damn refinery burned for eight days.
A third of the town evacuated. Martial Law. Looters.
Shoot-to-Kill orders. Gasoline in the sewers. And
news coverage. A friend of a friend saw it on a movie
newsreel in New Delhi. At night we went down to the Clark
High football field and sat in the stands, watching
across the marshes for gasoline storage tanks to go up
in orange mushroom clouds. Families brought picnic dinners,
employees of the very refinery, so as not to miss it
if a big one went. A month later a member
of Count Basie's band on hearing I was from Whiting
wanted to hear every bit of it. Imagine. It was, how
does a citizen explain this, reassuring and beautiful
watching our refinery blow up, sitting in the visiting team's
stands (they faced the fire) and being more amazed that
its heat reached our faces from a couple of miles
across the marsh than that the sun's did, from
wherever it was. The explosion, when she first blew,
broke windows in Michigan. Shock waves, we explained.
That was twenty five years ago and, my bet is, the last
time citizens of Whiting, Indiana, were,
to a man and woman, proud of that damn refinery.

Gypsies in Whiting, Indiana

Spring was when they came, every year.
Every year we were surprised. Why would a gypsy
live here, of all places, and in a storefront?
"They must know something we don't," we agreed.
That made us hate them, and be afraid of them.

We assumed they came for their usual—magic
and crime. Personally, we didn't admit to much
of either in Whiting. What's worse they came
at the time of year we started sleeping with
the windows open again. Now, under the traffic
and weather and railroad and factory noises
of our usual night, their presence was like a new
sound. Pain, abandon, lonesomeness, sex, joy,
magic—all together outside our windows now, the way
we heard confusing night sounds from our parents'
room. At the A and P you could buy a lemon,
take a seed from it, and sprout the seed in darkness.
That seed groaning single minded in its necessary
darkness was what gypsies sounded like at night
in Whiting, Indiana. A gypsy woman could drop her
skirt over your child and take it up into her.

They made us more confused about our bodies than even
the Negroes. In fact, they were darker than the Negroes:
they could know our minds. Their woman would take you
in her mouth and draw every thought you'd ever had—
that is, kept, as a secret possession. And she knew,
the day you'd die. In Whiting, lies were bright and
open faced. It was how we contrived to have a town
with each other. Candor was the dark thing. It came
and left town by rules of its own, rules we did not
want to know, or so we said. "They aren't breaking
any law," the Police Chief told us. But no one
really trusts a cop. He's half a gypsy himself, knowing
so many of our secrets, prowling the town all night.

One winter a doe wandered into Whiting. It grazed
on the evergreens at Sacred Heart Church during
First Friday mass. Snowflakes fell on its back
without melting. The doe behaved as if she'd stay
in the churchyard forever but Monsignor called
the police. She escaped capture and certain shooting,
left no trail into or out of town. One boy told
everybody she was Jesus and got sent to Sister Superior
to have his hand hit, with a ruler, ten times.

A True Biography of Stan Getz

"When you change the modes of music,
the society changes."
    Confucius, *via Gary Snyder*

"Place yourself in the background."
Rule One, "An Approach to Style," in
    Strunk and White, Elements of Style

1. 2013 Davis Avenue, Whiting, Indiana

The place of his first great appearance, 1950 or 1951. I was
doing the Forbidden in the bathroom: listening to the radio while
I bathed, heedless of electrocution and hoping for a jazz record,
on the Rhythm and Blues Gary radio station.

Stan Getz played "Strike Up the Band" and I was heart-struck.
I was, already, a heart-wreck, having seen Gene Tierney, her
face hitting the screen as a flash flood of light in LAURA.
Right then, at the Hoosier Theatre, I said (I truly said this)
I said, This is Beauty. I've been wreckage ("Wild to be wreckage
forever," says James Dickey) ever since.

(Hearing for the first tune that sound, the long and many
noted phrases of it, but the sound itself carrying those long
phrases out to the ends of breath as if Stan Getz's lungs and
heart would fall in on themselves, wreckage. And Gene Tierney's
face filled one entire wall of the Hoosier Theatre and like
the bathroom radio—electric, fatal—could not be touched.)

2. Hoosier Theatre, Whiting, Indiana

"I can have that Beauty," I actually thought against all the
evidence Whiting had to offer. The thought, I thought, was
in itself all the evidence I needed.

3. Indianapolis, Indiana

Now we are up to 1953. Thanksgiving Eve. Stan Getz played "Lover Come Back to Me" standing out front of Stan Kenton's band. I snuck in the Circle Theatre stage door and watched from the wings. The end of that tour, I believe, he was arrested for a drug store holdup, gone crazy attempting to withdraw himself from heroin and him arrested in the picture that appeared at Walgreen's Drug Store in Whiting where DOWNBEAT, the jazz magazine, was purchased. Riding the midnight bus in a snowstorm, my cornet up on the luggage rack, I was an agony unspoken: how do you say music in a Greyhound or anywhere else, to anybody? How do I remember now the exact sound and precise music of one Thanksgiving Eve?

Hill above Bedford

Carved stones legend us human and dwarfed on this hill
where the serious dead, divine in their ugliness, lie;
snail-horned stones drink the rain quietly,
and we who have felt the thirst of minerals and the hunger
    of animals at dusk
resign ourselves to contemplation of the holy perfection
    of ugliness;

what is beautiful is completely human,
and a stone is not a thing to plant
unless hard wishes have worn away
and nothing is left but love;

our fathers' land is poor, the timber second-growth;
all their tall illusions are cut down;
their walls are broken by cries of foxes and crickets;
and we who cannot build because we must sing in summer,
our minds made intricate by the sickness of music,
have these stones to stare down vanity;

here moments cannot stay, but fall trophies away
    like the wings of dinosaurs;
we cannot enter these stones, placed at the center
    of chance and innocence,
only a white monotone of instants that belong
    to life, and its quick going;
dressed fit to kill, we walk on this hill,
    Cain among the gravestones;
here pain moves leisurely, and cannot be put by;

serene in their ugliness, our fathers' uncharmed clocks,
with precise indifference to our humanity, are silent;
dressed in black cloth, satin round the arm,
we walk all afternoon, lame and beautiful,
knowing these bones and flowers we carry perish
    and shall not come again;

in a cedar tree, chants of young doves resume
    as we pass;
the fence rails are black, the burdocks green
under the blowing rain of spring; we listen.

Indiana

North from Louisville
The window blind is brown
in my window night
falls from a tower
holding a clock
across the river a city
glows, and beyond
fields of winter wheat
church spires and silos
bodies measure shadows
no words are heard

the rented room is quiet
the ping pong game in the hall
stopped at eleven
the pale girls have gone
to the White Castle
here silence is like
Dreiser dead, with a landlady
bent over his corpse
while her radio plays "Stardust"

I never draw the blind
whenever light comes
I do not want to miss it
light is my profession
it accustoms me to nights
when rats chew orange peels
in the wastecan near my desk,
and I stand at the window
where smoke from the flues
settles blue on the pane

the bridge looks handwritten
I draw my initials
the way you trace your identity
when you are not thinking
where my hand has rubbed,
light, not my name, comes through.

Robert Hazel   **89**

Harrodsburg: The Cemetery
The highway runs ahead of my injured eyes,
seeing only the concupiscent angels frozen:
the intuitive shame of motionless things,
the absence of consciousness and memory
    in the permanent grin
praise comes without honor, death without dignity;
the finite insult of prayers
takes no account of the distances
a live hand tapped electrically
in a red brick station against a green hill

an ingenuous painting might show a steam engine
    and gondolas paralleling a river
as on a ping pong table in a basement
a group of women suggests patience
while town clocks measure the distances
from rail yard to courthouse to coal-bucketed kitchens

but nowhere is the recognition that love or grief
    can be real.

Indianapolis
The policeman's whistle is clear and thin
at the white island of monuments on Meridian
Street, weighted with tableaus of frontiersmen:
Clark in green bronze, sword drawn,
leans towards Vincennes, and pale green
water booms from the fountain
and settles to a stillness under the reign
of blue-and-gold State banners on aluminum
poles that face the tarnished Capitol dome
above six Corinthian pillars; the limestone
wilderness stretches, treeless, to the open

arcade of the bus terminal, a slam
of light down Market Street to the Harrison
Hotel, under a long red-and-white sign

gamblers with dry faces and sallow skin
ravel in the weaving walk of equal blacks with brown
expectations; the Circle Theater kills time
with a film based on a Lloyd C. Douglas novel shown
in technicolor; and under his white helmet a modern
gladiator from North Vernon
creates Speed, a flying
red horse stenciled on the blue racer's engine,
while at the roller rink caryatids in
flesh-colored stockings support the roof, go nowhere in a din
of lucky wheels; on stage at the burlesque, near the wing
an Irish boy sings "Mandalay"; a bronze woman
with torch, on the monument's peak, faces south down Meridian.

Bloomington
The same way prayers end,
letters always begin

Dear Myself,
    Today
I heard music, drowned
in sunlight and slaughterhouse blood
and a strange sense of rubber
tires rolling around
the speedway without cars
or drivers, because tonight
after Hoagy Carmichael went back
to the piano in the gym
and Wendell Willkie returned
to the Law library

Robert Hazel

my father called me in
from a war to put on the earphones
and listen to Berlin
I had to listen then
because tomorrow everybody
would be in our attic,
my father's workshop,
to listen to the first
short-wave receiver in town
and hear the romantic music
of central Europe as if
it were one inch away
in Berlin a band was playing
from under the workbench
the color-coded wires
sped into the world.

Milan
In the darkened houses
they watch television
Their walls are scrolled
with Christian mottoes in red wool

Coal piles by the railway
are dense and odorless

The county held the world's record
for corn yield per acre

Mechanical cornpickers stand like giraffes
Sheep make few night noises

Clocks are meaningless

Before a train arrives the switchblock
obeys a steel instinct for direction

No lives are suddenly sidetracked
Loss is criminal

A black standpipe wears
orange letters: STATE CHAMPS, 1954

Young cars ease to macadam
and accelerate with sexual squeals

The green glass of bottles
broken in the street

looks American

When Dreiser wrote he had no readers
When Willkie ran he got few votes

My cousin in blue jeans wept for Dean
and raced her Chevy the wrong way

down all the one-way streets
in search of ice cream

I did not suggest she go to a doctor
Who is insane?

Labels are dead wonders

Who is free? I had a gray jacket
too tight across the back,

I strained against force,
my life confronted by perfect deadness

as I lifted the canvas mailbags
with brass padlocks, thrown from trains

I like to stand in the icy cones
of trains diminishing towards morning

It is not yet dawn
There is not enough light.

Robert Hazel

DNA in Indiana

In the morning, all along the shore
of the Atlantic, scores
of cone-shaped shells
dig themselves
into the sand,
camped out like fans
in line for tickets . . . or pilgrims
eager for a glimpse
of the holy martyr's bones
from the comfort of their spiral mobile homes:
little twisters that, when held
against the cloud-
filled sky,
reveal that they're inhabited by
a half a teaspoon's worth
of flesh that strains back toward Earth
where two of them are coupling in the surf, exchanging something
mysterious to us. How similar we are when my daughter
and my wife and I are clustered
in our beds, lying there like shells along the shore,
only no one can pluck us into the air
for their amusement or inspection
then casually drop us in the ocean,
unless, of course, you count
the occasional tornado or hurricane that turns things inside out
when what things want is to keep their insides in,
coiled like intestines,
coiled like the filament inside the light bulb that burnt out
on the porch the summer that we house sat for the man who thought
aliens were another way that humans could be
plucked out of their homes. For weeks, we couldn't see
what was crunching underneath our feet
on the front steps after dark, until the night
I finally changed the bulb, standing on a bench and looking

up to where the roofs peak seemed a ship's prow: me—the captain—steering
into darkness, untethered from the world
and feeling that, if I stared long enough, something would
unhinge inside me, but instead I stepped
down off the bench, flipped
the switch, and saw it wasn't acorns we'd been stepping on,
but snails, thin-shelled things light years from their ancestors in the ocean.
I prodded the reluctant aliens
(eyes on the ends
of their tentacles) back into the cockpits of their space crafts
and sent them spinning toward the safety of the grass
with the beneficence of a well-intentioned twister:
Tornado Dan might well be my moniker
among mollusk meteorologists,
because, let's be honest,
why should they be any less capable of predicting
the future than a weather satellite spinning
round the Earth or an Etruscan haruspex inspecting the entrails of a sheep
if it's true that everything we seek is buried deep
inside us, like the fetus of our daughter curled inside my wife's womb
upstairs in the bedroom
as I screwed
the light bulb in the socket on the porch, or like DNA (that's D-A-N anagrammed)
the "two long chains of alternating phosphate and deoxyribose . . . twisted into a double
helix." *Helix* as is in "any of a group of spiral-
shelled mollusks, including the common
snail." *Double* (see line 17)—use your own imagination.

Amaze

Don't forget when you
see the word, you whisper *maze*,
or lip it in your head
remembering, perhaps, the spring
it snowed so wet, so heavy
the maples and ash heaved
down across the highway,
branches crossed every path
in town so detours led only to detours
and everything was dead end,
but still the world was alive, warm,
crocus and daffodil poking out of snow,
magnolia buds fresh on broken limbs, tragic,
but amazing really, that labyrinth
the word refers to, pointing
after a few switchbacks to *daze*,
stupefy, the uncertainty one experiences
in short sleeves shoveling snow,
in trying to get from one place
to another without any clear view
as to how. We end up anywhere
but where we expect
such warm Spring days
like the one just after
we'd met. You had a secret
to tell me I already knew,
but I let you tell it anyway, your eyes
dark as branches
that moment I knew
we'd entered a maze
we live in still
where snow storms come
out of nowhere, incongruous
and absurd as children
we didn't expect, laughter
after death, anger cutting
its teeth on love, flowers
cutting up through ice.

Sanctuary

for the librarians, volunteers, and patrons
of the Putnam County Public Library on its Centennial

On a June 1903 afternoon when light
poured through the windows' amber glass
to change the air to gold, some slight-
built woman found a book to slide across

the desk of oak you stand at now with a book
to help you build or knit or sew or learn
your name in another language or look
into a world so like & unlike your own you can't discern

fiction from fact. That's why you've come here,
to borrow some little thing to change
your world. You open the book's hinge
to unhinge yourself, face fears

of what you know & don't. So imagine
that woman again come here (like you
today) a hundred years ago with some question
or quest already pouring over the blue-

black words in the book she's come to borrow
from this building of roman brick & amber glass & oak.
Now try to imagine the world without her or her book
or this sanctuary or the people who bow

and smile when you come no matter who you are,
rich or poor, man or woman, boy or girl.

Back Home Again

Coming home from our visit
to the grandma
my children
named "sand grandma,"
because she lives by the beach,
we cross the Ohio
and sing "Back Home Again
in Indiana." Even my youngest
knows *the sycamore, the candle light,
the new moan hay*,
and we sing
in that exaggerated way
part pride, part embarrassment
for being such Hoosiers
now home
from the ocean,
all sunburned and cranky,
from the long drive
across mountains
and hills,
that long stretch of white fences
in Kentucky,
but there's some unnamable contentment
in knowing there's a house
waiting, our vague belief
we did turn off the coffee maker
and it didn't burn down.

When we pull in
and see the ragged lawn
the shutters we need to paint,
I make a sigh I wish
for those
without a home,
simple air from a mouth
that is not about to kiss
the ground, just a sigh
that knows this ground
is ours.

Trying to See What Happened

Although I know I was born
in the Putnam County hospital,
and that my father was there, I always
imagine it happening at Dr. Ann's house,
in a little office in the front room,
on one of the Greencastle streets.
How quiet it was, just before 4 a.m.,
the dark thinning, not a car on the street,
the stars burning coldly.

My mother is at Dr. Ann's house, by herself,
and I have come so fast the doctor doesn't have time
to prepare my mother, doesn't shave her,
doesn't slice the skin to make a bigger door.
I slide out black-haired and bloody.
Dr. Ann catches me. It's quick
and easy, no screaming at this birth.
Already I'm behaving very well.
This girl will give you no trouble,
Dr. Ann says, wiping me off and handing me
to my mother, whom I imagine fully clothed
in her street clothes, something pressed
and stylish.

I wish I could remember how my mother smelled
when I first lay down on her chest,
what her voice sounded like inside her body,
whether she smiled or cried. I know she wanted me,
without thinking, the way women did in 1958,
in Greencastle, Indiana, in April,
on the 26th day of the month.

Those were the days when my mother used to laugh
so hard she cried, and the laughter broke
through her face like light.

Poem for Julie

Remembering
    1984. Our bodies above the river, voices
    a shimmer beneath god-toss of July stars.
What we loved
    was there, on the sandbar, the brown water
    rushing against us, under our talk
About fire.
    About thunder. Sparks
    from our fingertips, words
    whispered among plague-weed and stone angels.
And how everything
    that year came true! the shadows
    beneath the bed *did* grab our ankles, and somewhere,
    back in the woods, a cottage was built cookie by sweet.
We danced
    down the banks, we had not learned to be
    afraid. Our hands wove spells above the silver sand,
    we would cast our futures like runes
    and we would be fearless, we would!
Around
    our feet, the river rose and broke,
    murmuring the names of those
    we would someday lose; rising and breaking
    and not once
    did we hear our own names among them.

Academic Instructions

Don't write
about being black.
All that racial jive

is passé anyway;
no one wants to hear
how waitresses won't

serve you, how plainclothes
detectives follow you
in up-scale shops, fearing

you'll shatter or steal
one-of-a-kind china and crystal,
afraid you'll send property values

plummeting by stepping through
their revolving doors. And please,
no more poems on being a woman,

we get far too many of those,
and frankly, they bore us,
sullen tales of first menses

and lost virginity,
smug complaints about male
appetites, detailed renderings

of all those body parts
that should stay hidden,
instead of peering

from blouses, peeking
from parted legs.
And don't, for heaven's sake,

say a word about being both,
it's been done and we're tired

of it, tired of your constant

ancestor worship—your love
of strong brown women,
mothers who tilled fields

and birthed babies,
clothed and fed and loved
the sick, insane, and poor,

who made churchgoing clothes
from some rich lady's scraps.
No one wants to hear

what you call your history;
its naive and mundane,
full of scandalous blame

for everyone but yourself.
Come back when you are ready
to learn how to write

like the rest of us,
when you're ready to admit
all the beauty in the world

around you, finally wise enough
to know nothing you say clearly
can ever matter.

Shake Your Body
for Michael Jackson

This is the Michael
I want to remember:
full lips, Afro large
as life, lithe body
slim but not dangerous,
mouth imploring us
to dance, shout, shake
our bodies down to
the ground, his face
his own, untouched
by surgery. This Michael's
no freak show, his dancing
not reduced to crotch grabs
and pyrotechnics, skin
not powdered beyond
recognition to a zone
neither black nor white,
but phantom-like, pallid
as talc. This Michael
still glittered, still shone,
his nose broad across
his face, hair untouched
by chemicals that would
slick his Afro to a dead
sheen, greasy under
stage lights. This Michael
was on his way to being
a man, a black man,
someone whose albums
I wouldn't hide, whose
voice wouldn't turn into
mere vocal tics, tricks,
a parody of itself,
a joke we're all aware of
except for Michael himself—

who's left behind our
ghettos, our streets,
left behind Detroit
and Newark, Little Rock
and Gary. The Michael
I want to remember
blamed "it" on the boogie—
"it" the energy no one
can deny him, "boogie"
that irresistible urge
to dance—the dance
uncomplicated by the
dancer, uncompromised
as the face he used to possess:
broad, brown, African.

Wedding Party

I wanted to have a wedding
where a band called Sexual Chocolate
would play cover versions
of "Turn the Beat Around"
and "Got To Be Real," tunes
so disco everyone's forsaken them
in the oh-so-cynical '90s.
I wanted my bridesmaids
in orange tulle, groomsmen
in light green, their cummerbunds
so wide their waists became
some thick, enticing region,
regal as an alleyway.
I wanted folks to glide
onto the dance floor,
doing quaint, antiquated dances
like the funky chicken, Latin hustle,
polyester divas doing moves so fine
even Shaft himself would have
to stop, grin his approval.
I wanted finger foods
in snack sizes, a wedding cake
piled so high in gumdrops
and coconut that no one's
blood sugar level would be safe.
I wanted it crass, and big,
and ugly, bad enough
to make relatives shudder
whenever they remembered
my denim patchwork gown,
platform heels. Instead,
I'm here at the city clerk's office,
an ordinary woman in an
ordinary dress, marrying
an ordinary man in ordinary
shoes. Still, I know that party

is going on somewhere, if only
in the strange regions of my mind:
music and costumes
by Earth, Wind, and Fire,
catering by Momma and Company,
and the m.c., of course,
is a dapper black man
who wishes us *love, peace, and soul*,
our lives one everlasting ride
on the Soul Train bound
for Boogie Wonderland,
li'l Stevie's harmonica
blowin' us one last tune
in the key of life.

Photograph: A History of Maps

A young girl asks you to take her
picture, breath draws itself in through your ribs

as you shift your feet in the sand and consider
the colonization of ants. One culture

dealing another into servitude
is never a euphemism. One person's sudden love

for a stranger can solidify into eutectic
plates, harden the earth and snap. The rickshaw

that brought you here is not necessarily affection
but a map marking the rickshaw wallah's death

by age forty. Statistics never lie, your
records say, especially when they pertain

to mangoes. How three mangoes
arranged on a plate in Poona resemble

a woman, a man, and something androgynous. How
they form into a goitered wishbone

lodged in the throat of a heart
patient in Des Moines, count the country

orange and add cholera to your list
of fears. But you needed the ride,

needed to sit, like you need to preserve
this young girl's face for the empty place

on your office wall back home. India *is*
the other side of the planet, your textbook

tells, yet you sense a sudden growth
in Indiana oak and maple, even here

beneath Poona palms, hear, that is, a eutrophic
lake enter your spine and engage itself

in reducing and dissolving oxygen in ways
which nourish the basalt content

in your blood. Your cells limp,

your heart limps, your nerves clear a moment

to euphonium, to the higher pitch
of wind whenever violet appears radiant

in the forehead of a slowed, persistent breath.
But you need her smile, require

how her left foot turns that way on its side
with the shyness of goldfish,

with the patience of a mantra
strung out all through the splay

of the day into japa. With the care
in unconsciously hiding dirt. You scrape

your brain to hear its rich cortextual
pulse, wish you could offer her something

real, something solid, like your hand
in marriage, or your wife, or maybe a ring

of bandits who would see her home
after the bank, or even an x ray, say,

of your lower lip, which clearly
demonstrates the saline content

of your affection. But one question always leads to
the lake. One solution is to dissolve

into the ants at your feet, bust
the borders mountains make

of space. One person's culture
for a stranger can harden into curds,

into love, into the black crusts
of usury spread like broken bread

beneath you. Into a drawing in
of breath over the history of maps.

through minnow-holes in your ribs, which,
as you stand there waiting, do nothing but snap.

A History of Green

Green is for growth, fatigue, Fort Wayne, Indiana
spring, the burgundy of a smoke tree
slosh against horse chestnut and oak.
The centipede's blood, that green, incursion of lust.
The dark Aegean loneliness of Nikos Gatsos
green. Cricket scratch tugging anemic green
before the rain-stoked sky. Spark-stacked might,
the lightning green of haloes of violet
at first bloom of the infant's crown at birth.
Banaras green of sunset ox-carts, that lull
in a monk's left foot mesmerizing Ganges River green.
The paleness of curds cut by lemon juice
from goat or water-buffalo milk. The sudden gash
of aged cheese, of sun-bit trees, of the hosta back home
bowing darkened with cloud-crowded May.
The Stilton green of dead English smells.
Colonized fruit stalls in Jammu
and Rangoon. Mung bean, yarrow green, bull-rush
and reed, the scent of her clarinet
breast through bamboo. The momentary green
of all the water in the world.
and how everyone is everybody else
in a freshly shaved underarm
as she reaches for a dish or cup.
The Saturn turn of complete nothingness,
and your tongue stands scars
where might a star. Green of the circus tent
telling the juggler *yes* or *no* or *maybe one day
so*. Not just three or four pears in the air
green. Not the torn planet of sliced avocado
seed green. Nor Nikos or, even, Gatsos green
but Lorca green. Trench-lip green. Willow smoke
of motorcycle skid, husky green Granada.
The momentary Gobi retracted green
of every desert in the whirl, even the year
1936 back-hoed below sumac

shade of 1963 Indiana green, of all things
in reverse. The way Franco green
throws away the key, retreats
to repeat itself in black,
in blue. Green wanting green
wanting green (yes, Miguel Hernandez green)
to fall its onion tentacle shade-shift
self all the way through the earth
as an echo of ferns reaching further
into most moist starlight. Fade back,
that is, to a great pulsing
galactic placenta green, before love
or color, touch or color, tongue or
color, a great ghost-got green
far away from dark sound light
sound tuberculous seed, from *this* and *that*,
yes and *no*, from, even,
maybe one day so.

(after Charles Wright's "Yellow")

Convent Burial Ground
Ferdinand, Southern Indiana

Drawn to the peace of these graves
I find no evidence of individual achievement.
A recent burial still bears spade work scars
but grass invisibly mends unraveled edges
of any tear in this seamless blanket.
Identical thumbs of granite, each
with its own whorl—name and dates
of birth and death—give the year in which
this sister committed her life to God.
Mist silence is disturbed only by
footsteps doubling back to linger a while.

Today in Illiana

March soybeans up three quarters. Chance of sun.
Over the russet eaves of sheds and houses
icicles the size of soldiers' arms threaten
our beds of dark wishes: tulip and hyacinth bulbs.
On the kitchen's black-and-white the same country
church has been burning down for the last week,
the same faces saying "Somehow we'll make it" while
bodiless hands unpack Bibles from blackened boxes.

Someone should say, "I'm out of here. See you
in June." And maybe I do, passing through
the county where the prayer has one more word,
the town where the only light in months has gone
in for the year, taking her needlework and old jokes.
Maybe I make a bright coast by dawn.

In these gray states men who have grown up alone
open plastic bags of soup beans while the years
create themselves again: bland, half-written histories.
They did not gather at clear rivers to sing the native hymn
but here are their apportioned lots, no less
covered than the next with January's infrangible loam.

Do they dream of the sycamore in Grandma's yard,
it's creamy arms just short of picture book heaven,
the hollyhock as tall as a sister riding her tricycle
across the lawn? In this heat, does the hair loosen
into wisps from its winter bristles or does the oven
deceive us with its promise of rest and roasted bird?

Today in Illiana, Michiana, Kentuckiana,
the casserole of holiday leftovers
that a woman in plaid holds up against
the local TV station's painted shocks
looks more than edible under its gilded
skin of melting cheese. Our lives are almost
as big as her teeth, stretched into starved
fields for us by the camera's faithful eye.

It is 6 a.m., when such sleepy voices should still be
whispering their promise of valleys and honey floods.
Here, the breakfast dishes have been cleared
and the sidewalks are shoveled of the night's
new snow. Windows crowd with forecasts,
the hope, at least, that weather will come again.

Central Avenue
[*On my thirtieth birthday*]
after Elizabeth Bishop

In late dawn at last the garish rush has passed.
Salt-splattered cars and vans lurch at yellows
and the street is dry, the sidewalks gritty as cat litter.
Remembered, rather than noticed,
the quiet avenue doesn't guide anything,
a map so thin the place names are rubbed out.
One can see the pavement fading; Frank O'Hara
would find in it the death of Lana Turner.
The carwash grunts waxing at the end of the block
already have their boom box tuned to breakneck soul.
Bare trees loom enormous. Old oaks obscure
the Kroger with its persistent, flickering bulbs,
making, it seems, a jittery haze
the customers barely notice as they go and go
dragging their carts of redundant provisions.
Gray-black ash and stunted locust line a path
the locals have beat
to a Coke machine that beckons night and day
or lights a midnight rendezvous in shadows.
Drab delivery trucks keep circling the lot
with the tired gestures of aging lovers,
hovering at the loading dock with promises
of Red Dog Beer or Red Gold Salsa.
Across the alley is a half-renovated duplex
where, for most of August, two shirtless men
pounded with hammers and buzzed with saws
in a rage of neighborhood prosperity.
A few empty spools for wire still stand in rows
under boarded windows, holding the house
precariously against its foundation, shoring up the loose ends
as though the crew would come back tomorrow.
Central Avenue is a frieze of bankrupt starts.
Hiss. Hiss. Run the cars
that scatter the last grimy mouthfuls of snow.
The business day begins to begin
awkward and promising.

Wanting, Again

Old Point Tavern, Indianapolis

On Thursdays, we believe the dream retrievable.
The evening ripples. The doormat takes our names
like pebbles from the grooves of our boots. Even
the padded stools gleam. We know not to worry:
that freckled waitress in her mottled apron
will not scribble down our sins no matter
how venal, how obvious our smiles.
In this thick realm, we're seducers and seduced.

At half-time on the bar's omnipresent tv,
a woman bares her shoulder for the roaring
fire and velvet draperies of her drawing room.
Not Julia in silk but 317-971-LOVE
anytime at competitive rates. "I'm waiting,"
the girl surely mouths to the oblivious
crowd, "I'm your dream," but the Village
People have the body in hand, the band
of down-dressed co-workers grinning
like criminals in the tavern's platinum fog.
Raphael's cherubs hover where a chalkboard
announces the daily special with fries.

Such a liquefaction the night makes of us:
a freight train passes like a whisper or prayer.
A man drops a quarter in the chrome box
of a phone and becomes his old line, a trail
of crimson footprints blossoming in a gutter.
The brow beaten beat on chairs with their open
palms, the joke told again with liquor's voice
that makes the morning an opposing continent.
And how the swaying table widens between us
glozened under its sticky scrim of foam.

Do you see what the street is saying
with its eye like chiseled bone?
How can the quiet boy win?

Now I've spilled my beer on the windowsill
under a sign that reads simply BEER.
Down the block, a fifth story apartment
flashes on, then off, then on again brighter,
the cellophane novel stuttering to begin.
And you're in a haze of faces, floating
again with the girl you were sure was balloons.

Could all the piped and bent neon in the nation
undo the knots this laughter ties, the wires
the rising chatter slides inside my skin?

From the angle the walls make with a receding sky
those stars I see could almost lift us up.

O, how that glittering takes me nowhere!

He Sees through Stone

He sees through stone
he has the secret
eyes this old black one
who under prison skies
sits pressed by the sun
against the western wall
his pipe between purple gums

the years fall
like overripe plums bursting red flesh
on the dark earth

his time is not my time
but I have known him
in a time gone

he led me trembling cold
into the dark forest
taught me the secret rites
to make it with a woman
to be true to my brothers
to make my spear drink
the blood of my enemies

now black cats circle him
flash white teeth
snarl at the air
mashing green grass beneath
shining muscles

ears peeling his words
he smiles
he knows
the hunt the enemy
he has the secret eyes
he sees through stone

The Idea of Ancestry

1

Taped to the wall of my cell are 47 pictures: 47 black
faces: my father, mother, grandmothers (1 dead), grand-
fathers (both dead), brothers, sisters, uncles, aunts,
cousins (1st & 2nd), nieces, and nephews. They stare
across the space at me sprawling on my bunk. I know
their dark eyes, they know mine. I know their style,
they know mine. I am all of them, they are all of me;
they are farmers, I am a thief, I am me, they are thee.

I have at one time or another been in love with my mother,
1 grandmother, 2 sisters, 2 aunts (1 went to the asylum),
and 5 cousins. I am now in love with a 7 yr old niece
(she sends me letters written in large block print, and
her picture is the only one that smiles at me).

I have the same name as 1 grandfather, 3 cousins, 3 nephews,
and 1 uncle. The uncle disappeared when he was 15, just took
off and caught a freight (they say). He's discussed each year
when the family has a reunion, he causes uneasiness in
the clan, he is an empty space. My father's mother, who is 93
and who keeps the Family Bible with everybody's birth dates
(and death dates) in it, always mentions him. There is no
place in her Bible for "whereabouts unknown."

2

Each fall the graves of my grandfathers call me, the brown
hills and red gullies of mississippi send out their electric
messages, galvanizing my genes. Last yr / like a salmon quitting
the cold ocean-leaping and bucking up his birthstream / I
hitchhiked my way from L.A. with 16 caps in my pocket and a
monkey on my back. And I almost kicked it with the kinfolks.
I walked barefooted in my grandmother's backyard / I smelled the
    old
land and the woods / I sipped cornwhiskey from fruit jars with the
    men /

I flirted with the women / I had a ball till the caps ran out
and my habit came down. That night I looked at my grandmother
and split / my guts were screaming for junk / but I was almost
contented / I had almost caught up with me.
(The next day in Memphis I cracked a croaker's crib for a fix).

This yr there is a gray stone wall damming my stream, and when
the falling leaves stir my genes, I pace my cell or flop on my bunk
and stare at 47 black faces across the space. I am all of them,
they are all of me, I am me, they are thee, and I have no children
to float in the space between.

Hard Rock Returns to Prison from the Hospital for the Criminal Insane

Hard Rock / was / "known not to take no shit
from nobody," and he had the scars to prove it:
Split purple lips, lumbed ears, welts above
His yellow eyes, and one long scar that cut
Across his temple and plowed through a thick
Canopy of kinky hair.

The WORD / was / that Hard Rock wasn't a mean nigger
Anymore, that the doctors had bored a hole in his head,
Cut out part of his brain, and shot electricity
Through the rest. When they brought Hard Rock back,
Handcuffed and chained, he was turned loose,
Like a freshly gelded stallion, to try his new status.
And we all waited and watched, like a herd of sheep,
To see if the WORD was true.

As we waited we wrapped ourselves in the cloak
Of his exploits: "Man, the last time, it took eight
Screws to put him in the Hole." "Yeah, remember when he
Smacked the captain with his dinner tray?" "He set
The record for time in the Hole — 67 straight days!"
"Ol Hard Rock! man, that's one crazy nigger."
And then the jewel of a myth that Hard Rock had once bit
A screw on the thumb and poisoned him with syphilitic spit.

The testing came, to see if Hard Rock was really tame.
A hillbilly called him a black son of a bitch
And didn't lose his teeth, a screw who knew Hard Rock
From before shook him down and barked in his face.
And Hard Rock did *nothing*. Just grinned and looked silly,
His eyes empty like knot holes in a fence.

And even after we discovered that it took Hard Rock
Exactly 3 minutes to tell you his first name,
We told ourselves that he had just wised up,
Was being cool; but we could not fool ourselves for long,
And we turned away, our eyes on the ground. Crushed.
He had been our Destroyer, the doer of things
We dreamed of doing but could not bring ourselves to do,
The fears of years, like a biting whip,
Had cut deep bloody grooves
Across our backs

Birthday Poem

The sun rose today, and
The sun went down
Over the trees beyond the river;
No crashing thunder
Nor jagged lightning
Flashed my forty-four years across
The heavens. I am here.
I am alone. With the Indianapolis / News

Sitting, under this indiana sky
I lean against a gravestone and feel
The warm wine on my tongue.
My eyes move along the corridors
Of the stars, searching
For a sign, for a certainty

As definite as the cold concrete
Pressing against my back.
Still the stars mock
Me and the moon is my judge.

But only the moon.

'Cause I ain't screwed no thumbs
Nor dropped no bombs—
Tho my name is naughty to the ears of some
And I ain't revealed the secrets of my brothers
Tho my balls've / been pinched
And my back's / been / scarred—

And I ain't never stopped loving no / one
O I never stopped loving no / one.

Indianapolis, Indiana
April 19, 1975

The Deck

I have almost nailed my left thumb to the 2 x 4 brace that holds the deck together. This Saturday morning in June, I have sawed 2 x 6s, T-squared and levelled everything with three bubbles sealed in green glass, and now the sweat on my tongue tastes like what I am. I know I'm alone, using leverage to swing the long boards into place, but at times it seems as if there are two of us working side by side like old lovers guessing each others moves.

This hammer is the only thing I own of yours, and it makes me feel I have carpentered for years. Even the crooked nails arc going in straight. The handsaw glides through grease. The toenailed stubs hold. The deck has risen up around me, and now it's strong enough to support my weight, to not sway with this old, silly, wrong-footed dance I'm about to throw my whole body into.

Plumbed from sky to ground, this morning's work can take nearly anything! With so much uproar and punishment, footwork and euphoria, I'm almost happy this Saturday.

I walk back inside and here you are. Plain and simple as the sunlight on the tools outside. Daddy, if you'd come back a week ago, or day before yesterday, I would have been ready to sit down and have a long talk with you. There were things I wanted to say. So many questions I wanted to ask, but now they've been answered with as much salt and truth as we can expect from the living.

The Poplars

Half in Monet's colors, headlong into this light, like someone lost along Daedalus' footpath winding back into the brain, hardly here. Doubts swarm like birds around a scarecrow—straw pulled from underneath a work cap.

Church bells alloy the midwest sky. How many troubled feet walked this path smooth? Is it safe to go back to Chu Lai? She's brought me halfway home again, away from the head floating down into my out-stretched hands.

I step off the path, sinking into one-hundred-years of leaves. Like trapped deer, we face each other. Her hand in his. His blue eyes. Her Vietnamese face. Am I a ghost dreaming myself back to flesh?

I stand in the skin's prison. A bluejay squawks till its ragged song pulls me out into the day burning like a vaporous temple of joss sticks. June roses in beds of mulch and peat moss surround me. I hear her nervous laughter at my back, among the poplars.

I can't hear my footsteps. I stop, turn and gaze at the lovers against an insistent green like stained glass. I walk toward a car parked near the church. Birds sing and flit in the raucous light. I hear the car's automatic locks click, sliding like bullets into the chamber of a gun.

On Third Street, the morning's alive with coeds hurrying into the clangor of bells, Saturday night asleep beneath their skin. Flowers herd them toward Jesus—cutworms on the leaves, at the roots.

Surgery

Every spring, sure as the dogwood's clockwork, someone hacksaws off Odysseus' penis. And it lies dumbly at his feet, a doorknocker to a limestone castle, the fountain straying out a Medusa halo. In this watery mist, with a contrary sunlight glinting the bronze, there's only an outline of Eumaeus handing a quiver of arrows and a bow to him. Rivulets of water make the penis tremble, as if it were the final, half-alive offering to the gods.

Fifty yards past the fountain, on the other side of the quad, I step among lotus-eaters sunning in each other's arms. Mockingbirds and jays squabble overhead, dive-bombing Dutch elms. This unholy racket doesn't phase sunbathers and tree surgeons. As if they're fathering their destruction, branches fall into a pile, and the workmen pack beetle-eaten crevices with a white medicine, something like mortar—whiter than flesh.

I stop beneath an elm and clutch a half-dead branch. Momentarily, there's an old silence thick as memory. Claymores pop. Rifles and mortars answer, and then that silence again, as the slow light of tripflares drifts like a thousand falling handkerchiefs, lighting the concertina woven with arms and legs of sappers. Flares tied to little parachutes like magnolia blooming in the wounded air.

The sunbathers retreat into their abodes and the workmen feed the last branches into a big orange machine. The fountain's drained, and a man kneels before Odysseus. He holds the penis in one hand and a soldering torch in the other, his face hidden behind a black hood, beading a silver seam perfect enough to mend anyone's dream.

Crow Lingo

Can you be up to any good
Grouped into a shadow against Venus,
Congregated on power lines around
The edges of cornfields?

Luck. Curse. A wedding.
Death. I have seen you peck
Pomegranates & then cawcawcaw
Till hornets rise from purple flesh

& juice. I know you're plotting
An overthrow of the government
Of sparrows & jays, as the high council
Of golden orioles shiver among maple

& cottonwood. Your language
Of passwords has no songs,
No redemption in wet feathers
Slicked back, a crook's iridescent hair.

Mud

She works in the corner of the porch
Where a trumpet vine crawls up to falling
Light. There's always some solitary
Bridge to cross. Right hand

& left hand. The dirt dauber
Shapes a divided cell
Out of everything she knows,
Back and forth between the ditch.

I could take a stick and play
God. Soldier. Sadist. Nosing
Mud into place, she hums the world's
Smallest motor. Later, each larva

Quivers like bait on a hook . . . spermatozoa
Cloistered in a song of clay. So small
Only the insignificance can begin
To fill the afternoon.

The Robin's Egg

In soft grass underneath the pine
the egg is perfect, smooth and dry—
intact, uncracked, silent, still,
pale blue as Easter morning sky.
Hidden inside: clear morning songs,
a quick-cocked head, bright black eyes,
a jaunty bounce across the lawn,
twilight murmurs in tree leaves.
Like my own child's first child, the bird
inside, all wrapped in newborn blue—
that tender, terrible hue
of yarn, shawl, shroud—

Daughter, I bring this egg to you—
another life we never knew.

Raspberry Gathering

Blood runs a red current
between us, we know
what we know without saying.
Each of us keeps her own secret,
a seed in its silent red cell.

My sister will never admit
to a lover, nor will I discuss
my husband's other woman,
and our mother won't even try to explain
what became of her father
who disappeared
when she was twelve.

Today, we'd rather pick raspberries,
and so the three of us go
to the raspberry farm,
where children run in sun and wind
just as we once did,
climbing the hill behind our house
where raspberries grew wild.
We filled tin pans, filled our mouths,
laughed when juice ran down our chins —

Now another summer's ripe
raspberries fall, all afternoon,
into our hands, and finally, we taste
warm fruit, clustered together
at a wooden table, touching
each other's fingers,
eating berries from one basket.
After decades of pulling
apart, we're together—
mis-shapen fruit, but whole.

I do not have to ask the others
if they feel as ripe in the sun as I;
if they taste the richness,
in this moment; if they sense
our final folding in of petals
before the blossom drops.

Barbara Koons

A Face of Winter

black coat
black hat
black scarf
black boots

he is a beauty mark
climbing the white hill

what if
you knew him
eyes, beard
and hair
black, black
and black

the sky that was blue all morning
has gone milky all afternoon

now the milk darkens

in snowladen pines
a red bird flickers
and goes out

the man has gone over

but the hill
a white beauty mark
climbs the black sky

Etheridge

At two a.m. a darkness
like a lion walks the shadows
between streetlights down
in Naptown.

Around the dusty trees
and rotted buildings
street light flows like
scars on the face
of a Mississippi poet

gone to North Korea
and back (or part way).
Talked his way out
of more than one hell
(or part way) rhyming
Naptown shadows
with the Delta sun.

True to the rhythm
of an inner drum,
purple-gummed, each year
he's won the Nobel
Prize for Peace and War
against himself, horse
dealers, jailers, black and
white hairsplitters and
bullshitters. Those scars

are stars that tell you
where he's been
with his love, coals
glowing in the cornered towns
and penitentiary nights.

Still he can't wear a poem
like a new pair of overalls.
A poem doesn't scare a Hoosier
cracker or those monkeys
jumping on and off his back.

But tonight there's po-cash
in his pocket and his mama
lives just up that street
from where he's climbed
out of a college car

at two a.m., a darkness
like a lion walking
up the paved and curbed
and guttered night.

In Such a Light

If you walked naked over the meadow . . .
        Donald W. Baker

The boast of sunlight, dancing on the watery diamonds
the moon left strung around the barn and up
the wagon road, flashed me a dare to take the poet
at his word, and I remembered how a boy crowed
from the highest branches of the tallest oak
in Indiana, once upon a time, then rocked the limb
in wildly supple arc and laughed at double-daring
friends left stranded in the shade below. His eyes
blazed wide as any summer day.

                                That challenge met,
day-dreamed again now challenged all the more. What
could I do, but drop the guise of being civilized
and step out of the safety of dark woods? I've rambled
half the way across this ancient bowl of birds
and mice, to stand here in the center of it all—
feet soothed by moss and lapped by linen grass,
legs wrapped in webs where brambles scrawled red
signatures, couch grass and foxtail tickling toward
my thighs. A cool breeze whispers of the usefulness
of loin cloth, but my chest takes to the sun
like armor and my back recalls Tecumseh's pride,
tossing his head, acknowledging his kinship
with the sky. If any neighbor boys are watching
from the woods, I hope they see my antlers
point the five directions of the eagle fathers' way.

That dreaming boy, one summer, took himself to task
to cure his fear of spiders—red and yellow lumps
with hairy legs, and fangs. While hunting them
through fields and catching them with jar and lid,
his hands so close, he calmed himself by learning
to respect their fears, and praise the able beauty
of their fatal needs.

Tom Koontz   **133**

Then, walking home, he'd talk
to cardinals, whistling with the male's fierce
flame. One day he came upon a pair of king snakes
on a sunny bank, ecstatic in the doubling and
redoubling ring of their embrace. Then standing
motionless, the long while that the sun passed by
and they were all themselves, he honored them
for parenthood. Each day he raised his hand
to give the war chief s signal to the meadowlarks,
repeating the sure sign they carried on their breast
that all is for the good. And though he could not
see an end, he knew it is the end that counts
and dreamed he lent himself to be a means.

He ran the golden path and leaped from day
to day, like Thoreau on the hummocks under Merlin's
acrobatic flight. If this were Walden, in this
morning light, I'd leap from hut to pond, from shore
to shore. I'd leap from dawn to dusk and back.

More likely, I'll have chiggers on my balls tonight.
That is their way. And, hell, it is their right.
They shine in golden nature too. Their bite
is Buddha's bite. All things must live, in such a light.

From the *Indianapolis City Directory*, 1916: A Tally

Only one war memorial, two full pages of labor unions:
    Asbestos Workers of the World, Federation of Locomotive Engineers,
    the Musicians' Protective Association, and International Brotherhood
    of Book Binders

Fifty-two secret societies: the Odd Fellows, Order of Owl,
    Tribe of Ben-Hur, Masonic Temple (colored), Sisters
    of the Mysterious Tent (colored), Woodmen of the World,
    and the Improved Order of Red Men

Both a Prohibition Commission and two socialist parties,
    a Vacant Lots Cultivation Society
    and the Deutscher Klub und Musik Verein, Kurt Vonnegut, President

Schools included No. 3 Mary Turner Free Kindergarten (colored)
    and The Brooks Preparatory Academy for Boys,
    adjacent to the Home for Working Girls

An advertisement on every page:
    Fresh Beef, Veal, Mutton, and Pork,
    Indianapolis Abattoir Company
    Endorsed by the Butchers Ladies Society

    Brevort Hotel, European Throughout,
    Rooms with Bath, $1.00 and Up

    Glide Bicycles, California Disappearing Bed Co.,
    Beatrice Du Valle, Lady Chiropractor

    Terre Haute Beer We deliver to all parts of the city
    Try our Champagne Velvet, an ideal table beverage,
    or Radium, our effervescent, popular brand of the future

Miss Victory (1895)
Monument Circle, Indianapolis

You can't fool us, Miss Victory, queening it
over the roofs of this city, one hip swishing
toward the long sword you cock
like a walking-stick between your calves.

Girlfriend, who welded that eagle to your scalp
and posed you with the liberty torch
like some bridesmaid's lucky catch?
Miss Victory, why you're a certified virgin of war.

Your waist isn't wasp, there's no rumble-seat
festooning your behind. In the lingo of the parlor,
not the brawl, you remind us how we pussywhipped
the South. Are you trying to start something?

Your pectorals are rippling through your dress
and you've squared your Julius Caesar jaw.
To those shoppers down below
you're just a mannequin of camp.

No blood stipples your bronze bodice,
the polished cones of your breasts. Truth is,
you make war a costume drama, a tease,
your left hand flaming, the other hugging the hilt.

Return of the Prodigal

Old upright piano, she says, I'm home.
I'm home, shellacked bass, flying
above us on your plywood plaque. I'm home,

sloping floors tacked with red carpet
Oh Matisse, if you had been born a Hoosier
perhaps you would have lived in this

shotgun house, you would have loved
the flocked wallpaper and extravagant
cats. I am home, weeds up to the knees,

little crescent of boat in the swamp
outback, silver cloud of mosquitoes!
Old Blue, you half blind mutt with ticks

like bloated berries in your ears—
can you hear? It's me, I'm home.
And I'm here for you, daughter,

my poison bundle of calamine and Tiger Balm,
and you, my bearded husband,
my sullen bird dog, my hunter

with the golden eyes: your prized
Canada has returned Stroke the quilted
nap of her feathers, and take good aim.

Elizabeth Krajeck ❧

A Considerable Consciousness—Shell Station at 49th & Pennsylvania

Although Tim is the detail man on Hamaker Corner, it is easy to lose track of the cars in his life. He describes bruises, hazards, accidents and falling in with the Ohio River monster—also known as the Indiana alcoholic rat ravine. Originally from Columbus, the carburetor gods in Indiana rescued him. Memory follows the road to Indianapolis but at the end of I-70 West, the words stop. He shifts into neutral, pauses and the meaning of his universe comes into consciousness. I take notes. A writer knows a sentence can tell only so much truth. At the end of the sentence, only at the end—I grasp what he tells me. I am grateful. He tests the brakes. Tim stopped drinking when he ran out of gas. Writing in a careful orderly manner is one way of listening. Doors to the shops along this street open and close on faltering conversations. The flowers, tools and medicines for sale are both familiar and fascinating. I learn that as long as he is sober, he is the most blessed man on the corner. As long as he is blessed—he is alive. He tells me that every minute he is alive is a universe. In the right-hand wing mirror, he sees a fresh field. He is busy. The fuel-warning light is on. Those are the details of life on this corner.

The Piankashaw in the Sycamore

Somewhere I once read
that after the first Europeans
arrived in what has come to be
known as southern Indiana,
from Kentucky or Virginia,
an Indian was observed stretched
out on a big branch of a tree,
perhaps an ivory sycamore,
that hung out over the waters
of a bend in the Patoka River.

This was some time after
the Piankashaw had left
the area behind. Something
must have been terribly wrong,
the author implied, for this
man to return to the area
where he was born and make
himself so vulnerable.

What could have happened,
the author wanted to know,
to make the man risk his life
just to crawl up the trunk of that
ancient tree and stretch himself
out on a branch that dangled
over the waters of a river that
had flowed through the middle
of the life of his people for who
knows how many generations?

What could have happened
on or near that site to pull
the man back? Was it memory
of his people and their history
tied to that spot that made
him return and lie down
so high above the ground
above the flowing sacred waters
and spirits he knew remained?

Had he returned to pay tribute
to the unmarked grave of a relative,
gather medicinal herbs, and perhaps
offer tobacco to Lennipeshewa,
man panther who dwelt in the depths?

Was he given over to the power
of spirits connected with this tree
and the bend in the river where
he and his clan had fished
when he was a boy?

Had he lost the desire to live
in some other place he knew
was separated from the spirit
of those who had come before?

Was he preparing to enter
the spirit world in which
those who had once lived here
would welcome him there?

To Obscure Men

This is a belated letter
to lonely old men like
the uncle who taught us
how to hunt, the neighbor
who took us on our first
camping trip, or the friend
of our father who organized
the excursion to our first
big-league ball game
in Cincinnati or St. Louis.
This is an inadequate,
belated letter to old men
everywhere who, after we
grew up, moved away from
the town, and never wrote
back, sustained themselves
for a few years on bitter-
sweet memories of laboring
in factories, sweating on
county road gangs, or working
the earth on hand-me-down
farms.　.　.　. A long overdue,
unsuccessful letter to
unhappy old men who withered
away in parlors, hanged
themselves from two-by-four
rafters in garages, or shot
themselves in smokehouses
with the twelve gauges
they'd hunted with for fifty-
five years.　.　.　. An impossibly
late but nevertheless contrite
letter from those of us
who have just grown old
enough to begin to remember.

Sisters

for Mary

My first sister
was born without
ever drawing a
breath. I heard
my mother cry
and my grandmother
scold her upstairs.

When my second
sister began to cry,
my mother breathed
a lot easier. My
grandmother smiled.
The dolls we kept
clapped their hands.

Gary, 1961

Years ago, in 1961, we saw them—
my cousin Leroy and me,
boys in the grit and soot of Gary, Indiana,
watched a wedge of Canada geese
cut the air above the toxic dust
that settled from the steel mills
to coat trees,
swing sets
and clotheslines
in my Uncle's backyard.

You could see Gary all the way from Demotte back then,
and smell it all the way from Crown Point.
You could see the orange cloud the steel mills made
billowing like an angry genii
granting the wishes of industrialists
for wealth and power
but spitefully scattering acid
on the ground below
as ribbons of steel ran
and the furnaces created poisonous salamanders
who burrowed down into the soil
and thrashed in the waters of Lake Michigan.

He and I were enraptured
watching the perfect wedge of birds cut
the clear air up above,
geese honking,
going north to cleaner nesting grounds,
rolling their wings slowly
above the patch of foulness
where we stood,
our feet soaking up the death
of PCBs and sulfur dioxide,

gums bleeding from heavy metals
noses constricted and lungs aching
from coal and lime
filtering, silent as death,
into our blood.

Leroy's dad, my father's brother,
died of lung cancer
even though he retired to a
warm clean-air refuge in Arkansas.
Leroy's wife would kill him with a gun
years later
during some drunken, pointless lover's quarrel.
The mills in Gary are shut down now,
the air even a little cleaner
than it was back then:
no more orange clouds
or pollutants that would dissolve
my Aunt Geri's nylons if she hung them
outside to dry.
I wonder if the geese have found another route
or if they still cut their way
in the shape of a sideways V
up above it all,
above the sin and pollution,
up where everything is colder but clearer,
where human folly is only a smudge
on the landscape far below.
And I wonder if boys still stop
and gaze up at them
and marvel at their airy symmetry.

For the Love of Gerald Finzi

Spider Mums

Not these, I think, stroking
with my forefinger the outermost petals
of the individual I have selected, I think: *Not these splayed
phalanges,*

*cream and smooth, first out, now
farthest apart, sculptural* . . . Rather, it's the
innermost petals that intrigue me, those in the formative stages:
something in

the way they minutely
grip, curl, they're preparing for something later,
they're enduring the tension, the desire to do something, somehow make
the part that

feels the desire obtrude:
a young girl in her skirts squats to pet the cat
who lies on his side for her, a kind of girl: lonely, adult. Often
I address

figures I feel close to,
sketching under titles like "Girl in Full Skirt,
With Cat," addressing in the second person feelings I know: "You wish
your legs were

stems of such slenderness,
you could twine them together, tighter, tighter,
tight almost to the bursting point, tight as silk cord twisted into fringe
for velvet

cushions, or draperies
like those at "Grand-maman's." *Something needs to squeeze*
or be squeezed to extinction, doesn't it . . . [I name her] *Julie?* She says:
Yes! And, and

"it's nothing to do with
my talented mother or with my mother's
talented menfriends, nothing to do with my pastel chalks, or with my
violin

either!" "No," I confirm,
"it's wholly outside those things, but it's something
to do, to do with gripping/squeezing/pleasure/pain, like talented men,
like the chalks

themselves, like the very
paper, whether cream and toothy, or slick and white
to sooth the sharpest pencil, like the rending violin itself." Still
chartreuse, these

Not-yet-tendril-like . . . I
ply them, these inward petals, with my left thumb
away from the center's minuscule round yellow rug, I feel their urge
to go right

back where they were, so tight,
so inside-gripping. But I could tell them what
they better face: even the most secret vulnerability is
obvious.

Riddle

Tending to squatness,
                    my bottom is broad.
On top I offer
                his hand a curve.
Both flat and round,
                    I spread heat,
marry what he draws
                    with what he breathes.
Curious, he lifts
                the part that covers
my opening, his fingertips
                    encircle its knob.
He picks his time
                by his own thirst
but too, by the sound
                    I make losing pressure:
then doth he grasp me
                up altogether and pour.

the crime wave of nineteen fifty-eight

out back of Woodlawn Avenue, where a creek ran through
and crawdads darted in watery shade
in the cicada-steeped summer of 1958
a gang of Hoosier schoolboys
made tunnels through prickly brush
and built ourselves a weedy warren empire

we took turns trekking
with scraped-up pennies, nickels, dimes
to the comer store
where oiled floorboards creaked under lazy fans
pop bottles clinked in a cold bath
and pickle loaf and head cheese languished in a case
flattered close to edibility by the dim light

for our parents, we said,
we bought Winstons, Kools, and Swisher Sweet cigars
for ourselves, we said,
we bought Baby Ruths, pork rinds, peach fried pies
then sauntered out the door, cool as cucumbers
and hustled back, hearts pounding
to our waterfront den of iniquity and ease
to munch and puff the day away—
an orgy of chocolate, lard, and nicotine

a foraging member of the tribe
filched someone's special magazines
from under a porch on fourteenth street

their pages, mildewed, carefully peeled
revealing worlds of mythic wonder
like postcards from El Dorado
and with guidance from the older boys
we shucked our jeans and learned to tingle

for weeks our blissful spree raged on
and then, a whisper of doom:
"No tobacco without a note from your mother."

we pow-wowed posthaste
and settling on pre-emption, cleaned house
and invited Roger's Mom
—the coolest, all agreed—to visit Shangri-La,
and see that all was well
in the Land of Innocent Children

she came, said little, and days later
a bush hog and a John Deere devoured our domain
driving us out of Eden
into the pitiless shadow of September
and the tragedy of lives that peaked too soon

Michael List

Site Report

Burials 20 and 21/W-ll-A
"... the secondary burial between
the legs ... lightly burned
after deposit."

Predominant skeletal structure.
fully on the back
facing
upwards.

Arms and legs recognizable, assembled
vaguely. But from femur
to ulna, each full-boned
limb bent

into deliberate angles,
arms right triangles
from the crushed rib cage.

Bleached phalanges
splayed
near his hip:
one undisturbed hand bleached and visible.
The adult, Mississippian
male. Oriented Northeast.
Unremarkable save

the woman, somehow dead and de-fleshed
into a funerary bundle, the cloth
sack of her
lightly burned
and buried
between the diamond
of his legs.

Yet the carbon isotopes of her bones
and teeth ground
flat demonstrate
a different diet:
hickory nuts, deer dropped down
with spears in autumn
territories

much farther north.
   Not *Zea maize*
   of this Midwest village
   agriculture taken

in her mouth as a girl. Not cultivated
   green stalks
   stretching in fields
   to litter her childhood

   periphery.

   To be cautious
   with this story,
   make notes of
its deltoid-shaped points and unperforated
   pottery discs,
   its evidence,
   its beads.

   Wild bamboo,
   may grass,
   duckfoot
if she had ventured beyond the village
   wall. Near the river,
   touch-me-nots,
   even then.

   The sky
   glimpsed
   through willow
and cottonwood so like
   her own sky.
   Did water lapping
   at the bank's edge sound
a dialect she could answer? She was forty years

elsewhere, some suspect. Yet if her pelvis
   can't name children,
   her jaw
   has forgotten

   tongues.

Voodoo Meat

*Question asked by bioanthropologist friend at public
reading: Should you have told the audience that this
is a true story?*

*Answer given by poet: But should I have told them it is
equally invented?*

A shaman lives outside
town whose mansion shines
like coin. He's on the veranda
pinky-sipping espresso
chatting with his women
while an ensanguined NY broker
wanders naked in a nearby field,
because arteries showered him
when cut, the twitching neck held
just so, and blood in the sun smells
of an iron you can't get
in the city. Mr. Shaman is cool
and purifies for a fee. He fans himself
in the shade (because his white
skin burns), manicured fingers decked
in rings. Mr. Voodoo-
Man remarks on their client's tongue
that rested thickly in his mouth
like an eel. His watch face glints
that Rex's truck should dust up
the property line soon
because months earlier
when the answering service
said an archaeologist needed 100 jaws
for a study, he could be generous, thinking
fewer carcasses for the women
to bale: *Sometimes*
as many as four sacrifices
a day Weekends only. Often goats.
but sometimes sheep. Always
young. The meat

is good, not stringy, not gristled.
like you'd think. We will serve it to our friends
as a wedding feast. Have summer dinner
parties on it; anthropologists
will leave our nighttime, wind-down house
with one haunch each. ("No scape goats,
please.") And we will guffaw with them
over beers more than once this story
of counterfeit sacrifice-because
how else could Mr. Voodoo-Man's
Indiana estate get so rambling and so fine?
But when the calls come,
I know what I will be directed
not to see: the ornament
of stripped flesh tied by hooves visible
through the ajar outbuilding door.
Intestines Rex lifts out, heavy
and precarious, those marbled
sacks of waste. His bloody saw
rattling out its sound through bone

She Hardly Ever Says a Word

Weakness has no lilt, really. No fainting
spells. No housebroken eclipse. No wild sighs
into handkerchiefs. A baby sprawled open
all plush & nap-fattened: his strength
comes through like teeth. *Quietly.* These rooms
are asleep, the pipes not speaking, water
rests in their elbows. *Silently.* (She pins up
her hair-fanatical crown of pentecostal
cursive-& wields her unsung tongue
over underbite: 30 crooked birds
perched in a shut place. They sing only
of things too fragile to hold in your pocket.)

Crooked County (At the Bluebird with You)

Belly to the back of her double bass, 7 months
pregnant & hot as hell—swat, pluck, wail

& make me jealous. I want to be that baby.

Old Slew Foot, Jr. I want to be borne of that
bass-belly into this tavern smoke & tied by her

mean strings. And you, you sit behind me: you

& your shit-eating grin & your tapping foot &
your dare whispered into my ear to write a poem

of all things before I pass out tonight drunk

& over-toked at 4 a.m. when the rest of the world
is usually chasing me out of their dirty chat rooms.

You point out the girl who gave you something

you can't get rid of. She sways shyly to a cocaine stomp.
I used to be jealous but all I worry about now is your bike

outside without a lock. On stage the baby kicks & I

cross a bridge to momma's sloping shoulder. Her
fingers sting & she sings about falling into rings of fire.

Buddy, you got to know I want you but I'd trade you

in half a shot to have that whiskey voice, *big around
the middle & broad across the rump.* Looks a lot like me.

A. Loudermilk   **155**

Thinking of War on a Spring Day

Redbud stars tree-dance
in the April wind. In Faluja
a mob drags the bodies of dead
Americans through the streets
before hanging
two charred corpses from a bridge.
I don't believe in heaven. I hope
they do, both occupiers
and occupied.

Outside, my deck brims
with the wind-tossed sleeves
of hundreds of magnolia
blossoms. Some pink, some
white, some rust-stained, the color
of dried blood. If I could sew
them together, I could make
a silk train to Paradise, if Paradise
were other than the erratic
flight path of this cardinal
as it darts between crimson bud
and burgeoning purple flower.

A Swarm of Shadow

Illness came, though we could not
see it that spring, through the trees
with their green palms opened.

Could not hear the letters of your name,
chewed on and spit out as far thunder;
nor imagine that familiar rumble would

come back to haunt us as particular
and forewarning. It did not seem that
you could be so singled out from all of us,

row on row of other choices. That spring
we could not see beyond the promise of
the yearly change, the year unmasked

as sorrow. A swarm of shadow
moving across the moist fields towards us,
with its steady eye of purpose on you.

Cornucopia

To have the autumn afternoon
sun split the thinning pin oaks
with angled light, and the wafer
thin air, and a sweater you forgot
for an entire year, like a newfound
broken-in second skin,
and a Saturday unlike an other
day of the week, and your brother
still alive, sitting at your kitchen table,
talking about his nearly grown son,
and your own daughters moving on.

Swimming with the Old Broads

We've met at the pool for years
without knowing much, only

that water is a room we love, and movement
a sleek and slippery pleasure.

Going back, there were stronger strokes
and less use of the ladder, in and out.

But now is now and the pool stand ready,
so we move towards what we crave.

Afterwards, we steam up the shower room,
and a young one wanders in, drawn to the herd.

The Doctrine of an Axe

Of all times, now is not the time,
given the world's old vague condition,

to hang in my mind the plumb-bob weight
of original sin and watch it twist

around like a tire at the end of a rope
looped over a tree branch. Once

my sister came within a hair
of getting bit by a snake asleep

in the tire she'd hooped around herself.
She was wearing a dress, my friend, just home

from church; her patent leather shoes
kicked at the air just twice before

she shed the tire and screamed. I chopped
the copperhead to pieces. What kind

of parents allow their child to play
with an axe? Well, mine, I suppose. I made

them proud that day. The sin was how
I let myself be proud, a pride

that wore like whitewash from a fence.
Now you might think I'm being stern

and unforgiving. After all,
I was only six and could not have known

about sin. But I did; I knew it like
a nursery rhyme, or the Now I Lay Me

bedtime prayer. I once got drunk
on a Sunday morning; I don't know

if that was sinful, but it proved
that nothingness is absolute,

a naked shameful nothing left
beneath the shade tree in my heart,

the rusted axehead long since stuck
and buried in its trunk, a bone

caught in its living throat, a wound
I made in its side and can't undo.

We should both be doing something good;
we should be kind to someone now.

A Psalm to Bring Remembrance

I had a friend when I was little;
he went to a different school because

he was a little slow. He lived
with a giant man and woman who weren't

his parents, and six or seven more
he called his sisters and brothers. He had

a dog named Sister. We played in the woods
and tinkered on our bicycles.

One day, an older girl took off
her shirt and told us we could touch.

He did. He waved his hands around
as if he were trying to catch a bird.

The older girl was a Catholic,
I believe; her name was Mary; I

was a Presbyterian, and he
was nothing. Another day, we broke

a woman's window with a rock.
He got the tar whipped out of him.

I mowed the banjo player's yard
all summer to pay my share. You God

up there who saw it all, I hope
his life got better, but I doubt

it did. If he is dead by now,
I hope he's resting in your bosom.

Do not be slow. Remember he was poor
and needy, more than me.

This Close and No Further

In a canoe one afternoon we drifted across the flat
    reflection of a false lake that filled the trees beneath it
with green light and sun a broad lane under our keel
    trembling forward with the ripples that led in small
steps across the whole fetch unhurried silver pebbles
    laced with soaked weeds marked the shoreline
ragged with brush and gulleys on the north side
    while to the west the land lay back in an estuary
of winter-broken rocks on sand mounds scuffed by early
    summer growth already gold among broken blackthorn
sticks it was a place of rough edges of slow
    accumulation behind an unseen dam the point of the gathering
water lifted the surface in silence year by year until
    what was distant became what had been
all at once close to the bank our canoe turned gently
    into the shallows stepped a doe her hide held
a scattering of scars drawn along her withers in tan
    dashes lighter than her rich brown coat that
flexed over her well-fed body and she lifted her head watchful
    of us our blunt upright trunks our strange craft pointed
toward her she snorted ducking her head and
    waited we were still the canoe wavered forward the doe
stomped twice once with each forehoof the sounds syllables of
    wet mud the deer beautiful as determination we tilted
our paddles on each side to begin to take a stroke to back
    away turning as the wind caught our shoulders and the
blades of the paddles as we leaned both off-balance and flipped
       into the water its warm chill skin smelling of mineral
earth its light of ochre glass and its fingers ruffling scalp hair
    curiously in slow movements for a moment before the air
broke in again and we stood it was shallow the deer was
    gone and we began to gather what was floating around us

Withdrawal

—for Rik

The middle-class truth has begun:
rehab mantras are chump change
compared to H's smooth nod.
The result this time is mom's new
car, bent into a fist in the middle
of I-465. *I blacked out*, as you
stutter up cold steps to the house.
The snow is proof April
is unforgiving, junkies and clucks
breeding from Indianapolis concrete.
Transformation has begun:
middle class to middle of a needle
and spoon nightmare. All mom's
suspicions spread, collectable
saltshakers on the breakfast bar.
The kick took mom kicking
you out of the house. Two weeks
spasming. Some dry heaves.
A week's construction work
in Nebraska that made Indianapolis
seem like a birthday party.
After, you wanted a motorcycle
more than heroine, a free-wheeling
ride to Florida. The kid who
never learned to ride a bicycle
because training wheels weren't
cool, balancing 130 horsepower.
Indiana spring or Florida humidity,
a junkie is still a junkie.

Divine Order
—Jazz Kitchen, 1996

In Indiana, improvisation is using
a balled-up t-shirt as a basketball,
so jazz has no love for the Circle City.

Or maybe it's the other way around—
a downtown with high-rises
as spare as fingers doesn't need

half notes or quarter tones,
even if J.J. Johnson and Wes
Montgomery learned what music

can be while living in the state capital.
There they were, a couple of kids
with orange push-ups and loaner

instruments, sweating in the Indiana
heat that sits immovable, like a trombone
case on the long walk from school.

There they were, on Martin Luther
King, Jr. Boulevard before MLK
had streets named after him.

They had to find that music somewhere
in this town. Jazz has no love
for Indianapolis, but one night, Terence

Blanchard played the Jazz Kitchen—
the one all-jazz venue left in the city.
After introductions, Terence

walked on stage, hankerchiefing
his trumpet as if a horn with more shine
could muffle the cheers from Hinkle

Fieldhouse a few blocks away.
The music has got to come
from somewhere, but this is Friday

in basketball country. Gripping
the microphone, Terrence announced
"Divine Order" and a woman

in a dress so sequined she seemed
like a spotlight stood. She said:
We love your trombone, Terence,

while her companion tried sitting her
down by her wrist. *It's all good, baby*,
Terence smiled, *They're all brass*.

For Years I've Been Prohibited from Mentioning the Moon

So now the cedar-scented moon, and moon-
glow encasing the sky in lavender velvet,
clouds splotched on a moon-radiant sky
and a sickle moon raking a field of violets
and the moon and sun in Joseph's dream kneeling,
and how years ago we could've been on the moon
watching the city from an airplane,
the stadium lights a diamond necklace,
and she was there, a star singing,
but we wished to be back on earth to know
the measure of our loss, to see
a star singing, her voice drifting beyond
a necklace of light tilling the city's dim streets.
How many times, though for years I've been barred
from mentioning the moon, how many times
have I switched off the lights to gaze at the sky,
the moon full or receding, holding court,
how the breeze itself changed the light,
how I wanted to weep at the sight of the moon rising
from the hills of Indiana brightening a frozen stream?
How many times have I turned into this subdivision,
the pipes stacked like a tangle of pythons,
the fire hydrant, tall as a man, exposed, its lower pipes
to be buried under pavement and sick lawns?
I know this hour, the thick lament to come,
the thousands churned. I know this laughter
tearing at my lungs, because seeing the moon
is no consolation for what was to be lost.
But here's what really happens: I see the moon
surrounded by the rubble of conquest
where there are only old stars and dead wolves,
and I am moved again by something I felt before,
shaken, but without an atom of pity in my body,
filled with a transparency capable of bearing

the whole world, a void that takes in the moon
in the sky, the pipes and the evil they gush,
and the poisoned water, and the lead-laced dirt.
Only the moon and whatever spins within me
as I worship all that remains, each speck of light,
every crooked ray beaming from my chest.

The Bus Driver Poem

I wasn't driving
just crossing a street
with trees, leaves mustard
yellow and ketchup red,
when a low ranking employee
of an insignificant bureaucracy
gave me the finger.
Did my face foretell
seven years of drought?
Did I remind him of
Don Kirshner. The Bee
Gees, the Cold War?
As usual I was lost
between the stuffed
tomatoes of my youth
and a future that says tick
tock boom boom.
Lost because I was living
the now of hurried afternoons,
the present that makes me bark
"No, I don't need help"
to the teenager bagging
my groceries at Mr. D's.
So when the bus driver
gave me the finger,
I gave him the Italian arm.
Brakes screeched, people inside
jerked around like carcasses
in a hot dog plant. He stepped
out shouting, big mouth
flashing. I couldn't hear
a sound. Still
I screamed fuck you,
fuck you, and the present
became a rabbit searching

for its severed head.
I mean the now was Reba
McEntire crooning to Sid
Vicious biting on a slide guitar.
Then the present burned
a heap of old calendars —
June 23, 91,
March 4, 92, the smoke
of all those days!
I didn't look back
but watched my life
from a helicopter
or a sewer hole, my heart
pounding 140 fists a minute.
Look at me, look at me
fling hours at the universe,
headbutt my old friend fear,
knee the wide skirts of hope.

Khaled Mattawa

The Bloomingfoods Promise

For the ugly man who buys bell peppers,
eats them raw before talking to himself,
for the widow who loves prunes because they're tender
as lips, for the Saudi who comes wearing a jalabia,
his face easing, not afraid of being stigmatized,
his veiled wife ahead of him telling him what to do
the only time this week, for the red haired cashier
who believes in her beauty, the gorgeous plump blonde
who shaves neither armpits nor legs, for the day manager
who prices apples according to his mood,
for the mounds of wilting tofu, the Moroccan olives
crispy with sand, the barbecued setan, nori maki,
organic tomatoes, four-bean salad, celantro,
Indian frozen foods, for the meatless pate, countless
boxes of couscous and falafel mix, jars of eggless mayonnaise,
sacks of whole grain teff, liquid aminos, anise extract,
and seaweed crunch, for the biodegradable shampoos,
Burmese healing clay, and tiger balm, for all
the small compromises you plant in the concrete,
the wholesomeness you pluck from chaos, for all this
my love and I will break in through the window
near the record store, french kiss all the kiwis and plums,
fondle mangoes, bananas and pears, empty coconuts
of their milk, stuff our faces with tabouli and lentil soup,
eat almonds, raisins and cashews out of each others' palms;
we will dip sticks of rhubarb in cayenne pepper
for a taste of hell, and purgatory—the rush
of the acid bitter juice, then paradise:
swigs of orange blossom water and spoons of honey
from Tibet; we will dye our hair with Indian henna
in the kitchen sink and glow under the light seeping
from the street, dance our way upstairs to sitars
playing in our heads, and next to the buckets of granola
and flavored coffee beans, we will make a mattress of kale

and Boston lettuce leaves, rub our bodies
with extra virgin olive oil, sip demitasses
of aphrodisiacal teas, and like Adam and Eve in their bower,
we will make love, our touch warmer now, our limbs
glistening and slick, Ah the soul ascending to the crotch,
the moist feverish pudendum, the throbbing of the hasty cock;
we will have known nothing like this, never experienced
such joy. In the morning you will find us radiant
with innocence, behind our eyelids butterflies,
starfish, and pearls; you will wake us, tell us
the ghosts of Buddha and Marx and the think tank
of meditating angels who invented New Age Zen have bestowed
upon us a kismet of unparalleled bliss, that from now on
our sweat will become holy, that we will fly over villages,
continents and streets sprinkling the world
with blessings, that mothers will heal their ailing
babies with the mist of our transcendental rain.

Khaled Mattawa

Spring

At the intersection of Third and Dunn, the magnolias
are doing it again, the whole gang of them lined up
along the sidewalk, giggling girls in extravagant finery,
branches displaying luscious blossom cups, white/
purple/pink tossing in the fickle last-day-of-March wind, yes
such gaiety, such outrageousness, this yearly flaunting,
this daring of the elements.

Found Poems

Freedom Ltd.
Sign at Ed's Bait Shop reads:

"One Nation Under God
Indivisible
With
Liberty and Justice
For All
Mon - Sat
8-5
Sunday
Noon-5"

Spring Break Special:
Breast Augmentation, $3,950.00

Spring Break is icumen in
Lhunde sing swimsu

Sliceth knife and passeth coin
And Springeth the breaste nu

Making of the Rivers and the Prairies

Before, a rhetoric, an epigraph,
gushing of the ancient, unheard waters all along
the terminal moraine. Before the melt,

Maumee ice flow inching toward a Wabash
where no water ran, a Saginaw
into a dry Dowagiac. Before an unbound Kankakee,

glacial borders pressing ice lobes out
to flood the valley where no valley was, to spread
the drift two hundred feet and more above

Coniferous, Devonian and Trenton rock.
Before the flood, copper manitous locked up in stone
on distant islands not enisled

before the miners who would dig for them
where no mines were and build the pregnant mounds
by forest trails that were not blazed.

Before the forest trails, before the oak & ash,
path of the moraine: sand & boulders,
quartzite, clay and till . . .

Before the Potawatomies. Before the French.
Before the Studebaker &
the Bendix and the Burger Chef. . . .

                 10,000 years ago
the Erie ice, the Saginaw,
the Michigan converged just here.

Hills and ranges fixed the contours then.
Basins formed, and runoff made
two rivers wider than the Mississippi.

Tributaries broke through lateral moraines.
The Elkhart and the Yellow rivers
drained away the last of Maumee glacier—

no waters yet could run off to Desplaines.
When they did, the two great rivers
slowed—silted up their valleys with debris

and changed their names.
Turning on itself, Dowagiac became its former
tributary, flowing to Lake Michigan.

Kankakee at flood time
emptied into the immense abandoned channel,
flowed on to St. Joseph, left

an ice gorge, then a sand bar and a bluff
here at Crum's Point.
Drainage opened to the east

all the way beyond the lakes to the St. Lawrence.
Water levels fell, channels
slowly narrowed, and the River of Miamis

took its present course. Curving to the south.
Flowing to the north.
Rising where it fell in the beginning.

So Crum's Point burst its ice-dam and
the Kankakee flowed mostly with the stronger
new and narrow river now.

Silted up to fourteen feet, the site
of a confluence sealed itself with rock
and sand and soil: made

a watershed on the continental divide.
Above, the level sand plain. And below, the marsh:
Seignelay south-west, & Illinois.

From a millennium of glacial drift, the prairies
now had formed: Portage, Palmer
Sumption . . .

Terre Coupee. . . .

      But on these waters:
Could you sail a ship?

And on this land: *Found an empire now*

    surrounded on the north and east by oak & hickory? On the south adjoining: scattered clumps of alders, willow bushes native to these soils. The prairie reached from portage landing two and one half miles, three & more from the nearest eastern verge. To the west & south, the vast expanse of grass and marsh appeared as one great plain. Deep into the west, a stretch of rolling timber. . . .

Swimming at Midnight

[*Near my grandparents' home at the outskirts of town, a stone quarry was established, then abandoned, nearly a hundred and fifty years ago. The early blasting hit water, and after many soundings were taken, the management concluded that they had uncovered a bottomless lake, fed, they surmised, by a sizable underground river.*]

Under a pine and confusion:
ah! Tangles of clothes: (come
on, silly, nobody's here:) and
naked as fish, a boy and a girl.
(Nobody comes here: nobody looks:
nobody watches us watching us
watch.) Except the police.
Thighs slide into the moon.
Humbly, into the stars: Mirrored,
flashes a father's red eye, a
blue-bitten mother's red lip: No
Swimming Allowed In The Quarry
At Night. (Anyway, nevertheless
and moreover: feel how warm!) here,
among the reflections. (Feel the
water's mouth and its hands, feel
them imitate mine: can there truly
be any danger?) danger allowed in
the quarry at night? can people
really have drowned? (Now my body
is only water alive, and aeons
ago you were a fish growing
legs—) well, dust to dust, a
curious notion. But quarry water on
dust green with seed! Quarry water
forbidden on land after dark! What
young forms of vegetation emerge.
What new colors of light.

Reception

When the tired old poet's genuine modesty
and quiet life in the small university town
had finally made him all but invisible in the larger
world of literature, his former friend arrived

out of the past for a visit between readings
and appearances on television talk shows.
When the old poet's wife thought she heard
the condescension in the faint praise

the famous writer offered of what would be
her husband's final book, she took him aside
to fill up his wine glass and quietly said
You know, Ernest's poems have always been

better than yours, which are full of
bombast and pretension. Although I wasn't
meant to hear that, I did. Remembering it now,
I also think of Ernie telling me one night

about the way Eileen, young and pretty then
and not just some professor's wife,
used to dance like Carmen on the tables
of a local Polish bar. . .

We walk into Mundy's for the Meaning of Life

The waitress smiles. She's anticipating us.
"It's *all* meaningful," he says to me
eyeing the salad bar
"Who is the woman who put this pink
in the cottage cheese?" I ask.
The waitress brings over her
high school smile
and never stops telling us
the specials here.
We think she smiles like she
knows something we don't know.

She places the paper mats
in front of us. He looks
over at me and reads the questions:
Which product requires the most milk
to manufacture? (cheese, ice cream, butter)

I order a vanilla malt
and today's special.

Whole milk is 50%, 77%, 96%
fat free?
What's your dream?
He asks all this before
the fried chicken comes,

I look down at our mats
and read: WE'RE STILL FOR
(with the picture of black and white cows grazing)
REAL.

So is this it:
the way the cows
stand at sunset
by the road

and take the peach sun going down—
chewing, chewing
like they always have since
cows were born—only the dance
changes, the choreography
from under the apple
tree at noon to the fence
at twilight.

Oh what is my hunger
to say America
your salad bar is
pink cottage cheese
and green jello with grapes
in Plymouth Indiana at Mundy's
where I look into a new lover's
eyes and he says what is your
dream and we look down at
the place mat and it says
"WE'RE FOR REAL."
No wonder
the waitress smiles
and takes our
money.

Human Nature

"We are embracing artificial versions of nature as we
watch the real nature diminish." Carolyn Hughes

Even the angel's usual
chatter from the power lines
is mute down here where painted dogs
stare at you behind the fence,
dumb-nosed guards among the fake
menagerie of eagles, deer, turtles, and bears.
Where farmers' hills slope
up and over the horizon in a fine
brown Boxer fur, you can buy the fashion
in barns full: cows on green slabs, pink
pigs, Little Bo Peep's sheep, and wishing wells.
Where backs of billboards portray
the weathered art of Indiana, geese
parade in green hats, frogs embrace on a bench.

Corn stalks rustle.
Foxtail grasses bend to each other—a game of
telephone. What was the message?
Are we not lonely among these statues of the lost
farms and wilderness on green manicured lawns and pastures?

I know a man who moves his white ducks everyday across
his yard, strategizing like a game of checkers.
I know the pink flamingo draped in bows and wreath
on wire legs in the landscaped garden.
I know the curious goat who trots over to my camera and
poses between two lifesize African elephants.
I know the plastic deer safe in a thicket and the buck
sprawled fresh down that street.
I know two bears, harmless under porch light until a child
dreams and the raccoon, who after a few corn kernels thrown
to the road, now lies dead, intestines unwinding like a red yoyo.

On Road 52

I am in this silver diner thinking
about the extra "s" in dessert and the "men"
in menu, and how I learned from my Mother
a woman is a spoon—a woman can
live in a soup pot or a pie, serving up,
day in and day out the sugar and salt—
love is a meal, memory its bone,
and how a pink towel outside on the line
lifting to sky can be a day's work for some
and for others passing by, it is an inspiration
from the wind before the next junction.
I know we hold our lives taut as the clotheslines
of our childhood we vaulted over like circus acrobats
into the baskets of whites.
What will this daughter of mine twirling
on her red seat in the parade of silver dollar
stools at the counter say she knows?

Traffic Jam on Highway 41

Maybe it's because I miss my dog today, the mutt-bred one
that used to nuzzle my arm when we both needed a long walk,

the one the vet put down last Tuesday when her kidneys
quit working or because the woman in the red Dodge

next lane over scolds the bare seat on her right, finger wagging,
head nodding, tongue lashing at no one, that I think of Carl Jung

explaining from the swirling midst of madness how all people
over thirty-five suffer from loss of religion, how we search

in unlikely places for nourishment to fill our empty,
aimless hearts, expanding roots along the desert floor of life

like the Joshua tree until we strike a patch of wet, lush soil,
suck it dry, and begin that same sycophantic crawl believing

there's somewhere useful left to get to. Yet, it could be what
Jung missed in his *creative illness* that keeps us all creeping

forward in this god-awful traffic, a homeless pair along
the highway's shoulder. The man, rose in hand, guides

the woman toward a vacant barn in hopes of romance.
She smiles, pleased to trade her deadened body for his concern.

Hopping a Freight Train

More than forty years ago Jerry Miller tore
the wind in half. Arms pumping, legs churning
like pistons on the freight train he ran beside, Jerry
struggled along the tracks until that single instant
in time when the best we do no longer fulfills
our need to do. Then, he flew into an open boxcar
as the train switched gears, lost his balance
and slipped under a sextet of wheels, trading his foot
for legend in our local high school.

I'm standing where he started on a patch
of honey-combed gravel when the whistle sounds
a Charlie Parker wail along
the snare drum rattle of tracks and ties
as the Southern rounds the bend near my home.
Even at the age of fifty, I want to run with this train,
seek an open boxcar and leap headlong into darkness.
I want to balance Jerry's failure against my own need,
that voice increasing in my brain that says *don't give in*,
don't walk through a doorway while there's still a wall
to knock down, a woman left unloved, a city unseen.

My father used to say, "I'd like to be young again
and know what I know now." But, I'm not seeking
youth, not even immortality. I'm no Ponce de Leon
in a jogging suit. I just want to hold, for as long as I can,
the unbearable ecstasy beyond the fear of death rising
in my throat now like a growl as the diesel fumes draw near.

Why I Hate Realism

There are always plenty of viruses
to go around. Everything is reasoned
out to hopelessness, and no realist
ever committed *Sleeping on the Wing*
to memory because memory is a way
of picking out a joyless scientist, a harsh narrator
who spends no time looking out the window
underneath clouds at the man
across the highway, watching the traffic
from his white chair, a whip in one hand
and a diet Coke in the other. Sometimes
a whip, sometimes a violin out of tune.
Gregory Peck never wins Audrey Hepburn
in *Roman Holiday* though the story behind
the story turns out okay considering in realism
you never meet the love of your life
and too many drinks is just too many drinks
and a headache. The map of Indiana
on the coffee table is just a map of Indiana
and not a mansion or a tonnage of Clue
leading to cures, there aren't any miracles,
all the Replacements recordings are at the bottom
of a big, muddy river so we're left with
a legend without an echo. In realism, O'Hara dies
of something completely unludicrous. No one goes
walking out of Denny's real casual-like
with a pot of steaming coffee in one hand
while the other hand waves a goodbye
that isn't a goodbye as much as it's a wink.
Nothing of flight, only something
like flight which is really not flight at all.
The good part survives in order to instruct you
on how bad things realistically are.
You always walk out of the Sistine Chapel

alone, full of rue and reduced as you pass
a beautiful woman wondering if she's the other
love of your life but she isn't because in realism
there is no love of your life and your mathematics
are devoted to decreasing pain at the risk of
never rushing awkwardly, mistakenly,
right into pleasure. *Jouissance* is just a word
the silly French made up. Now always makes up
its mind to be worse than Then. Appearance of flame
means only loss, disintegration, the fight
between the boy and the girl as everyone leaves
the baseball stadium results in her
getting into a stranger's car right in the middle
of slow, heavy traffic, and then rushing
back to Ellsinore, yelling some more
and then getting into the stranger's car again,
it never shakes itself into anything other than
the inability to know another, no redemption,
Joi never sees a ghost there's no such thing
as ghosts, no spirits, no spirit, no soul, no fuse,
no 8 year old girl asking me plainly, wisely,
What is *incisive?* What is a *quadrant?* when
she's really asking Are things like they say they are?
What can you tell me in the time it takes to eat
dinner at my house? Don't believe one of them,
Courtney—they're scared you won't be scared.
Courtney, once I caught my shadow.
I let it go because it asked to be released
and there was a horn section nearby
can you believe it? A horn section and somewhere
an organ and I felt like I wasn't *just* walking
and would never have to again.

Surrender

Voice of Patrick on cell phone:
thin, pointed, the wand
a conductor raises and drops and waves
sidelong and diagonally in tempo with
Brahms' first movement, fourth symphony,
which is exploding from his car stereo.
Patrick's a wind gust. He says,
"This movement's a civil war
battle. Listen: hear that, the misery,
the courage, the fear, a creek, something eerie.
It's there, you just gotta listen."
Or Patrick's a young palm tree

in a wind gust. Brahms is among many
who move Patrick thus. Once,
listening to him play "Parable for Solo Viola"
on CD, I heard him breathing
during rests, between notes,
between something like despair and
something like resignation,
breath strong enough to bend
a candle's flame without extinguishing it—
but Patrick's words remind me why I called:
three weeks ago, he broke the Sacred Knot with Anna,
so I ask him how that is because
I need an update and I need him to know
I haven't forgotten. His voice—
that wand—summons one cello
bowing two notes, the song
of a deep, quiet howling.
He says, "I'm glad it's over"
and I can't believe it
but then he adds "Talk about a fight,"
which he punctuates with a "Ha!"
which bleeds into his trademark "My God!"

which lingers in the quiet
like the quiet that hangs above a plateau,
a quiet descending from regret
to reverence to relief, a quiet Brahms erases
with four measures and a string section.
And then Patrick describes it:
"corpses shade the hillside
from which smoke lifts in curls;
cannons sit quietly, mouths closed;
a male chorus too lucky or too cursed sing
a nearly inaudible lullaby of moans and gasps;
and the sun ascends once more from a maroon pool,"
which is when Patrick stops with a sigh
that suggests he has dropped, temporarily,
the baton that is his voice.
Before I can ask him a question,
he picks it up again, only to tap it this time:
"We were fine despite the distance—
but then the troops marched in
and we had a thousand reasons to hate each other,
and each reason had a gun.
I'm still alive, I think,
but you know it's hard to tell
sometimes. It's hard to tell."
And with that he puts down the baton
as though, finally, he had measured out
the length of some sorrow he'd kept inside,
as if it were the long red handkerchief
a magician pulls from his mouth
until all he holds is a square
the color of a mourning dove flying away.

Some Very Important Business

This morning I sit on the front stoop
and watch ants pick apart a beetle
who is easy food because
only half of him remains: his head
and his abdomen to which
his two front legs are still attached.
Too bad for him, I think,
because he is still alive, on his back.
About every twelve seconds,
he reaches his legs up, as if to grasp
something—maybe his beetle soul—
so as to pull it back before it slips
into this cool October ether.
And now—too bad for him—
there are more ants than before,
each one carrying beetle pieces
back to headquarters. I ask the beetle,
"Should I contact a family member?
A friend? A man of the cloth?
Do you have any last wishes?"
The beetle does not respond,
just reaches his legs up again,
losing his grip. Were the beetle
a person, some would say,
"God has his plans," or
"He'll be better off in Heaven."
I say, "This is the way
God wants to eat you today."
This doesn't help, so I try Poetry.
"Rage, rage against the dying of the . . ."
And the beetle rages and rages and
reaches his legs up, reaching for
the light switch. Then I say,
"I'm sorry for not knowing

what to say as you lie here."
As I say this, I lean in, look
for eyes to look into. I hear
ant voices screaming,
"Come on!" and another:
"They found a robin by the oak."
The beetle moans. I lean in closer.
His guts smell like rotten potato.
I lean in more so that I am only
millimeters from his nose:
He wears a thin silver mustache!
which matches the silver in his hair
which glistens in this morning sun.
And his jowls hang there like an old dog's.
hanging there like wisdom,
hanging there with too much
familiarity. So I can't help what I see
Next: grandfather giving in
to the cancer, the cold creeping
behind his eyes and cheeks.
Afraid the beetle recognizes me, I talk
about the weather, the economy, baseball,
and then I remember that this scarab beetle,
which I've always known as a June bug,
is still alive with only half its body
and the small black ants
moving to and from the beetle
like an animated dotted-line
are not nurses nor doctors.
I consider blotting out
with my flip-flop the illusion,
but it's too late for that now,
I know, as I kneel over the scene,
mesmerized by those diligent ants.

WNDU

I am your anchor, and my spouse is another anchor, and this child
made up like a blind boy imagines his future bride
dressed as a candyshop
        besieged by a cloud army
                armed with mascara-wands
is also your anchor. Look how I run my motor in this storm
authorized by our Stormteam, and how your porch
caves in every night around a truck
like a sad mouth at last granted gleaming dentures
shoved in the wrong way. For an afterlife of grinning down your own throat
plus the weather.

This solemnity
's thick, it pours in lashings from the boom mic and my greased hair
splits on a dime. How many Michianans say no, no, goodbye
and how many say stay 'til the morrow, my dove, my windfall
of unmarked pre-tax dollars, my heap, which is a helpmeetful
of happenstance? And, viewers, who would suffer it.
When we return.

Pissarro's *The House of the Deaf Woman and the Belfry at Eragny*
A painting in the Indianapolis Museum of Art

What he really wants to paint
is behind him,

but the solitary sound of a bell
at the wrong hour turns him
toward the belfry.

It is a song he can no longer
avoid. But it isn't only
the mournful song of a bell
that calls to him,

it is the cloud's lament, the ripe
agony of trees, grass,
all living things.

He knows nature is so mysterious
he cannot embrace it.

Nothing is immobile.
Nothing is without sound.

He knows that a canvas that does not shimmer
will not stir even one fiber
of his soul.

Only Pissarro paints a music
so mournful, so beautiful
it can make a deaf woman
fall to her knees.

Where You Are

Our lives are loft and ballast, lift and drag,
high from the thrilly clouds of travel to deep
in the glacial till of home. You pack a bag
and feel your feet lighten, caught up in the sweep

of going away, which would bewilder
every time if you let it, as you gaze down
at each square of farm, each leaf-vein river,
each night-time glimmering circuit-board town.

Some satellite photos paint this place as though
our cities were purple, fields pink and waterways
lime green—the White and Fawn, Eel and Ohio,
the Wabash, the Little Blue—all a bright glaze

of iridescence. Before you unpack again,
the earth will have to grow larger for you
and more muted, coming back to the tan
of bark and soil, the silver of streets, blue

lake, stream, pond, pool. No matter how tanned
or weary, work-worn or free, your welcome
will be familiar—the look, then feel of the land
under your feet. Here is where you come home.

Poem She Sent

when the cutout
paper
fold it
up and
tape it
shut sheep
I gave
you came undone

the back
legs flew
back and
tabs sev-
enteen,
18,
19,
20
slipped out
of their
slots and
the back
flap sheep
butt stuck
up high
and all
you could
see was

how

empty
the in-
sides were
and are
and will
be world
without
end

Mark Minster   **193**

Clang

A woman stands in a cornfield at the end of day.
Nowhere does the "extensive totality of life"
bear down with such menace as in southern Indiana.
These are not just rocks by the side of the road.
It is not just a pleasantness of trees
that gathers here. The man out back
raises a maul above his head and brings it down
with enough force to change the course of a life.
It is the straight green grain of black locust,
and like a good life it sings when it's split.

The leaves come down off the trees in the fall,
and there's a moment near dusk when you don't know
if it's the last of the swifts racing
for its hole or the first uncertain bat
launching its night-long raid on the bug life,
which may be the true life, of this wrinkled
republic, this land careening down a hill
of river bottoms, ox bows, limestone and mud.

Four-Hundreth Mile

I am 83 miles north of Indianapolis on I-65.
A few clouds are out and the corn stands
dead on its feet on either side of the road.
It is dusk and the light leaps up
to take its last look at the world.
It is September, early September, and the leaves,
though they feel the soft stroking of the air,
shiver slightly.

I am driving my four-hundredth mile of the day,
alone now, and calm, the lights of the oncoming cars
beginning to sparkle in the dying light.
Huge flat-sided semis, as the night comes on,
pass like immense untroubled animals,
like the sides of houses in a flood.
How many times have I been here and not seen
the width of the sky, the slow curve of the landscape
going away, the tiny wire trailing after?

This is the place and this, undoubtedly, the way.
As much of the sky above as there can be,
as much of the earth beneath.
This, is the place where the world appears
in its robe of night and day,
where the dirt road travels with us a ways
and then turns sharply along the ditch,
disappearing down interminable rows of corn.
This is the place where you can see forever,
where pure emptiness hangs on outspread wings
circling above a field.

The soul ranges everywhere and everywhere finds
what it needs, a stick, a fleck of matter on the tongue.
The bird at the top of the dead tree will fly
before I can see it, so I will see it fly.
The cow in the truckbed in front of me looks out
at the world and, if I'm not mistaken, sees it.
The car makes a steady wind-ripped thrum, the glow
of the dashboard rising into my eyes like dust.
I am somewhere between exits. The promising sign,
"Vacancy," flashes above trees in the distance.
I am in no hurry. The only thing in front of me
is home, a few stars, and another night.
I have tried to love what I thought was the world,
but the world moved. So I will love the move.

The Quickest Way to Get There
for the Lotus Festival, 2003

That's Jackson Creek that slides down
into Yellowwood Lake, mumbling
to rocks it finds the sides of,
weeds it likes to lick. It's quiet there
but never silent. In the reeds
at the north end, red-winged blackbirds
scrape their untuned fiddles. Turn left
at the eight-stone graveyard, and you take
Tulip Tree Trace up into places
so local only the maps know
their names. Sol Pogue Hollow for one.
When you reach Scarce of Fat Ridge,
look back. That's Dubois Ridge
on the other side. At the north end of it,
where a nameless feeder creek
cuts a clean arc along the bottom
of Pattys Garden Ridge, a steep slope
of shagbark hickory, sycamore,
musclewood, green bramble and grape
spreads like a bolt of the woven earth.
The quickest way to get there, though,
is some version of a jig the Shenandoah
brought from Scotland that a Mongol
taught a Turk in the Dardanelles.
It's apt to have the rasp of a cross-
cut saw, a catbird's fiery clarity
and jump, but you wont mistake it: song
that wraps the globe in unmowed field.

City of Back Yards

A sprinkle of ash on the lip of the wood stove
like a burped baby. This is the only place I've lived
long enough to have burnt the fence.
Here the rug lies down like an old dog
and the unwashed light piles up in the corner.

No one I knew ever lived here. None
ever drove through. I stick my seeds in the ground
each spring and cut down a wiry assortment
of grasses, wildflowers, ground ivies and weeds
to keep it from disappearing.
I know the cracks in my sidewalk exactly,
which root of which tree passed through,
the place where the water slipped in one March.

The alleys threaded through this town,
worms in an odd compost,
end in a tumbled wall or rotting garage.
Poles sizzle on summer nights
lugging their tonnage of volts
to the wheezing air-conditioners.
This is where garbage and cars
and the weekend gardens,
the half-built seesaws and broken lamps
shoe boxes full of old letters,
albums of forgotten friends,
are put on display for the curious rain.

I look at the staid, plain houses
of the people who lived here once,
the brick stacked up in its bricky way,
the wooden lintels, the back doors snug in their jambs.
Forget-me-nots cluster in the shadows of stumps.
Unleashed forsythia bounds up from the grass
for the twelfth time, thirty feet away.
And here, seven mail boxes
are nailed above the broken doorbell.
Seven samples of soap are newly placed there,
seven gestures of hope.

Why We're Here

Before we can properly excuse ourselves,
I am sitting in the shade under the oak tree
talking about farming with the old man,
and my wife is out among the flowers
with his wife. I know nothing about farming,
but the words fall effortlessly from my mouth.
My wife comes back holding an iris clipping,
and they join us in the shade with the flies.
We are suddenly members of the family,
rocking and swatting. We talk about things
as though we had waited all winter long
for the snow to melt. A bluebird
flies into the box on the fencepost
as we talk, and a rabbit hops lethargically
across the driveway down by the car
where I left the mower I brought
to be sharpened. That's why we're here.

He is the last man in the county
who can sharpen a push mower.
And he is not easy to find. And,
he takes his time. We have found him, though,
and he is taking most of the afternoon
to tell us he thinks he can do it
and for how much. We shake on it.

I am getting my mower sharpened
by first having my flaked faith in the ways of people
touched up and my disinclination to old age
abated. It is costing me eight dollars.

The Daguerreotype

This, then, is she,
My mother as she looked at seventeen,
When she first met my father. Young incredibly,
Younger than spring, without the faintest trace
Of disappointment, weariness, or teen
Upon the childlike earnestness and grace
Of the waiting face.
These close-wound ropes of pearl
(Or common beads made precious by their use)
Seem heavy for so slight a throat to wear;
But the low bodice leaves the shoulders bare
And half the glad swell of the breast, for news
That now the woman stirs within the girl.
And yet,
Even so, the loops and globes
Of beaten gold
And jet
Hung, in the stately way of old,
From the ears' drooping lobes
On festivals and Lord's-day of the week,
Show all too matron-sober for the cheek,—
Which, now I look again, is perfect child,
Or no—or no—'t is girlhood's very self,
Moulded by some deep, mischief-ridden elf
So meek, so maiden mild,
But startling the close gazer with the sense
Of passions forest-shy and forest-wild,
And delicate delirious merriments.

Fountain Square Mama
. . . In Heat

"There she goes again," they said. "Red," the aging Maureen O'Hara
look-alike, once-upon-a-time beauty, parading up and down her cracked,
littered sidewalk in furry slippers and see-through nightie—Hot Pink, of course.
"The nerve! In broad daylight!" they said.

This time she ventures across her narrow century-old avenue, dodging show-offs
poppin' wheelies and a dog with no name, setting her sights on
The Alley Widower. Lookin' for love. Doin' what 'cats do best.
Underage hoods hoot and holler as she sways and sashays.
She's feeling 21 again. Well, maybe 30.

From his rusted metal chair on his cluttered front porch,
Old Harold watches with freshly-lit pipe in mouth as she
opens his gate and eases toward him. Rising,
he shuffles before her, they silently enter his
musty bungalow, void of a female's touch,
and the screen door bangs behind them.

Illinois, Indiana, Iowa

Austrian food is not served in Vienna,
and people in Paris drink Coke, not wine.
Lebanon has its Little League
and Warsaw its Civil War cannon.
Carthage is full of blondes,
and Cairo divides, American-style,
into white and black, money and rage.
Gnawbone keeps teasing, a tricky riddle,
and What Cheer defies punctuation,
but Stony Lonesome is all that it says.
I have seen Hindustan—Hoosier twang,
no belly dancing allowed—
and I have been in Arcadia:
one street by a railroad track,
blue chicory, golden rod.

    O telltale country, fact and mirage,
    coat of many colors
    stitched in homesickness, threaded with dreams,
    land of seven fat cows,
    is it finished, your poem?

Scenic Route

For Lucy, who called them "ghost houses"

Someone was always leaving
and never coming back.
The wooden houses wait like old wives
along this road; they are everywhere,
abandoned, leaning, turning gray.

Someone always traded
the lonely beauty
of hemlock and stony lakeshore
for survival, packed up his life
and drove off to the city.
In the yards the apple trees
keep hanging on, but the fruit
grows smaller year by year.

When we come this way again
the trees will have gone wild,
the houses collapsed, not even worth
the human act of breaking in.
Fields will have taken over.

What we will recognize
is the wind, the same fierce wind,
which has no history.

Pigeons

Like every kingdom,
the kingdom of birds
has its multitude of the poor,
the urban, public poor
whose droppings whiten
shingles and sidewalks,

Who pick and pick
(but rarely choose)
whatever meets their beaks:
the daily litter
in priceless Italian cities,
and here, around City Hall—
always under foot,
offending fastidious people
with places to go.

No one remembers how it happened,
their decline, the near-
abandonment of flight,
the querulous murmurs,
the garbage-filled crops.
Once they were elegant, carefree;
they called to each other in rich, deep voices,
and we called them doves
and welcomed them to our gardens.

A Grackle Observed

Watching the black grackle
come out of the gray shade
into the sun, I am dazzled
by an unsuspected sheen,
yellow, purple, and green,
where the comb of light silkens
unspectacular wings—
until he, unaware
of what he means at this one
peculiar angle of sun,
hops back to his modest dark
and leaves the shining part
of himself behind, as though
brightness must outgrow
its fluttering worldly dress
and enter the mind outright
as vision, as pure light.

Lisel Mueller   **205**

Letter to California

We write to each other as if
we were using the same language,
though we are not. Your sentences lap
over each other like the waves
of the Pacific, strictureless;
your long, sleek-voweled words
fill my mouth like ripe avocados.
To read you is to dismiss
news of earthquakes and mud slides,
to imagine time in slow motion.
It is to think of the sun
as a creature that will not let anything
happen to you.

                    Back here
we grow leeks and beans and sturdy
roots that will keep for months.
We have few disasters; *i.e.,*
no grandeur to speak of. Instead
we engage in a low-keyed continuous struggle
to get through the winter, which swallows
two seasons and throws its shadow
over a third. How do you manage
without snow to tell you that you are mortal?
We are brought up short by a wind
that shapes our words; they fall
in clean, blunt strokes. The birds here
are mostly chickadees
and juncos, monochromes
bred to the long view
like the sky under siege of lead
and the bony trees, which hold
the dancer's first position
month after month. But we have
our intimations: now and then
a cardinal with its lyric call,

its body blazing like a saint's
unexpectedly gaudy heart,
spills on our reasonable scene
of brown and gray, unconscious of itself.
I search the language for a word
to tell you how red is red.

Hoosiers (2)

I grew up short, slight, and a step slow,
where iron hoops hung from most garages,
and rusty bracket holes claimed
almost all the rest. What they now call
"walking" we called "steps," and
palming the ball was among the major sins
we knew. With two or three
we played H-O-R-S-E, spelling out jumpers,
hooks, and lay-ups as the days shortened
and a twilight chill blew in off the lake.
With four or more
we faked and passed
in ad hoc alliances,
breathing in
the fading light
and breathing out
warm clouds and truancy,
forbidden by the code of the alley
to go home and break up the game.
Better to face an inquisition
than be mocked for the rest of the week.

That was Northwest Indiana in the Fifties,
in the shadow of smelters, refineries,
and Branch McCracken,
so no chance of avoiding it
any more than an occasional fight
or the neighborhood grit that made the ball
unruly. I was never any good, of course,
but to be in the right place at the right time
to screen for the sure-handed and the quick,
a natural at going from slow to stop
so the game could go on and on. Jackets
in a heap, we scuffled into suppertime
and the wrath of our fathers,

dribbled and drove until fingers tingled
and sweat made us shiver,
until darkness came on
and the rim we shot at
was just a memory
and a sound.

Crossing the Line, 1955

I got to Chicago from an Indiana sandlot
by way of a state-line Calumet City bar—
a convenient game-day rendezvous, but
a jurisdiction apart, as scofflaws, Lake County
fugitives, and Dillinger himself knew well.
Dreaming of baseball and nursing a Nehi
while grownups made small talk,
I wandered into musty shadows and neon fumes,
spun bar stools, encountered a blear-eyed early-bird,
examined cigarette displays, and pondered
calendars and posters of robust ladies with rosy cheeks
promoting alcohol, auto parts, and friendly talk.

Jostling in game-day traffic, we squinted
in the sultry glare, winced at acrid emanations from
the Lever Brothers plant. My father muttered at the pace
and (now more than several miles from home)
even swore. When we finally entered the ballpark's shade,
four front-stoop lurkers exacted South Side tribute
for parking where they lived. The concourse
to the upper deck was a gaggle of inflections, an urgency
of curious urban smells. The loudspeaker droned,
"Welcome to Comiskey Park."

As twilight came and the players hustled toward history,
elegant parabolas glowed in the hazy night. But
guttural epithets and beer beneath my shoes
invoked the sweet darkness of Calumet,
stale smoke and liquor on a stranger's breath—
my introduction to the next town over,
a neighborhood away.

A Promise

One day I'll get around to this or that,
and have a night to celebrate, to brag
about the clutterless house, my essay on hats
(published!), the waxed car shining like a battleship
in the driveway. In the morning I'll beat up
perfect omelets, flipped
just as the sun's cooks flip her up.
I'll squeeze oranges and squeeze you too,
I'll even ask about your mother,
stalking through the house like a man
who gets things done.
I will open like a sack of peaches
and shake my fuzzy organs out
for you to squeeze, to inspect for flaws
passed on from seedy ancestors—
sailors, criminals, gents . . .
But there are oceans of errands to be done,
spools of chores:
the dishes, the oil change, the rent.

The Bowling Alley

Sooner or later we have to face the fact
that if God liked us, we'd all be rolling perfect

games; not every time of course—then
there would be no thrill—but at least once

or twice a year. What a dim reflection of heaven
we are tonight, staggering toward the pins

like bullies to a bar fight. We blame our shoes,
the music, the slickness of the lanes, the booze,

then keep hurling, trying to understand
why singers ever sing of human deeds,

and how we can have faith with all we lack.
Then, when hope is almost gone, a strike!

The seven sliding by to clip the ten—
a tiny joy before the whispered prayer. *Again.*

An Afternoon to be Filled with Kicked Snow

Neighbor boy, it's time I looked you in the eye
but you career drunkenly, walking on your hands
by the rusted slide, rolling in the snow
under the swing that hangs from a broken chain.
The snow turns to rain pelting your face.

Your glasses have fallen through the wet crust.
Fish them out—your hands hurt,
lenses drip with slush and dirt,
fling them at the porch.

I've seen you often in the yard alone.
Now at the end of November
you shower Mary and Joseph with stones.
Donkey and cow, a baby with a bone-white face
lie under a plywood roof in the rain.

Your hot wheeling glance is not for them
but arcs like a searchlight
to clouds, to the ground.
Boy in a drift with rain in your mouth,

pack three balls with slush and grit
and juggle them high in the heavy air.
You and I, we belong to the same
runaway circus though I traveled
without you in the old days,
when I thought that I was dreaming.

Small Town Ceremony

Junk man,
write your own song of farewell,
before summer comes,
before the undertaker stands
on the soundless carpet
polishing your casket with a snowy cloth
while his mind wanders to dinner, the rush
of ice falling from a machine
in a motel two towns away
where his girlfriend paints her nails,
hand poised in the light of the screen.

Tonight the March ground sends up its raw smell
and before he takes you in those smooth hands,
enter the shed, stoop, stumble down steps to the dirt,
run your hands over old forks and spoons,
a broken wheel, the washer you've saved for parts.

While your wife sleeps before the T. V.
walk the aisle that barely parts this jumble of junk.
The ground sends up the cat's smell—
He's arched against a box. As your cramped hands
move over the Braille of old sockets,
nails, mildewed straps, your fingers relax.
The slap of the planks on the dirt,
the ring as a chain uncoils to the floor
when the cat springs from the rickety table—
you answer with a long whistle and a tune
tapped out on the empty freezer.

Two towns away, the undertaker snores,
his girlfriend's flicking the dial.
The sound's turned down, a moon pulses blue.
Now she's up, counting headlights.

Grampa's Liquor Bottles

Stiff in our black funeral ties and jackets,
my brother and I crept out the kitchen door,
escaping the crowded family room, far
from the somber drone of voices and Grampa,
hands positioned on his motionless chest.
We crossed the yard, went straight for the corncrib,
and nosing behind a cobweb-covered plow
we found a row of bottles—ancient bottles,
green, and when held to the light, glazed with dust.
We lined them up along the window ledge,
and from the other side of the barn threw rocks,
most landing in the green sea of cornstalks
beginning to brown in the late July heat.
Before long we remembered our 22's,
nearly forgot the funeral inside.
We took turns exploding the thick green glass,
wondered aloud if Grampa would get buried
with his false teeth in or if they'd stay
in that bathroom jar, magnified forever
to the size of horse teeth. The bottles shattered as if
from inside themselves, sides bursting out, necks
toppling over, and suddenly Dad was there
standing beside us. Our hearts jumped with fear,
our faces braced for rage. What happened next
mystified us, because it was Dad's dad
that lay dead inside, and because of that death
we came to the family farm, full of grieving
strangers and unfamiliar family members,
and Dad stood almost unrecognizable
next to the disused corncrib, his face pale,
so pale in the morning shade, and expressionless.
"Make sure you pick up every piece of glass,"
was all he said and headed back to the house,
sparing us our awkward imitations.
of grief and letting us get back to the work

of boys with mercifully protracted childhoods.
We lay down our guns and lined another row
of Grampa's liquor bottles under the sun,
let them fill with light one last time
and glow with phosphorescent life, and then
we shot them to slivers in the oily black dirt.

Mistakes

Coach called them learning experiences,
and we sucked them up like dirt does rain, the fistfights
and pregnancies. Alvin, the smartest kid in school,
got drunk on margarita he stole from Chi-Chi's
and drove his hatchback into the Ohio River.
We were parched for learning.

                              When we grew older,
we made more learning experiences, ended up
divorced, in rehab, in jail. Now, our shoulders
stooped with learning, faces creased with experience,
we stand on the concrete bank where Alvin drowned
and try to think of what we learned. You can
never drive into the same river twice?

But it's easy to call the game from shore or sideline.
Even when we were losing, Coach would always
give the scrubs a shot at learning experience,
a chance to play and get chewed out next practice.
I was a scrub, and my name has never carried
the same thrill as when the coach picked it
out from our line of hopeless benchwarmers
and tossed me into the roiling experience,
heedless of whether I learned anything or not.

Coins

My change: a nickel caked with finger grime;
two nicked quarters not long for this life, worth
more for keeping dead eyes shut than bus fare;
a dime, shining in sunshine like a new dime;
grubby pennies, one stamped the year of my birth,
no brighter than I from 40 years of wear.

What purses, piggy banks, and window sills
have these coins known, their presidential heads
pinched into what beggar's chalky palm—
they circulate like tarnished red blood cells,
all of us exchanging the merest film
of our lives, and the lives of those long dead.

And now my turn in the convenience store,
I hand over my fist of change, still warm,
to the bored, lip-pierced check-out girl, once more
to be spun down cigarette machines, hurled
in fountains, flipped for luck—these dirty charms
chiming in the dark pockets of the world.

Joe, Born 1895
Near Bean Blossom Creek, Indiana

I. Laying the Fence Row

Your dad woke you in the dark. The smell of creosote
drying on the rails. Hands stiff and bruised.
Head to head you held the posts between you
and set them in their holes. Sister cut
tupelo gum; mother hauled out cold chicken
and well water. Stripped to the waist, grown men
doused themselves and shook like calves.
After a hard winter when children died and graves
were dug through frozen ground, no one complained
about the heat. Help came and went. Four of you
worked past dark winding the wire taut, eating
and sleeping the wire taut: having said about
everything you could think of, knowing exactly
what needed to be done, you worked
one beside the other, as if you were alone.

Excerpts from: *The Seasons at Walden Inn*

February is faith in things unseen, Spring waiting in the womb of an aging Winter. Its gift to us is the pleasure of anticipation, the heart and soul of romance.

July in Putnam county is an acquired taste. It has certain elements in common with the swims I used to take in the Irish sea as a boy, done not so much for the teeth-chattering experience itself, but for the subsequent feeling of well-being that came from being fully clothed and warm afterwards. It is the same kind of impulse that inspires a jog down the country roads about the Inn in the broiling sun in order to experience the sensation of sweet, fresh water from a fountain dousing a head and neck already drunk on the wine of its endorphins.

October, we take a break from the work in the kitchen, sitting outside the back door on milk crates, feeling small beside this display of nature's sorcery, witnessing the magic in every turning leaf.

December's mixed emotions steal like the shadow of the sundial across the face of another year. We are thankful for the opportunity to paint the four seasons from the palette of our pantry. We are sorry for the year we must surrender soon like the orchard's last apple to the gravity of time. The Inn, contented in its rug of Christmas color, dozes like a dreaming dog in the flicker of its own firelight.

William Orem ❧

Turning Home Late

The night is dark like lake water when I leave,
one a.m. Bells
from the Protestant church bring out
their soft shivers,
long sleeves of curling sound.
And this walk across town
is past coldness; deep constellations

stand in their one fixed moment.
Everything about me is closing down,
I know my tiredness
like the ice-clotted root.

But the air is fettered with crystals tonight,
and the spreading ways of snow
come back to the eye with that minuscule
flutter in stars.
This whitened country is soft
and receives the foot kindly.
I will walk past my home,

and past all this town;
I will take myself out where the silence of pines
and the blue of their stillness
are one.
The walk is not far. I have time.
Already I begin.

Avalon

I was in the country in a dangerous time.
 The county fair was in full swing, a wheat field knocked down
to hold the staggered vans and trailers

in their erratic rows down the ditch's muddy line. A fire-drunk dusk
 enwombing the river and pitch
and machine silhouettes butterflying angles into the sky, across the flattened stalks

 and weeds, grease and powdered sugar
steeping. Hoping to make out with a stranger, or drink the evening slurry,
 but it was a dry fair, heavy with the parking lot tramps

who'd sneak a glove-box flask and toss a grin your way
 like a lesson in the vagaries of lust.
The knitting-bee spinsters were cloistered in the judging tent awaiting sentence,

 their polychromic quilts erratic
with fractal logic, as if a rural conference on chaos theory unreeled within.
 The spirit of evening was drunk

and kept stumbling into me, struck by the sodium lights. July didn't matter.
 It was giving up with missed phone calls
and early goodbyes. In rabbit hutches pinned with cheap ribbons.

 Every night brought another departure.
And my sterling engine, oh Meredith, shh, let's not argue. I was never any good
 in a fight. No, I should have promised

to wait in that field, until the hour would come when the moon could convince me
 that she is blameless
in all of the folly she's illuminated, an unwitting accomplice.

The End of Free Love

And wasn't the drunkest mania we'd ever caught
    like a bad crush
on merlot: days wrapped in wash-dulled sheets, no matter

    the hundred miles
between our cities, their factories like monuments to folly,
    producing only smoke.

It didn't matter that you wanted us to fight in bed,
    urging ourselves
beyond temporary wounds and into permanence; that I was

    unable to admit
reluctance for the mornings I couldn't raise my left arm
    without wincing,

the memory of your teeth a ring around my clavicle,
    a familiar pattern
surfacing. And weren't our complicities like a remedy

    for love, absolution
from the butcher's work those memories would exact? Our bodies
    weren't built to last.

The elaborate mythologies we'd bury in each other
    wouldn't stay put,
rising as bruises, as ravenous ghosts, as inadequate courtesies.

Quarriers

Just south of Oolitic, in Walter's Bar
and Grill, run by an ex-prof and Jill
his alcoholic wife, a half-dozen men

with skills as rare as a three-legged dog
wash down the 99-cent special: two eggs,
home fries, and one of Jill's cinnamon rolls.

No apologies to wife or child or any
smart-alec kid for taking limestone
as a life's work, their joints flaming

from decades of standing knee-deep
in winter seepage. They drain a last cup
before sliding off cracked, red-vinyl stools,

even the smallest of them heavy in boots
and overalls, each with a hot thermos
maybe laced with something eighty proof

to keep them true on a Tuesday shot
with sun and flurries as they measure,
cut, and crane the gray walls of stone.

Near Gessie, Indiana

Someone's dog, not quite home,
is grinning in the weeds below
a sign for Stuckey's pecan rolls,
one mile. In the quiet light
of dusk, shelves of ice protrude
from the muddy banks of a ditch
that runs between the road
and a field where blackbirds rise,

their cries glass breaking over
rutted stubble, the only other sound
the white noise of traffic,
now and then the random buggy
or phlegm-throated motorcycle.
Up ahead, trucks and neon,
Judyville, maybe the same song
in someone's head as when he left.

The Best Looking Man at the Funeral

It was the wife of the deceased who said
I was the best looking man at the funeral.
And I did look rather spiffy in my blue
blazer, light blue shirt, dark blue tie
and pants of a complementary hue,
a proper ensemble sliding to a dark closure
of black wingtips with a slightly cleated,
selfishly comfortable sole, though nothing
disrespectful or inappropriate.

I blushed at her words, more so when
she followed up with *When's your next movie?*
as if I were some sort of Sean Connery
or Kenny Rogers, with whom, I'm told,
I share certain features. Speechless,
her husband lying just beyond the crowd
of mourners moving slowly past the casket,
I stepped back and merged with the other suits,
my face blood hot, burning still with mortal pleasure.

Washington Street, Indianapolis at Dusk 1892–1895
after the painting by Theodore Groll

It certainly wasn't this world we live in now, with its
whirr and swish of traffic, the overpowering boom of
car stereos, police sirens, emergency sirens. Then it was
mostly the lone wail of freight trains, bells of churches
and horse cars, the whinnying and stomp of animals,
voices of people closing shop before walking home.

At dusk one could smell the sweat of closing day,
with workers still in shirt sleeves, drivers stabling
their teams for the night, the faint sharp odor of dung
in the street, while above, the sky faded through
the blue haze of coal smoke, as gas lamps were lit,
flared on these first mild evenings of autumn.

Later, up the street in a tavern, men singing over their
beer remembered the Fourth of July picnic, the big parade,
veterans of the Grand Army of the Republic marching down
Washington Street and not knowing what to make of what
they read, about war-rumblings between the Cubans and Spain.

Yet the rest of the world was mostly a world away and
Victoria owned almost half, but not us of course. In London
creepy Jack had finished his bloody work while in France,
Paris splashed the world with new color, frolicked at night in
the Moulin Rouge. People did not hate each other so much then
as those dynasties, where nothing was spared to preserve power.

No rock and roll or hip-hop, but brass bands in parks, barbershop
quartets, or a piano in the parlor, or even string quartets played
by some new German folks—just off the boat. While on
nights, across town where the black people lived, came the first
sweet hints of ragtime and jazz, and on Sunday mornings
the sounds of salvation, voices raised high in praise.

New Indianapolis was small though no one thought so,
through the haze of coal smoke and coal oil lanterns, looking
down from the edge of town (no suburbs then), to where
Fall Creek and the White River met. It was a days journey
by horse across the county, and sky bloomed huge behind a new
capital dome, with red streaked clouds, smoldering shadows . . .
purple and rose following brick streets back to where we lived.

Perfect Relationship

Love, love, love, love, love, love, love, love, love, love,
love, love, love, lave, love, love, love, love, love, love,
love, love, love, love, love, love, love, love, love, love,
love, love, love, love, love, love, love, love, love, love,
love, love, love, love, love, love, love, love, love, love,
love, love, love, love, love, love, love, love, love, love,
love, love, love, love, love, love, love, love, love, love,
love, love, love, love, love, love, love, love, love, love,
love, love, love, love, love, love, love, love, love, love,
love, love, love, love, love, love, love, love, love, love,
love, love, love, love, love, love, love, love, love, love,
love, love, love, love, love, love, love, love, love, love,
love, love, love, love, love, love, love, love, love, love,
love, love, love, love, love, love, love, love, love, love!

Sizzling Happy Family

    The mother and father
who brought me into this life on the cusp of the Crab and the Lion
    now forget

to eat. They line up their dozens of pills on the formica
    counter and swallow them
with over-diluted orange juice concentrate. When we visit, I find nothing

    for dinner but three frozen chicken
pot pies. I take my two children grocery-shopping and cook for all of us
    my own bastard version of Sizzling

Happy Family, that ancient Chinese meal of pork, chicken, beef, and seafood
    grilled together
with vegetables. My wife and I eat no meat, so I sauté tiger shrimp and garlic,

    scallops, squid,
summer squash, red peppers, asparagus, snow peas, and Maine
    mussels with bunches

of cilantro and purple basil chopped. I season it with coarse sea salt
    and fresh
ground pepper, and serve it with a pyramid of corn on the cob picked

    that day. My mother
and father stare at this steaming platter of smells and colors
    harvested from the earth

and ocean, cooked for them in desperation and hunger
    by one of their two
middle-aged sons. Slowly, tentatively, they help

    themselves
to this strange food. My mother picks up a mussel in its shell
    steamed open

like an iris in late April to reveal its blue-and-white-enameled
    inner petals.
She teases out the plump sexual meat and chews its tender

    saltiness. My father
reaches for the corn, then spears asparagus and shrimp together
    on the tines

of his trembling fork. "Remember," he turns to my mother, "Napoli,
    that little trattoria
where we ate linguini with artichoke hearts, and how we saw

    octopi hung on clotheslines
with the day's wash?" My mother holds up a sunburst of squid
    like a wild wedding ring

and stuffs it whole into her mouth. "Yes," she replies, "and the red table wine
    cheap as water
and us on Pegasus, our Harley, cruising down the Costa Brava

    after the war
past the entire Third Army on maneuvers, all those catcalls!" They laugh
    together and have forgotten

us. Sixty years slip like an avalanche from their shoulders. It is
    another country.
They live on kisses and calamari, tasting everything

    the waiter puts
before them—seviche, its raw scallops, onions, and green peppers
    over which my father squeezes

lime juice bright and astringent as sunlight, then fritto misto. Keep eating,
    I want to tell them. Remember
how hungry you are for all of this. Belch. Throw down the napkins

    stained with the prints
of your lips. Order coffee and the pears with rum. Have them flame it.
    Don't leave the table. Not yet.

Summer Arrhythmias

Weak heart, fist knocking on a door that doesn't open,
    have patience.
Keep banging against my ribs. One early afternoon or late summer

    night that has already
been recorded in a hospital chart, God will swing the door
    wide. At first

you won't know what to do. You will stand there
    foolishly knocking
on nothing. The blood slows to a shuffle

    from atrium
to ventricle in its felt slippers and hushes along the starlit
    arteries. Death

is our neighbor. Do you come here to borrow a cup of flour,
    some sugar, an egg?
Stand there on the worn threshold over which

    everyone passes. Outside
the crickets are a digital clock's small alarm. Dawn comes with its crimson
    lipstick streaks. Stars

dissolve. The sky opens its one gold-lidded
    bloodshot eye.
Step through. Leave the body. It has been good,

    all of it—
both the pleasure and the pain you, stammering heart, have given and received
    though not

in equal measures. It doesn't matter. Now, shorn one, you must learn to fly.
    Who will wear the paper
wings my daughter once constructed in kindergarten and gave me

    as a birthday gift? They have purple
and yellow stripes and resemble the blades of oars. They got torn. They won't
    lift me up

in this air I row through now. The only way to go is in and down
    and out.
Heart, you keep hopping like a toad before the power mower.

Cartwheels

That truly the body is a wheel
    in perpetual
motion, that it was never meant

    to stand
upright on two flat feet rooted
    firmly

to the ground, but instead
    to bend
sapling-supple at the waist and hurl

    itself down
and sideways so that the limbs
    spread out

like a starfish's arms from the hub
    of the solar
plexus and become spokes

    that connect
to an invisible
    circumference,

rim that keeps rolling
    the body
around our living room,

    is the
unlikely theorem that my daughter
    proves over

and over. But how long
    it took her
to master the cartwheel's

    fluid
geometry, days, weeks
    of flailing

legs, bruised knees, palms
    burning, her
torso wobbling and toppling

into
a tangle of limbs! But then
    that moment

when the body, which had been
    a teetering
top, suddenly came

    into true
and the center of balance
    shifted

a few millimeters and she
    was
cartwheeling our worn

    kitchen
linoleum, where I stooped
    scrubbing

the crusted dishes and sighing
    over my dying
parents as she

    showed me another
way of walking
    this weighted world.

Following the Calves

Stones grow, the calves stumble
down the bank sloped dusty
toward a residue of green,
toward the brown whips of brush
which swirled beneath water
when it ran here.

This is not for herding,
but following the herd
of young—their amble,
the dust's cloud,
a perfect flowing.

Reaching the other bank
one calf turns back, his body sensing
something his eyes do not—
eyes like moons, yellow
on black, cratered
by spots of sunlight:
his eyes reflect the settling dust
the vanished water
the heredity of rock.

Sometimes I wish for eyes like his,
slow eyes that see
before they know,
measure before they judge,
leave the moment be
rather than absorb it.

I wave and the calf
turns away and trips—
there are stones on that side too—
then trudges up the bank,
dust flowering at his hooves.

Whooping Cranes Near Muscatatuck

Put the picture
where you will always see it,
the dance of an endangered species
at the beginning of the century,
the same floating graceful dance
they felt in their bones
before you came along to watch them
to marvel at their size and grace
to take pictures of objects
you might have once taken in
to the bone. Put the picture
where you will have to see it every day
nature dancing in the face of danger
dancing in a farmer's wetland
in front of a handful of awed people
creatures who have flown so far
on an impulse in their blood
creatures dependent on nature
creatures blowing on their cold hands
walking back and forth
on a gravel road already forgetting
how to dance for their lives.

Indianapolis

It is so cold today, no one runs past my house
to shave off a pound of last year's fat. They cherish
each ounce as coating for the aching bones.
It is late January whose two-faced god
looks to both the past and future. And it seems right
to me to worship anyone who gets me beyond
the misery of the present. Then a whisp of steam
comes out of my neighbor's dryer duct.

It rubs against my window like a ghost that wants in
and I begin to pity steam and half-think I'll open up for him,
when the next ghost rises and, I swear, I see
a face I seem to know . . . and am startled
to recognize mad Willy Blake, Prince of the Eternal
Present, come to check out our chartered streets.
But no one in this city is mad enough to be out
on a day like this: "Only ghosts like you," I tell him.

"Maybe if you wander Indiana Ave. you can find
some of those brothers of Jazz or fathers of the Blues.
We destroyed their haunts. But they're still there,
just as in the old days, little praised and little honored,
but persistent. Or some gust will carry you
like Jesus to the top of the State House dome where D.C. Stephenson
might offer you his kingdom of the Klan for just a genuflection."
Then as if propelled by Blake's own voice, it is I
who am transported to the Wheeler Mission where men,
who look like ghosts, and women, barely alive, vie for a meal.
They were out all night. My heart sinks and I hear old mad Willy whisper
"marks of weakness, marks of woe," and I remember those jazzmen
hammering at the manacles our minds have forged, and those blues riffs
that formed, from the cold, their own long lines. But it was only when Blake's ghost
refused to enter my house, and took his place among the poor, I saw on the window pane
a halo of ice around my breath as if the cold itself were the holy place.

Crawdads

Just west of the barn—
    three storeys fallen in on themselves,
    maple saplings and Virginia creeper
    sprouting, splitting its stone—
a pond once lay.

A pond where men landed bass
as big as buckets or barrels or boats,
depending on the teller.

Drained now of all but legend,
its lone channel cuts through the field,
quenching willow whips and blackberry brambles,

Along its banks are the moundbuilders'
fireless volcanoes,
pebbled mud lava spilling down cones.

The builders have steam shovel hands
and eyes that grow on stems.

Landlocked, they await the tide's return,
the swimming backwards into time.

3/1/04

the road is quiet
in Claysville by the Lost River

the missionaries of 1814
are still there
on the narrow level
between bluff and river

what luck have you had
missionaries
sunlight and dark
averaging themselves out
the old years loose in the air
flying slow like crows
off along the high ridge
near Claysville by the Lost River

This Afternoon

I walked over the cemetery
to the oldest part at the back and higher
where the weeds had been knocked down
and the bare fieldstones on the slave graves
looked like shoulder blades sticking up

their names their birth their sorrows
wrongs and work and wonder and words
for it and mouths to speak minds
to call back and look forward
what they built and carried and knew
what was in their pockets or whispered
back at them with a smile before sleep
and their names are in a register closed to me

the stones are sticking up
someone has cut the vines back
and brought down the saplings
sun and shade go by in turns
birds fly over on their way
not far to an unseen shelter
when I hear the cars
over on the road go by
it sounds like someone's life
slowly escaping

"Such Was Our Garden"

That is all, merely
a matter of poised
cups and fragile
wafers—

the fallen
    flowers of the trumpet vine
    lie in fragments
    of bloody daggers
    about your feet,

and the hollyhocks
    are like beribboned,
    aged virgins,
    sentimental
    with reservations

as the architecture
    they complement,
    as a flirtation
    on a moonlit
    doorstep.

That is all—
    our lives are
    measured with tea
    and almond cakes in austere
    gardens,

and we
    shall strive to ignore
    the insistence
    of decaying
    crimson daggers—

        fleshy,
        and phallic.

Red Maple Leaves

The maple leaves are brilliant
Over the tree lined streets.
The deep shade is filled
With soft ruddy light.
Soon the leaves will all have fallen.
The pale winter sunlight
Will gleam on snow covered lawns.
Here we were young together
And loved each other
Wise beyond our years.
Two lifetimes have gone by.
Only we two are left from those days.
All the others have gone with the years.
We have never seen each other since.
This is the first time I have ever come back.
I drive slowly past your home,
Around the block again and once again.
Beyond the deep pillared porch
Someone is sitting at the window.
I drive down by the river
And watch a boy fishing from the bridge
In the clear water amongst
Falling and floating leaves.
And then I drive West into the smoky sunset.

A Discouraging Model

Just the airiest, fairiest slip of a thing,
With a Gainsborough hat, like a butterfly's wing,
Tilted up at one side with the jauntiest air,
And a knot of red roses sown in under there
      Where the shadows are lost in her hair.

Then a cameo face, carven in on a ground
Of that shadowy hair where the roses are wound;
And the gleam of a smile O as fair and as faint
And as sweet as the masters of old used to paint
      Round the lips of their favorite saint!

And that lace at her throat—and the fluttering hands
Snowing there, with a grace that no art understands,
The flakes of their touches—first fluttering at
The bow—then the roses—the hair—and then that
      Little tilt of the Gainsborough hat.

What artist on earth, with a model like this,
Holding not on his palette the tint of a kiss,
Nor a pigment to hint of the hue of her hair,
Nor the gold of her smile—O what artist could dare
      To expect a result half so fair?

A Variation

I am tired of this!
    Nothing else but loving!
Nothing else but kiss and kiss,
    Coo, and turtle-doving!
        Can't you change the order some?
        Hate me just a little— come!

Lay aside your "dears,"
"Darlings," "kings," and "princes!"—
Call me knave, and dry your tears—
    Nothing in me winces,—
        Call me something low and base—
        Something that will suit the case!

Wish I had your eyes
    And their drooping lashes!
I would dry their teary lies
    Up with lightning-flashes—
        Make your sobbing lips unsheathe
        All the glitter of your teeth!

Can't you lift one word—
    With some pang of laughter—
Louder than the drowsy bird
    Crooning 'neath the rafter?
        Just one bitter word, to shriek
        Madly at me as I speak!

How I hate the fair
    Beauty of your forehead!
How I hate your fragrant hair!
    How I hate the torrid
        Touches of your splendid lips,
        And the kiss that drips and drips!

Ah, you pale at last!
    And your face is lifted
Like a white sail to the blast,
    And your hands are shifted
        Into fists: and, towering thus,
        You are simply glorious!

Now before me looms,
    Something more than human;
Something more than beauty blooms
    In the wrath of Woman—
        Something to bow down before
        Reverently and adore

Lotus

The Lotus World Music and Arts Festival. Bloomington, IN

Music breaks us open
scatters us like seeds
rich autumn hues replace
the pale summer sky
in this small Midwest place
the world swirls: zithers and reeds,
voices of deserts, voices of rain,
congas and castanets
common as heartbeats
call us to dance.

We move ribboned in languages
latitudes and longitudes,
dance with strangers and friends,
flamenco, zydeco, samba,
dance until time and place converge
into this shared harvest of song.

I believe it is possible to transform,
to shimmer with light,
to hold the sounds of the world
on our tongues like cherished nectar,
and then, for our hands to open,
tenderly, like a lotus.

Midwestern Summer: My Dead Mother as Muse

My mother doesn't
like me nosing into her life
   in the afterlife

   any more than she
liked me nosing into it
   in this one. Witness, the

   ratcheting buzz of the cicada—
that's her way of saying,
   Bug off.

   Josie gets to do it. Her mother
loved her. She made a little shrine
   with a skull knife

   on it and her mother
knocks the knife down, says hello. My mother
   teases me with thistle fluff,

   wafting by my windshield
as I sit stalled in traffic on I-94
   in Chicago. I am dying

   to go to the bathroom, creep
inch by inch for two hours. Thistledown,
   nonchalant fairy, drifts unharmed

   between the twin axles
of a Mack truck. On the prairie,
   my mother lures me into watching

   the beautiful dragonfly,
brown bars embossed on its
   glistening transparent wings,

   its little white lobster
tail curled under; she lets me think it
   a shining emissary from the

   other world, then laughs
when I open the folklore
   reference book and discover

that the dragonfly, often known
as the "mosquito hawk,"
    is also nicknamed "the Devil's

    darning needle" and likes to
sew children's mouths shut—their nose, ears,
    and whole heads, too, if

    necessary—when they speak
out of turn. Likewise, the bronze diamond-patterned
    snake reclining in the path—

    she lets me mull that one
over, as I leap three feet in the air.
    The orange monarch with black

    and white spotted regal
head resembles her. It lands on a sprig
    of golden rod, looks at me

    priggishly, asks me to pay
obeisance. The petals of each lavender cone flower
    chirp *love me*, *love me not* through the

    whole damned meadow. I never end up
with the petal I want. Goldfinches follow their
    zigzag radar, while I lurch off

    in search of the new ripe
blackberries my mother leaves for me
    every day on the bush

    under the horse chestnut.
Then suddenly a bramble pops
    up from the path

    and hooks my leg:
"Do you think it's a picnic
    here in the Bardo?"

    Purple lupine, black-eyed Susans.
The shining hip-high grass. Coming around
    a curve in the newly

mown path, I flush a flock
of wood thrushes. Among them is a blue bird —
gorgeous, preternatural.

I remember the new
black silk pantsuit I wore at my mother's
funeral, as if I could ever

approach the dead's
iridescent splendor. I hear the sound of
birdcall, my mother's

laughter, watch the exotic
bluebird vanish down the creek bed
into the thicket of

the other world,
leaving me to choke
on the dust of this.

November 15, before the Frost

That's it, like
a light on
or a light off,
like that tree glorying
in the damp
coolness out there—
you know how
they mysteriously
brighten in the rain—
then shedding, still
glorious,
while I sweat it
out inside,
then boom
the tree
is indistinguishable
from the others,
the yard, the gray
sky, leaf
rot, no,
longer standing
out.

Her Wealth of Shells

Back home again in her heartland she's picked out her best.
She arranges them on a sidetable like a showcase of jewels.

She remembers the night she wakened to the bay water
shaking the air, its whole body a froth of whitecaps,
its bare fangs tearing at the sand and the seawall.

The next morning it wallowed in a bath
of sunshine. Its mammoth weight,
lolling about, lifted a gentle overflow
of ripples along the shore. And then

as if this salt-water monster had casually
tossed it to her, there at her feet
in the wet sand lay the prize
she's been looking for for weeks—
a King's Crown, perfect in every detail.

How could such a clumsy, amorphous
giant teach its little soft ones
to spin from their gelatin bodies these exquisite
private castles, hard as stone?

Now they are here, spread out before her:
ribbed, whorled, voluted, turreted,
in patterns artfully imprecise,
striated or speckled with bands and dabs
of color, smooth as polished gems,
or pebbled with whims of warts and pockmarks.

Granted, the elemental need to survive.
but why this excess, what need to be beautiful?
She tries to imagine how much her forebears
had to forget, aeons ago, while learning
to make her human. One by one

she fingers the shells with names she has had
to learn, like a child, from picture books:
cockle, pecten, whelk, coquina, tellin.
Those with punning nicknames sound
closest to her: tulip, cat's paw,
cat's eye, auger, worm shell, olive.

She watches the landlocked light wither
to mere husks the fabled treasure
she meant to bring home in her plastic bag,

yet says amen to the space that has been given
her in air, on dry land, where she has room
to love them if not to know them. She picks up
her King's Crown. The sultry midwestern
afternoon sweats salt in her hand.

A Brief Story of Time, Outside and In

When he comes face to face with the kitchen clock,
he crosses himself because he's old enough to know that early
or late it's time that threatens him.

And now he can sit and listen to the night outside.

What he hears first is the unceasing, merciless din of traffic
along the nearby highway punctuated
with dissenting sirens. And then from across the river

he detects the church tower keeping the faith,
storing each hour away, melodious quarter by quarter.
What is left for him to do is to listen for silences

within himself deep enough to resonate into one
inexpressible meaning the fury of the pavement
with the meditative bell.

Full Circle

standing near the creek
the last day on the farm
I pointed my camera
and clicked the old tree across the road
soaking up the brilliance of late october sun

moving slightly to the right
I pointed and clicked once more
then
moved
pointed
clicked again
methodically repeating my slow circular dance
until my first photo
became my last

five octobers later the stack of photos
still waits to be assembled into my panorama
titled the last day on the farm
where eyes will move
from creek to barn
past the house
down the hill
to the creek once again

the awful silence of the images
    an empty house starkly white against the sun
    no men wiping foreheads in the fields
    a barn without restless cows wanting milked
does not allow for the whooping and shouting child
running around that house
followed a world war later
by his whooping and shouting son

neither child could guess that someday
the son would mutely turn and turn again

picturing the unbearable

Little Brown Girl, 1927

On viewing John Wesley Hardrick's painting at the Indianapolis Museum of Art

looking into the future
does the seriousness in your face
tell us you know what is to come:
strange fruit in your own indiana
your four little sisters in birmingham
dogs ripping flesh
the voices
of medgar and martin
becoming untimely silent

or does it show
quiet amazement
at the rising of a people
you feared doomed
never to overcome

instead:
you see
laughing little brown girls
confident
prosperous

risen

Dennis Sipe ❧————————————————————————

Hatchery Trout
Gone as Wild as They Can Go

Three weeks after the truck
dumped five hundred trout into Jackson Creek
the corn and worm crowd have given up
and gone home.
They left Mountain Dew bottles and
white plastic cups like offerings
to the god of stupidity.
Their cigarette butts float swelled,
rafted up in foam.

I walk for three hours, hunting cut banks,
probing tree root weaves with nymphs,
before I find a pair of ragged-tailed rainbows
swaying in clear cool current,
swinging their pectoral fins
like ice skaters going nowhere against the wind.

They are where a proper trout would be,
in the funnel stem off the biggest, deepest pool,
only six feet wide, half under a hackberry
with roots like an old woman's arthritic hands
laced in prayer too many hours under an unforgiving sun.

These days, I need reading glasses
and a flip up magnifier
to tie on a dry fly smaller than size sixteen.
I still tremble sometimes, the same as when I was eight
so I make a little mantra to cut the shakes
enough to add two feet of tippet,
and clinch on one of Elwood's mosquitoes.

If he were here he'd say:
*"Just take a deep breath, Jump.
You'll do okay."*

I get a good enough drift over one rainbow.
It rises like god's promise that he will
no longer drown us in flood but use fire,
which cuts out any hope,
unless you are a flaming grayling
that can swim through fire.
But I am rusty and strike too soon.
I switch to my last Adams and
wonder why it is my last Adams
until I lose it in one of the little, overhanging branches
that waves, when I break off,
causing the old hackberry woman to call both trout
home into her dark, safe prayer.

Suddenly, I miss my children and my wife
and think it was enough to find and watch
two survivors of the put and take
that I wouldn't have taken anyway,
only let slip back into their chance.

I head up around the pool to cross the creek,
remember the sandwich
and bottle of beer in the truck.
Right now, I like this life and being me.
This is not Montana but it's okay—
maybe the best it will ever be.
Before I cut over to the road,
I walk down and lean against the hackberry.
When I look down,
dark, crooked fingers are all I see.

135 in Winter

This ridge road is like a frozen snake
caught before it could coil
as it crawled hunting mice
in grain fields that now are gold
and every shade of brown
like plates of rolled out cereal
laid out for hungry gods.
Ravens spread over the fields like raisins.
They raise their wings a little in the wind
slowed by hay rolls joined into giant rolling pins.

When dark settles down like a cold crystal hen,
hungry gods sneak past Pisces
going for the fishhook moon.
They sprinkle snow like powdered sugar
and dance until dawn while it covers their tracks.
They don't care if they step on each other's toes.
They never say they're sorry
and they don't look back.

Improvised Sabbath

New Harmony, Indiana

Two women walk in the town where *history*
is a word like *God*, quiet and huge.
One woman holds a camera, the familiar gesture
of a visitor recording the details of place.
The day itself is golden in a season of rain, of maple
seedlings that twirl and fall. Today summer
considers her arrival; the air so bright and full
the walkers begin to forget the cool spring.

I think too much, says one of them, the one
whose hands are free. They are mostly quiet, though,
walking past a walled cemetery with no markers,
walking toward the recent gate to a labyrinth.
When they stop near the lake, dark fish
like swimming ghosts, neither woman will say a word.

Morning

Between the cat-tails
and an old hawthorn tree,
down where the women gathered
wild strawberries
in the thicket just beyond
the edge of the pond, a child's body
was found floating near dawn
by a fisherman
who'd just said *Good Morning*
to his own son and daughter, *Good Morning*
over a plate of eggs and a slice of dry toast, *Good Morning*
only to find himself standing
in the early sunlight beside the body
of a dead child.
A dragonfly perched on the exposed
throat like a small pendant
his wife might have worn,
convincing him for a moment
it must be a girl, though when he knelt
closer, the narrow hips
and small bruises along the wrists
made him equally certain
it was a boy. The face
lay slightly to one side
like a piece of torn Styrofoam,
eyes partly opened
toward the sky where a cardinal
may or may not have been flying
at that moment,
a dog may or may not
have howled somewhere in the distance
as he noticed the child's small lips, closed
to hide the teeth, clenched
as if to hold back the tongue. *Good Morning,*
it would have said
had the day fulfilled its promise,
had he not found himself on one knee

in the muddy water
at the edge of the pond.
Without thinking
he reached out
to touch the child's hair,
though he would not
include this in his retelling of the story.
He would not describe
skimming over it—running
it through his fingers
like wet grass—not even to his wife,
though she would want to know
every detail, asking again
and again at night
in bed together.
He would keep that for himself,
the hair soft and shiny,
not mossy as you might expect,
but smooth like the water itself,
and later, returning with the other men
who had not found the body themselves
he would think of his own boyhood
as they lifted it
into the air together, the body
extracted like a cloud
from the belly of the pond, rising
then as only a drowned child
can rise.

April

My cousin April unveiled her freckled chest,
the pink nipples like my own, startling me
with our commonness, our bodies that were not yet broken
open, still pink and spongy. At night

under Grandma's satiny comforter, we played
Married, lying on top of each other in the dark, a boy
and a girl, like our parents but happier, her small pelvis
against my hip bone making a soft clatter

deep in its socket. In the morning we'd play
Dress Up, draping ourselves with grandma's
nightgowns and jewelry, a sapphire bracelet,
a rhinestone stick pin, strands of pearls,

the sample lipsticks left by the Avon Lady:
Carnation, Starshine Pink, Dusky Rose, ripe tokens
of womanhood worn by a boy and a girl painting
their nails in the kitchen beside the butter knives,

keeping a look out for my father who'd caught us
once, his temper flaring like the rouge on our cheeks.
Boys don't wear make-up, he'd said, so lipstick
became our secret, April powdering my face, April

whose name was spring, whose body was like mine,
unfinished, almost ethereal, thin as the shadow puppets
we made at night in the porch light, all those birds
and wolves coming out of our hands.

Strawberries

still make me think of David Freeman,
whom I was not supposed to love though I did
that summer, fearlessly, like a fish with a hook
punched through its lip, my teeth struggling
not to name what would be hated,

David, whose mother studied to be a nun
but who lived down the road from us smoking
Camel cigarettes and drinking rye whiskey from Dixie cups,
David, who gave me comic books and a red bandana
and cried in front of me when his stepfather
called him a little prick.

I loved him as I was not supposed to love him,
the two of us sleeping over at my house every night,
side by side, until once in the middle of August,
I kissed him and he awoke, looking at my mouth
as if it were a cut opening in my face,

David, saying I disgusted him, saying he hated me.
And though I asked him to stay, he walked home
anyway, the night pressing against me
like the burn of an exhaust pipe,
small and blossoming on my wrist.

When I finally slept that night I dreamed
of my brothers and the wild strawberries
we sometimes picked in the fields around our house,
which you could take as a sign of hope if this story
had turned out, in any way, differently.

Mary Ellen Solt ℘————————————————————————————————

s   k   y

                    rainrainrain
                  rainrainrainrainrainrain
                rainrainrainrainrainrCLOUDinrain
              rainrainrCLOUDinrainrainrainrain
            rainrainrainrCLOUDinrainrain
          rainrainrainrainrainrainrainrain
        rainrainraCLOUDnrainrainrainrain
          rainrainrainrain
          rainrainrainrain
                              rain
                    rainrain
                                        rain

                    a
                                        i

          r   n

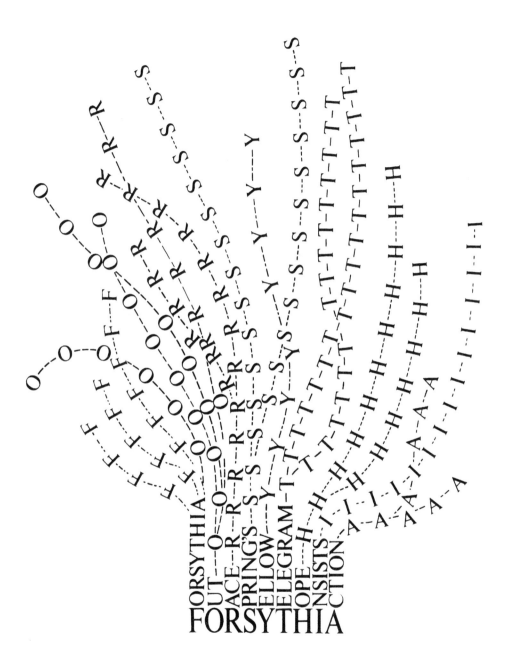

FORSYTHIA

Geranium

SUMMER
TIMES
MEASURES
GOD'S
SILENCE
EXIT
SUMMER
UMBELLAR
RESOUNDS
INTERPRETS
NO ONE
A CAPELLA
ANSWERS
RED
SEEN
EACH

Catharsis

A busy road: I hear a high-pitched wail
Above the traffic, and I catch my breath
To see a big raccoon—masked face, striped tail—
Calling her frightened babies back from death.

The indifferent cars don't notice our panic
As they stream forward in the early twilight—
My waves and screams, her bitter bitter shriek—
As the confused cubs run toward the headlights.

I cover my face. But when I dare look up
The mother's got the babies near the culvert
Under the bridge. I watch them all drop
Into the safety of the sewer, no one hurt.

The drama's over, but I can't weep or cheer.
Have I been purged, or learned a deeper fear?

Simultaneous

Halloween. Passengers on the propjet commuter plane circling
Chicago turn over pages in fat novels with embossed covers, or
murmur to one another about missed connections, or close their
eyes, thinking of home, the one they've left behind or the one
they're so close to, just down there below the turbulent clouds
that make their stomachs churn. The molded plastic purple skull
ring, worn for a joke, flashes on my finger as I gesture in the
classroom which seems to grow brighter as the sky darkens
outside, and thunder rumbles. In her office, a colleague looks
up from reading, thinking of her husband flying through such
weather. An angel with foil-covered wings, and a vampire in a
black rayon cape, each carrying a paper shopping bag, hurry up
the walk to my front door, but since I'm not home, no one
answers. A bolt of lightning makes the students at the seminar
table look up, laugh nervously, and pass around the paper plate
of candy corn and tiny marzipan pumpkins somebody has brought to
class, held during the town's official hours for trick or
treating. "Hurry up, you guys," a father calls out, while the
angel bangs harder at my door. "It's going to pour any
minute." A man driving on Route 55 spots a black puff of smoke,
and sees a plane banking sharply before it plunges to the
ground. The wind rattles windows and bends trees just as
someone praises the beauty of a certain line of poetry. The
angel crouches inside her father's car as the rain streams down
the windshield, her wings mashed against the car seat, while the
vampire takes off his mask, wet from his own breath, and wipes
the lipstick blood off his mouth. Thunder booms, and the sky
cracks with brilliant light. One of my cats claws under the
mattress liner, and burrows into the box springs, while the
other crouches in the dark living room, watching the front door,
her tail quivering. In a soybean field sixty eight hearts and
one hundred and eighty two pieces of luggage explode at the same
moment. My colleague looks at her watch, hoping her husband

will call soon. Up and down my street, rain extinguishes the candles burning in the grinning jack-o'-lanterns set out on front steps. Fourteen students and one teacher look again at a line of poetry, some of us agreeing that it is beautiful, some of us doubting it, and some of us just looking nervously over our shoulders at our reflections on the shaking glass.

Faux Deer

Once, hiking a ridge line in October woods,
I held my breath, surprised to spot a doe
turning to gaze at me. She didn't leap
across my path, and disappear in the brush,
so I dared a step, and then another step,
wishing I could stroke her velvet nose,
or murmur endearments into her big ears.
That's when I found she was a rigged-up decoy,
set up to fool the poachers. She'd been shot
over and over, her hide seared with bullets.
I shivered to think of someone sighting along
a rifle barrel from the ravine below,
and ran back to the trail, forgetting her
on the drive home. But today I remember
my spoiled hike as I read this news story,
DEER DECOYS CATCH POACHERS IN ACT.
Our state now has sixteen look-alikes
with detachable antlers that can revise
a buck into a doe, and other creatures,
fake owls, eagles, coyotes, hawks, wild turkeys
posing as game, hidden in the state parks.
In the AP photo, conservation officers
carry Artie out of the bare grey woods
for repair. He's in pieces, his antlered head
unswiveled from his lacerated trunk.
I stare at the scene, trying to match it
to some lost feeling, that dreamy moment
before I grasped the danger we were in
and simply stood there in childlike wonder
at the magic deer, unafraid of me,
who seemed to have stepped from a fairy tale
where animals talk, and humans understand.

And Know This Place | Poetry of Indiana

Winter Walk

One winter night, faces hidden in scarves,
We two tramped out across the snowy park
Down in the dumps about most everything,
When all at once we glimpsed a snow angel
Brushed into the hillside we were climbing,
A small, shallow shape just visible
In the moonlight. We stopped, and you exclaimed
You'd never actually seen one before,
Though I'd stretched out across a snowdrift once
To show you the technique. But I was heavy,
And jumping to my feet, left the outline
Of someone knocked down, murdered, dragged away.
But here was a perfect child-sized angel
(Boy or girl, no way on earth to tell)
Like a rare intaglio in the deep snow,
And we cheered up, thinking it an omen.
Next night, the weather still cold, we followed
The same path, and there it was, untrampled,
Though now surrounded by many boot prints
Of others who had stepped carefully around
On smooth or waffled soles. I thought about
All the people who'd paused here just like us
Looking down at the angel, so personal
(the child's cap had a tassel at its tip)
And yet, somehow, so strangely anonymous—
If we could only make a mark like that
When we die, whirling our arms into wings.

The Catch

Your college learn you be smart, talk fancy. You go with the
girls, talk fancy. You tell your mother, Ma, why you got the
bun on your head, old fashion. Your college learn you don't
respect your mother. Some college. Now you say this girl you
live together, marriage never mind, old fashion. Your mother
cry, and with the beads pray pray and pray. What you think,
she ask me. You know what I think, boy? I think if you was
pig we raise by and by we sell you for money now, not your
mother cry.

Midwest Fantasy

1. Winter: Red's Barbershop

Boys who played the games they've always played,
at nine years old, at forty nine years old,
the snow, the moose, the lake, the air so cold
it hurt to breathe, as someone said,
calling to his buddies up ahead—
he slipped into an icy ditch, and spilled
his guts caroming, but his rib-cage held.
He laughed and laughed. His buddies called him mad.

The barbershop is buzzing up a storm
of memories this snow-sharp afternoon, some boys
as full of liquor as they are of noise,
such is the fellowship that keeps them warm.
Later, back home, their women will cut loose
at them about that moose, that bloody stupid moose.

2. Spring: The Mourning Dove

The mourning dove, soft idiot on my sill,
pecks at the glass. Surprised it does not yield
he straightens up, and blinks his button eye,
and like a small parade struts back and forth,
then shows his white behind and flies away.

3. Summer: August

This heavy hour,
this ton of light;
the blinding pane,
all I can do is squint

at the garden with its look
of frost in early dawn,
where a cricket is making music.
The mirage cuts like a knife.

Then I stare as hard as I can
at the squirrel in the pawpaw branch

not three feet from the window.
He is heaving, heaving.

I think of the flameshapes of the corn,
tumescent and gold,
that point and point.
Where my dream walks they cackle.

4. Autumn: Indiana

Now the sheaves crackle
to the touch, like new dollar bills.
Glowing October. The irrigation pond
shimmers.

Like a stampede the stand of trees
in the distance shudders its green mane—
glint and ripple of shadow,
mist on the ground running silver.

The ditch by the road heaves with plumes.
A rock shows its head among the yarrow.
Poetry is a gun
aimed at the fat hare trundling across

the field. He comes to a stop,
sits up, ears twitching.
I have been at my window all morning,
my page covered with the showering thresher's dust
that flirts in the breeze like gauze,
like a flag.

At the Widow Kate's Retirement Banquet

The guest of honor sits, as patient as
the furniture, and listens maybe to our talk
about her service to the cold country
of working for a living forty years,
and raising up three kids without a man.
Among the cataracts of drapes, the cliffs of glass,
she gleams, the slender willow by the stream
of our smooth conversation, the fragile fact.
And old boys joke, and the Big Boss swoops down
from the eagle's nest of his democracy
to grasp her by the hand, and wish her well;
while all she does, like a willow by a stream
in sunlight, is to toss her flowing hair.

First Performance of the Rock 'n' Roll Band *Puce Exit*

If puce were sound not color,
    it would be us: Deep Purple,
though more confused and discordant,

our guitars tuned in electric ignorance
    of tone, key, each other—the word
puce derived from the Latin for "flea,"

as appropriate for pests in the hides
    of neighbors—our raucous weekend practice,
pubescent groupies lingering on basement steps,

first on the block to show hearing loss,
    first to wear paisley with polka dots.
And *exit*, of course, because music is

our ticket out. It's Peggy Wasylenski's
    fourteenth birthday party, a real gig,
her parents too cool, or simply so new

to America they're expecting something
    with accordion and banjo, not the freight
we unload from my father's blue Chevy:

amps, mikes, drums, Christmas color wheels
    for visual effect. We set up in the dirt
floor garage, our amps a wall of sound

maybe knee high across the left bay.
    Everything's plugged into a quad outlet
above the single ceiling bulb. Orange wires

cascade around us like a waterfall
    of blown fuses. We start, start over,
and start again, until we get right

the three drumstick beat and launch into
    an 18 minute version of "Satisfaction."
I'm howling "I can't get no!" even though,

in eighth grade, I'm not sure what it is
    I can't get any of, but it's something,
I am sure, I need as badly as any guy

ever needed anything, like "voice lessons,"
        the drummer screams. On break, we play
spin the bottle, Peggy flicking her tongue

and me choking with surprise, with glee,
        with adolescent resolve to improve
on the next round, which never comes.

Police arrive to pull the knotted plug
        and send us scurrying for the bushes,
guitars around our necks, though no one

is drunk or stoned on anything other than
        the rush of innocence soon to take a turn,
accelerating around the corner like Peggy,

three years later, first night with license
        and the family station wagon, her eyes
on the lit radio dial and not on the barber,

my barber, trudging home in rain, the scissors
        in his breast pocket soon to puncture
his heart beneath her tire's worn tread.

But none of that has happened to happen.
        It's spring, and the bushes we hunker in
make riotous bloom. They smell of sachet,

cheap pink tins scenting my mother's floral
        dressing table. Or maybe it's Peggy,
her breath against my still whiskerless face,

cops' flashlights, cymbals hissing as they spill
        in puffs of dust, and neither of us
in a hurry to leaven this sweet bouquet.

Adolescent Hemlock

Say you're 16 and your mother's dying in
spoonfuls of custard frosted around its edge
by your avocado refrigerator
green as the eyes she's dying in,
so while you're there you squeeze in
some Plochman's mustard yellow as the skin
she's dying in, and pitiless Vivaldi offers
endless winter because the turntable's needle
rides the carpet of dust we'll all become,
and since from dust ye came, you add a pinch
from the floor's corner the mop won't reach
when she kicks the bucket she's dying in
while redbuds shed their tousled blooms
as she does her hair, so you fist in
dropped blossoms for the color her cheeks
used to be, though at 16 you leave
things open as the bed she's dying in,
pink sheets and daisies, so petals and pollen
lend the blender a festive note as you ladle in
Liquid Drano—one cup, two—and press puree.

Say your mother's already half down
the drain, and your sodden father's passed out
upon the couch, and your footfalls fill
the small hall her bedroom spills in.
Say the mug's beneficence brims
its grim grin—this kindness, her letting go.
Say you give a shiver when guilt trills
its little a cappella in your seashell ear,
so it's 1-2 a gulp for you, 3-4 down some more,
5-6 you'll get sick, 7-8 accept your fate,
9-10 the end begins. Say the shocked doc's
plastic shunt salvages your burnt gullet.
Say a nurse hunts the beaded string she's looped
through your nose, throat, gut, and out
so your airway won't scar shut. Say you die
but don't. Say you dream then what you've dreamed

before: frosh gym, and Mr. Wooden splinters
his voice poking you up the knotted rope.
For once no snickers, no jock itch, not a single
twitch or bead of sweat. Say the air's as hushed
as the hospital waiting room. Say this time—
no, next—you'll reach the top knot's heaven.

First Day, Container Corporation of America, June 1972

When the bleak break-room smokers asked,
    "What you run?" I answered "the half
and quarter mile," to which response

they burst in furious, gut-clutching
    yucks and howls. "No, boy," one said,
"what *machine* you run?" and I got it.

Both the joke I'd innocently made
    and the joke I was: high-school-Harry
among the balding, unionized sublime.

"Slitter 66," I said, and their blue
    ballooning guffaw burst in rarefied air,
everyone exhaling Lucky Strike at once.

Eighteen, big-haired and mutton-chopped,
    brand new black pocket tee taut over
my still tight gut, I thought they saw

the future in me and shuddered
    at their vision. Or was it their past,
themselves before the war to save

democracy—resplendent in white shirt
    and dungarees—now pot-bellied and shot?
The young think things like that.

How could I know the guy whose job I took
    came home boxed from Vietnam,
a war I fought in TV news clips

and the peace marches of us blessed
    with high draft numbers? I ate alone:
mother's cold meat loaf, bruised banana,

a Coke that gave me the jitters.
    When the horn burped, I lit out for work
like the apple polisher I'd planned to be,

though not before those men
    who'd seemed too gray had heaved me
in a tin bin of cardboard scrap

and slammed the lid, their fists beating
    rhythm to the heart thumping my throat.
Whatever republic we were then,

its pulse beat among us,
    though no one would say
the word. Sprawled headfirst

among mis-cuts and discards,
    the dross of a process I'd yet
to learn—man, this was a start.

Our Armor

"Clothes make the man."

Where the sleeve cuts I've left to experts
in men's issues, say, how the break of cuff asserts
authority in this blue pinstriped looking-for-work.
To be a man is to labor with hard heart,
for cruelty is men's work, knowledge ancient
as declensions of the genitive plural, nuances
of subjunctive mood, that sorry scribe who scrawled
Vestis virum reddit and bade us remember
the chastened agent of virtue tested. And failed.
As when balding Miss Spalding, importuned
from retirement, so frantically thwacked
the black pointer on chalked verbs her teeth fell
from sunken lips not once but daily—pink debacle
jeered by the huddled offensive line and backfield
sketching dream play X's and O's
before half-ass practice they snoozed through.
Merciless, those starters and we who'd lie to be.

She stank of rank musk, or so we thought,
knowing squat of that region we'd wasted legions
of calories lusting after. She fumed at our ineptitude.
Spumes of foamy spit flecked desks nailed down
as nothing in our lives and all in hers. We hairy
howled at her gate, last castle in the kingdom
of union wage—fathers' Trojan horse, our birthright
the belly of a beast. So in season she was in season,
our weapons those we grew into: Gary's hand
that sloshed his cock around the lip of Miss Spalding's
coffee cup, 33rd straight she left class to slip
her teeth back in. Our hands that pinched
cheerleaders' cheeks so they gawked-blushed-giggled.
Hand behind the hand that shut my mouth as her lipstick
tattooed the cup of our belly-laugh, bitter grounds of cruelty—
word descended from Middle English, from the dainty French,
originally from Latin *crūdēlis, crūdēle,* "morally unfeeling,"

an inkling that comes to me now in the tri-view mirror,
the tailor dutifully asking "Dress left or right?"

so he'll measure the inseam without my flinching.
What makes a man? Can such a fool thing be said?
Not the rope hung between his thighs,
nor fist nor fart nor hairy arm. Not parts factory
nor burnt lubricant sweat. Not the mendicant
steward's pocketed pint of Beam.
Not a pencil-necked foreman grinning green.
Not the stench of smoker's bench.
Not overtime. Not the rusted lunch box
father hands to son. Not this cut of clothes.
Can't a fool say what makes a man? Speak up.
I wish I'd hollered before her lips met the cup.
I wish that huddle had kicked my chicken ass.

Reflections in a Furniture Store Window

In the furniture store window TV
plays all night. People are in their beds,
even the bad boys who ride skateboards
and the girls who stand with them in
the bank's empty parking lot, looking bad
in black dresses faces painted white
to light somebody's way into dark places—
they are all asleep in fugitive beds
under someone else's sheets.

This is the hour when the television plays
all night so that ghosts can hear race car drivers
sermonize on motor oils, watch violence and sex,
watch people opening wide the spigots
of their souls until back ooze pours out like tar
and the excited audience swills down like lemonade.

The ghosts are neither happy nor unhappy.
They are ghosts, they have nowhere else to go,
they cannot exactly distinguish between fast foods
and beer ads, and they are not sure if news
is different from these, or from the singers
who grunt out inconsolably.

Far beyond them, the girls in black
trail in the dreams of skateboarders
could tell ghosts this and much more,
but they're asleep in a country of amethyst
where everything floats in violet without abrasion.

Here, dresses are of skin that shimmers
like light, and the boys, not hungry anymore,
don't need skateboards to glide and glide on purple seas
under a purple sun, until a deeper current takes them,
and not even television interests them any longer.

Returning to the City of Your Childhood

In the framed black-and-white photograph
on the wall of your rented furnished condominium,
you imagine a hidden garden of blue cornflowers.
It drifts in the acid residue. In this black-and-white
photograph, the garden you imagine is beyond
a narrow passageway between two buildings.
For you, it exists in spite of this jerry-built
investment condominium. And you imagine
someone, perhaps it is you, in the hidden part
of the photograph; you, a child, are looking over
a plank fence to where surely, (you imagine),
a grandfather is nailing together piece by careful
piece an original wooden dollhouse
(not yours, it was never yours). In reality you once
watched him, that grandfather beyond the fence,
with your own trust in miracles, at age six.
In the room where the photograph (not yours) hangs,
a montage sharp as the odor of fresh sawdust.
You put your hand against the striated silence.
What are these things that draw toward us,
these visitors who hide among us,
who are as the air that enters,
giving and taking away . . .

Icons from Indianapolis

The fountain around the soldiers' and sailors' monument,
the mist from the splashing water, the Murat Theater;
it was there I waited for the young man I loved,
hour after hour. Often he would not come.
I leaned against the walls of a candy shop,
boxes of rubber chocolates in the window,
behind me buses snoring their pneumatic doors.
His thin bent-down body too tall
like the priest he went away to be but never was;
often exhausting even my compulsion to wait for him.
Once when he kissed me I swooned. His name was
    Mike Tarpey.
Even after I was engaged to someone else,
I would meet him in the park. I was not Irish. I would walk
past Our Lady of Lourdes, the sisters starched into archways
beyond the cement Pietà. I doubted even the Presbyterians.
I could see the older black woman in the bus station,
pus running down her legs, gushing out of her,
the policeman coming to take her away. What were hats
and fur shawls when I knew that? She never left me.
From that time I carried her like an icon.
In these catacombs also he lies in perfect condition;
age nineteen, black hair, his thin jaw slightly out of line.
Was it that Picasso-like shift in planes that I could never
look at enough? These go with me where I go.
I wrap them in linens without prayers. I carry them.

American Milk

Then the butter we put on our white bread
was colored with butter yellow, a cancerous dye,
and all the fourth grades were taken by streetcar
to the Dunky Company to see milk processed; milk bottles
riding on narrow metal cogs through little doors that flapped.
The sour damp smell of milky-wet cement floors:
we looked through great glass windows at the milk.
Before we were herded back to the streetcar line,
we were each given a half pint of milk in tiny
milk bottles with straws to suck it up. In this way
we gradually learned about our country.

The Provider

Several crows were lined up along the ridge of a quite ordinary house. "These ridge poles are a good idea," said a young one. "Who dreamed it up?" "This place of rest is a fortuitous gift from the moon," said a raven who was mixing with the hoi polloi today. "The moon is a relative of the roc, a distant cousin of mine. Believe me," he said, stretching his wings out to their full advantage and pushing the crows at the end off balance, so several leaped into the wind and cried "caw". . . "it depends on your original stock. I've got a piece of the roc." The moon rose spectral and drained, a gossamer imprint of her nighttime self, a reminder of crystal fracture, the load of swinging primitive stones, the ancient hairy arms with slingshots. A sudden explosion and the sky was defined with flapping and cawing. "What was that?" cried the young one who was addicted to awe. "Who knows?" replied the raven. "Often the moon demands a sacrifice. As a close relative, it is now my duty to go and eat the meat. For it is said, nothing is wasted; nothing is without purpose." And the raven rose and flew toward the hunters.

On the Farm

The evening of the day
Grandpa hobbled the back feet
of the black and white beagle with jute,
then lashed the cinched legs to a stone,
I watched the pond rise and fall,
as if to breathe.

I leaned against the sagging gate,
listened to the crickets throb,
the frogs grumble and splash,
and I knew a dog's nose pointed
to the wrinkled moon above the surface.

That night in the bedroom
after prayer and supper around the kerosene lamp
I first saw the darkness under my mother's eyes
and the pulsing of my baby sister's skull
tight against my mother's breast.

I floated my hand
softly over the smooth and powdered skin
to feel whatever thrashed there
and wanted free.

When We Were Young: A Brown County Memory

here it is again
surfacing as a stone from soil
whispering in the rain
that trickles down the window pane
pools in garden and lane   then
sings in narrow rivulets down the hill to join the spring
falling dark silver to the pebbly creek

at the end of the fruit cellar
path winding through plum and cherry
stand of pines
path we walked to deep and pungent woods
turning a furrow of wet leaves behind us
sun splashing through lace canopy of oak and beech
laying a necklace of light around us
on the forest floor

it rises as easily as crocuses and grief
where we'd been   oh!
how we breathed
our bright familiar air

Another Way

If you were immured in melancholy
and I gave you a field
of purple asters in autumn,
each mauve disc encircling a bright yellow center
like the light of morning,
a field of a thousand mornings,
would you take them with you into winter?

When the press of hours pushed
like harried crowds at your back
and I showed you to a wide shore
where blue waves curled in,
line after line,
scrumbling and swirling over boulders,
pulling back to re-form, fluently,
and I offered this rhythm
as my gift of time,
would you call me impractical?

If you felt as empty as a sketch
and I told you of an old field
where seed-rank-growth of mazy colors,
woven with webs and songs, overflowed,
and I said that you could walk in this fullness
and swell like a chrysalis
would you dismiss me
with incredulous eyes?

I know an old apple tree,
twisted and gnarled,
that bears sparse fruit.
If I made you a seat
beneath its thick and graceful limbs
to nourish you with its age,
would you smile
but think me foolish?

If you were subdued by grief
and I asked you to come with me
where waves rise and break like imagination,
could you sit silent, remembering,
until your sadness became
the cry of seabirds?

And if you grew haughty
and I asked you to leave
your cities of glittering props
and stay alone
in a shadowless forest night,
could you wait
for the splintered light of morning?

Thomas Tokarski

Lucky Life

Upriver from Metropolis, its flaking
Superman square-jawed in heavy Illinois
spring, the Ohio's spilled past levees,
dirty water kissing the legs of stilted

trailers leaning back longingly toward
Kentucky from the Indiana shoreline.
The Evansville roads drive right down
to the river, trails disappearing any

season into back-eddying currents
as if submerging is the only answer
to the life these swampy bottoms offers.
Imagine: a boy or girl scrambling up

or out of the aluminum shelters, all
smudgy arms and legs speckled with
the bitemarks of fleas and mosquitoes
breeding in the stagnant backwash:

what technicolor paints the days and
nights this child passes? A few spindly
antennas crown metal roofs, electric
possibility channeling in *The Price*

Is Right, *Wheel of Fortune* opulence
shaping these lives to an All-American
mold. Huddled about the pixilated fire,
cartoon promises guarantee *That's all,*

folks! with piggish glee, but is it?
Downstream Merv Griffin's riverboat
casino rests moored between its nightly
cruises back and forth from debt and

its release, but the short odds belong
to the house. Trotline runners and
would-be farmers gather here with
the semi-pros to rearrange slick chips,

the ruttish numbers spinning orderly
behind the smile of the pit boss.
Captain Fantastic won't be here tonight
or any night, so these luck wranglers

rustle one another, hoping to herd
together a clutch of compliant faces.
Flood or drought, the land sinks here
beneath the economy's tide of desire.

Indiana Marriage

The state did not require my blood
and yours had passed all inquiry
this county seat demanded, so we
hurried back to find the cashier
before she locked up for the day.

It wasn't bad once we figured out
the maze of offices, and, as she
checked our forms for accuracy and
completeness, you noticed half
the fee went to a fund for battered

and abused spouses. The judges
were all booked for end of the year
ceremonies, the mayor and vice-
mayor out of town for the holidays,
so we settled on the city clerk

and waited for the weeks to pass
until my parents and your sister
could get away to witness our vows.
A gray day like most that December,
you wore a purple dress and I

slipped on a sweater, and we drove
the few blocks to the city office
building that looked more like
an old elementary school, orange-
brick facing the only festive touch

of the afternoon. The assistant
city clerk showed up in her tennis
shoes—the clerk a victim of that
winter's flu—but she brought along
a robe for an official touch, and

she led us back to where they kept
the vows, xeroxed sheets where names
were scratched or whited out and
replaced time and again as each new
couple registered their vows and

joined the temporary lexicon. We
chose innocuous words, quick and
direct and without vestiges of
overt possession or obedience.
There was hardly time for my

mother to tear up before we both
said "I do," and we were done.
Two friends who hoped to witness
the event were five minutes late
and we met them and hugged,

and then the wedding party—
such as it was—drove to the town's
only seafood restaurant where
my father treated us all to shrimp
and crab and so-called catch of the day.

As we toasted with our water
glasses raised high, the waitress
brought out a thick slice of Key
lime pie, and we fed one another
a bite of its tart sweetness.

Center of Gravity

The man beside me stares up at television
replays of races that ended three days ago

while paramedics try to hold his son's leg
together. The boy's friends left him pinned

in a car—better not to call the police, he was
drunk, a second DWI worse than death to

them, more real—and the man says he can't
wait to get his hands on them. I skim *Popular*

Science, try to find something in the pages
to convince me of anything more than

the smallness of this place, frustration I don't
want to share with the guy in the DeKalb cap

whose girlfriend's telling the police everything
except, *He hit me. He doesn't mean to, but*

he hits me a lot. When he walks out with her
later, her face shiny with bruises, she stops him

from opening the door, says, *It's too late*
for that, just loud enough for any of us left

here watching Championship Wrestling to hear,
but we're too good at not listening, the only art

any of us has mastered. The nurses won't tell me
how you're doing—*nothing's been determined*—

and they sit around with their coffee and
tell one another how busy they are, how they

can't believe so much is happening here.
No one else in the waiting room and I'm

tempted to turn off the ball game, remember
a friend who said baseball is the perfect game

—no time limit—played perfectly by both sides
a game would go on forever, and I think about

these players giving every last strain to end
things and keep things going. It's a terminal

world, the center only a shifting mass of jello.
Popular Science reported this—researchers

creating computer simulations, astronauts
completing experiments in space observing

globes filled with silicon. They're pleased
how the two appear similar, another proof

in a universe of guessing. They also found
new matter, quasi-crystals that shouldn't exist,

but do, despite expectations, breaking rules
we once thought applied. If they'd just

let you out, we could go home and I wouldn't
think about these things, just hold you against

the pain, bring you water and poppyseed cake
and re-enter an orbit that makes some sense to me.

Cicada Sonnet

for Ashley

Mud chimneys after rainy weather—a sign that something's
afoot. White cicada pupas with bright red eyes burble
underground. Biding. Temperature's secret handshake
signals a munching eruption, soft bodies boil from tunnels
like bubbles in simmering rice. All at once a screech—
seventeen years of swallowed squeal—releases, sprung
sprocket, hilarity of air and sap. Tympanum mad to prattle,
chatter up this host of neighbors, find a mate to hitch with,
grapple abdomens, babble. Best of all, the shedding.
Flip backwards out of straightjacket stricture, jettison
exoskeleton. We're here to find their brittle alien armor
in the evening, crackling with lack, the hollow whirring
of absent wings, wings we'd like to sail off with, trade
brown husks for translucence and a flood of wind.

The Lucky Bamboo
Tipton, Indiana

You'll find it next to the Ti-on Lounge
in a town named for the general who oversaw
the 1838 "Trail of Death." In this jungle
of styrofoam crates stacked full of bamboo
stalks, rhizomes resting in shallow pools, spiked
tongues shouting their green language
of chlorophyll and life, I follow a scent of water
and silt through shelves of potted bamboo and
bonsai along stained carpet paths that wind
like sand trails in a Zen garden while outside,
the geometric grid surrounding the yellow stone
courthouse stirs in summer heat with an erratic
pulse of traffic. I listen to the owner
who tells of how bamboo replaced
cut flowers as an offering to God because
it could store water and endure while across
the street, the decaying marquee of the Diana
proclaims its coming attraction, Legally Blond II.
But what have bamboo and bonsai
trees to do with this town of McDonald's
Diners and hardware stores? What if
General Tipton had climbed the rock face
of this bonsai pedestal and sat on the precipice
against the braided trunk with this miniature
figure of a Chinese sage whose white beard
flows earthward toward some wellspring? Would he
have tendered an offering of bamboo while
beneath him the shrouded Potawatomi drifted
past, and above him the foliage of the bonsai
had already begun to turn brown?

The Topeka Auction Restaurant
Topeka, Indiana

We sit at a table for two perusing place settings
with blocked ads for Eastside Enterprises "New
and Used Buggies" and Deisler Chiropractic
Services "For You and Your Horse." On the back
wall, a blackboard proclaiming the "Haystack Special"
interrupts the procession of brindled cows
and bay horses affixed to a faded border.
The August sun casts a spotlight on my pale
arms and face and my Cardinal baseball hat
flashes its red blush in the company of sweat-streaked
Massey-Ferguson and Wellman Feed caps
while a parade of well paunched farmers trust
invisible feet to troll the "All You Can Eat"
Buffet for fried chicken and country fried steak.
Outside, Amish buggies soak up summer,
the frothy shanks of horses ripple almost
imperceptibly as they paw the earth like a man
kicking off dirt before crossing a threshold.

Across the street at the Topeka Seed and Stove
we admire the wood stoves, the heft of their
black haunches, boulders fastened to kitchen
floors. The salesman spots "a live one" and launches
into a homespun legend of wives placing premature
babies in the bread warmers and I imagine
fetal forms rolling toward some boiling baptism,
the family recipe for rivel soup. In the sale barn

our bare legs blaze neon as buyers spread
their girth over bleachers, rooting themselves
to floors stained with manure. As the auctioneer begins
a cicada chorus that washes over this wooden
ark like wind over wheat, glass-eyed bulls stagger
across straw and sawdust floors under the scrutiny
of these immutable Noahs whose every
flinch inflects the cadence. We are stowaways

here; we sit with backs hunched, our anxious
hands cuffed to our knees, but as the song swells,
our restless limbs relax, our bodies sag back
in search of support as we begin to feel it
calling us home like cattle who have strayed
too far on the hill.

Chuck Wagner

Anti-Slavery Cemetery
Westfield, IN

These stones have names
the rain rubs into silence: Bales,
White, Hiatt, Sumnar, Moon—Friends
of conscience who hid
the refugee behind a false
wall or their own plain
bonnet and veil, who fed
the hunter and the hunted
from the same cast iron
skillet, who led families
on foot, at night, through Dismal
Swamp, then crossed back
alone. One strayed
from his theology, raised
a stout stick to save
a child. Eleven went
to war, relinquishing
the perfection they sought.

All are gathered now,
in this solitary space,
beneath old trees
and broken stones. All
are gathered and all
are gone, but the light
remains, the light
that traces the indentation
of a life
and remembers.

"Washington Street, Indianapolis, at Dusk"

(1892–95) / Theodore Groll
Indianapolis Museum of Art

It's not merely that the sun
dissolves into the northeast
nor that the State House broods
too near the street, something else
is not right and the dog with a boy
at the end of a leash
knows it. He braces hind legs
and will not budge.

Could it be the bearded man
brandishing his brass-headed
cane to hail the Blake Street
trolley who causes the dog
to bristle, this man with
a face cold and precise
as a pocket-watch, who stands
oblivious to pedestrians bartering
or loitering closer to the foreground,
their countenances bearing
the blur of hurried brush strokes?
What deception does the dog sniff?
Or does he detect some danger
further on, past Park Theatre,
its liturgical line of hansom cabs,
to where Washington recedes
into a sulfuric haze
of electricity and gas? Maybe
the dog is tired. Maybe
he does not want to step
foot into the future
but, instead, would follow
trolley tracks back
to an avenue of porches
and his own ragged rug
by the hearth. The end

Shari Wagner

of a century and he surmises
what those looking askance
are too preoccupied to foresee:
when the mules turn the trolley,
they will proceed to vanish,
as will the wagons,
the vendors,
the fish-tainted barrels,
the scent of horse sweat
and bread.

Maybe his dog sense tells him
this one truth: that from a distance
nothing matters, not
a dog, not a boy,
not a dingy street, nothing
but the ethereal theatre,
or rather, its facade,
illuminated by a light
almost lurid.

The Junior High School Band Concert

When our semi-conductor
Raised his baton, we sat there
Gaping at *Marche Militaire*,
Our mouth-opening number.
It seemed faintly familiar
(We'd rehearsed it all that winter),
But we attacked in such a blur,
No army anywhere
On its stomach or all fours
Could have squeezed through our cross fire.

I played cornet, seventh chair
Out of seven, my embouchure
A glorified Bronx cheer
Through that three-keyed keyhole stopper
And neighborhood window slammer
Where mildew fought for air
At every exhausted corner,
My fingering still unsure
After scaling it for a year
Except on the spit-valve lever.

Each straight-faced mother and father
Retested his moral fiber
Against our traps and slurs
And the inadvertent whickers
Paradiddled by our snares,
And when the brass bulled forth
A blare fit to horn over
Jericho two bars sooner
Than Joshua's harsh measures,
They still had the nerve to stare.

By the last chord, our director
Looked older and soberer.
No doubt, in his mind's ear
Some band somewhere
In some music of some sphere
Was striking a note as pure
As the wishes of Franz Schubert,
But meanwhile here we were.

A lesson in everything minor,
Decomposing our first composer.

The Shooting of John Dillinger Outside the Biograph Theater, July 22, 1934

Chicago ran a fever of a hundred and one that groggy Sunday.
A reporter fried an egg on a sidewalk; the air looked shaky.
And a hundred thousand people were in the lake like shirts in a laundry.
Why was Johnny lonely?
Not because two dozen solid citizens, heat-struck, had keeled over backward.
Not because those lawful souls had fallen out of their sockets and melted.
But because the sun went down like a lump in a furnace or a bull in the Stockyards.
Where was Johnny headed?
Under the Biograph Theater sign that said, "Our Air Is Refrigerated."
Past seventeen FBI men and four policemen who stood in doorways and sweated.
Johnny sat down in a cold seat to watch Clark Gable get electrocuted.
Had Johnny been mistreated?
Yes, but Gable told the D.A. he'd rather fry than be shut up forever.
Two women sat by Johnny. One looked sweet, one looked like J. Edgar Hoover.
Polly Hamilton made him feel hot, but Anna Sage made him shiver.
Was Johnny a good lover?
Yes, but he passed out his share of squeezes and pokes like a jittery masher
While Agent Purvis sneaked up and down the aisle like an extra usher,
Trying to make sure they wouldn't slip out till the show was over.
Was Johnny a four-flusher?
No, not if he knew the game. He got it up or got it back.
But he liked to take snapshots of policemen with his own Kodak,
And once in a while he liked to take them with an automatic.
Why was Johnny frantic?
Because he couldn't take a walk or sit down in a movie
Without being afraid he'd run smack into somebody
Who'd point at his rearranged face and holler, "Johnny!"
Was Johnny ugly?
Yes, because Dr. Wilhelm Loeser had given him a new profile
With a baggy jawline and squint eyes and an erased dimple,
With kangaroo-tendon cheekbones and a gigolo's mustache that should've been
     illegal.
Did Johnny love a girl?
Yes, a good-looking, hard-headed Indian named Billie Frechette.
He wanted to marry her and lie down and try to get over it,
But she was locked in jail for giving him first aid and comfort.

David Wagoner

Did Johnny feel hurt?
He felt like breaking a bank or jumping over a railing
Into some panicky teller's cage to shout, "Reach for the ceiling!"
Or like kicking some vice president in the bum checks and smiling.
What was he really doing?
Going up the aisle with the crowd and into the lobby
With Polly saying, "Would you do what Clark done?" And Johnny saying "Maybe."
And Anna saying, "If he'd been smart, he'd of acted like Bing Crosby."
Did Johnny look flashy?
Yes, his white-on-white shirt and tie were luminous.
His trousers were creased like knives to the tops of his shoes,
And his yellow straw hat came down to his dark glasses.
Was Johnny suspicious?
Yes, and when Agent Purvis signaled with a trembling cigar,
Johnny ducked left and ran out of the theater,
And innocent Polly and squealing Anna were left nowhere.
Was Johnny a fast runner?
No, but he crouched and scurried past a friendly liquor store
Under the coupled arms of double-daters, under awnings, under stars,
To the curb at the mouth of an alley. He hunched there.
Was Johnny a thinker?
No, but he was thinking more or less of Billie Frechette
Who was lost in prison for longer than he could possibly wait,
And then it was suddenly too hard to think around a bullet.
Did anyone shoot straight?
Yes, but Mrs. Etta Natalsky fell out from under her picture hat.
Theresa Paulus sprawled on the sidewalk, clutching her left foot.
And both of them groaned loud and long under the streetlight.
Did Johnny like that?
No, but he lay down with those strange women, his face in the alley,
One shoe off, cinders in his mouth, his eyelids heavy.
When they shouted questions at him, he talked back to nobody.
Did Johnny lie easy?
Yes, holding his gun and holding his breath as a last trick,
He waited, but when the agents came close, his breath wouldn't work.
Clark Gable walked his last mile; Johnny ran half a block.

Did he run out of luck?
Yes, before he was cool, they had him spread out on dished-in marble
In the Cook County Morgue, surrounded by babbling people
With a crime reporter presiding over the head of the table.
Did Johnny have a soul?
Yes, and it was climbing his slippery windpipe like a trapped burglar.
It was beating the inside of his ribcage, hollering, "Let me out of here!"
Maybe it got out, and maybe it just stayed there.
Was Johnny a money-maker?
Yes, and thousands paid 25¢ to see him, mostly women,
And one said, "I wouldn't have come, except he's a moral lesson,"
And another, "I'm disappointed. He feels like a dead man."
Did Johnny have a brain?
Yes, and it always worked best through the worst of dangers,
Through flatfooted hammerlocks, through guarded doors, around corners,
But it got taken out in the morgue and sold to some doctors.
Could Johnny take orders?
No, but he stayed in the wicker basket carried by six men
Through the bulging crowd to the hearse and let himself be locked in,
And he stayed put as it went driving south in a driving rain.
And he didn't get stolen?
No, not even after his old hard-nosed dad refused to sell
The quick-drawing corpse for $10,000 to somebody in a carnival.
He figured he'd let *Johnny* decide how to get to Hell.
Did anyone wish him well?
Yes, half of Indiana camped in the family pasture,
And the minister said, "With luck, he could have been a minister."
And up the sleeve of his oversized gray suit, Johnny twitched a finger.
Does anyone remember?
Everyone still alive. And some dead ones. It was a new kind of holiday
With hot and cold drinks and hot and cold tears. They planted him in a cemetery
With three unknown vice presidents, Benjamin Harrison, and James Whitcomb
    Riley,
Who never held up anybody.

Looking for Nellie Washington

My job in a hard time
Was to bring those people down
To the small loan man
For a mouth-to-mouth discussion
When they'd fallen far behind
Like Nellie Washington
Who lived up a street across
An alley at the top
Of a crooked stairway through
A fence in a side yard
High-stepping down concrete
To a drain behind a basement
Garage you know by the cans
Against the incinerator.

When I finally seemed to be
Somewhere I asked somebody
Or other whereabouts
Is Nellie Washington living
Somehow around near dark
Any more the manager
Would dearly like to see her
Immediately at the latest
Or at least sooner
To talk if possible
In person the whole thing over
On the telephone tomorrow.

Then nobody I could name
Would say she headed south
Or north to a neighborhood
Next door to a home far away
In bed going to work
In school after the wreck
On the road to the hospital
Except for an hour ago
Yesterday just last week

She was downstairs in the front
Of the back in number something
As far as they could forget
To say what she looked like.

In back of the front I almost
Saw through a crack in a door
A shape moving beyond
A strip of stained wallpaper
Banana-peeled to the floor
Like a window shade unwound
To the edge of a curled carpet
Something maybe like her
One black hand turned light
At the frame to flip good-bye
A moment before it faded
Away shut gone for good
Forever like her credit.

Does her bad-account-chaser's card
Wherever it went still say
Nothing Nothing Nobody
Called Called Again Nellie
Washington where are you now
That your better business number
Was up to be disconnected
Down in black against white
On the dotted line of the Man
When you didn't come on in
Come out wherever you were
Supreme as mysterious
Unlimited beyond me
As God the National Debt
With interest so long forgiven
As I owe you I quit.

A Valedictory to Standard Oil of Indiana

In the darkness east of Chicago, the sky burns over the plumbers' nightmares
Red and blue, and my hometown lies there loaded with gasoline.
Registers ring like gas pumps, pumps like pinballs, pinballs like broken alarm clocks,
And it's time for morning, but nothing's going to work.
From cat-cracker to candle-shop, from grease-works along the pipeline,
Over storage tanks like kings on a checkerboard ready to jump the county,
The word goes out: With refined regrets
We suggest you sleep all day in your houses shaped like lunch buckets
And don't show up at the automated gates.
Something else will tap the gauges without yawning
And check the valves at the feet of the cooling towers without complaining.
Standard Oil is canning my high school classmates
And the ones who fell out of junior high or slipped in the grades.
What should they do, gassed up in their Tempests and Comets, raring to go
Somewhere with their wives scowling in front and kids stuffed in the back,
Past drive-ins jammed like car lots, trying to find the beaches
But blocked by freights for hours, stopped dead in their tracks
Where the rails, as thick as thieves along the lakefront,
Lower their crossing gates to shut the frontier? What can they think about
As they stare at the sides of boxcars for a sign.
And Lake Michigan drains slowly into Lake Huron,
The mills level the Dunes, and the eels go sailing through the trout,
And mosquitoes inherit the evening, while toads no bigger than horseflies
Hop crazily after them over the lawns and sidewalks, and the rainbows fall
Flat in the oil they came from? There are two towns now,
One dark, one going to be dark, divided by Cyclone fences:
One pampered and cared for like pillboxes and cathedrals,
The other vanishing overnight in the dumps and swamps like a struck sideshow.
As the Laureate of the Class of '44—which doesn't know it has one—
I offer this poem, not from hustings or barricades
Or the rickety stage where George Rogers Clark stood glued to the wall,
But from another way out, like Barnum's "This Way to the Egress,"
Which moved the suckers when they'd seen enough. Get out of town.

Their Bodies

To the students of anatomy at Indiana University

That gaunt old man came first, his hair as white
As your scoured tables. Maybe you'll recollect him
By the scars of steelmill burns on the backs of his hands,
On the nape of his neck, on his arms and sinewy legs,
And her by the enduring innocence
Of her face, as open to all of you in death
As it would have been in life: she would memorize
Your names and ages and pastimes and hometowns
If she could, but she can't now, so remember her.

They believed in doctors, listened to their advice,
And followed it faithfully. You should treat them
One last time as they would have treated you.
They had been kind to others all their lives
And believed in being useful. Remember somewhere
Their son is trying hard to believe you'll learn
As much as possible from them, as *he* did,
And will do your best to learn politely and truly.

They gave away the gift of those useful bodies
Against his wish. (They had their own ways
Of doing everything, always.) If you're not certain
Which ones are theirs, be gentle to everybody.

Brooklyn, Indiana

This boy his blue
10-speed bicycle dumped on the ground
buries the dog right there yellow (you
can smell it as you drive by twice)
where it died
along Centenary Road.

Riverside Auto Parts trailer sky turned
over shatter 1972 tornado new Ford and Chevy
truck parts tiny purple flowers broken Plexiglas.

They send him out to clear off flowers and flags,
every month he piles them pink and yellow
silk with beer cans,
medicine jars and grass clippings
green behind the cinder block shed.
A wood chair inside there tiny and sharp
in shadows (to torture the living?)

The dead here talk in junkyards
listen to shapes of faces
in windshields.
Sideways school buses on fire
the plastic seats melting red.

You step on their black toy guns
break them up in dried mud.

City

Smells of almond oil the light
from the black bathroom and her eyes glow.
Inside my body the silver city streets
night clouds low outside. New Jersey Street
sleeps with its eyes open. *Soft* I say
white and she is touching me. Swallows me
soft and drowning in milk to drink. Inside her
I burn truck tires. Next to me eyes closed
she breathes evenly asleep warm like a child.
I think about the years she breathed back into me.
She leaves in fear in desires in shadows in long black cars
all under motel pools police stations. She leaves
with a kiss. Taste her tongue her cigarettes
her small hands. She won't walk back to me
through the city rain. The angel's wings.
And I look out my windows
wet everywhere. Nobody walking drunk
and driving. Nobody thinking about killing.
No grass out there. Nothing alive out there.

Late Afternoon

Webbed and banded by sunlight
Swinging intact in a basket
of sunlight; bleached and golden
as autumnal grasses or as pears hanging
gilded with sun-dust in thickets of leaves
the afternoon drowses in meshes
of interlaced light.

Twirled by dry wind, day lapses,
it dwindles toward evening and darkness;
but still the ropes hold, the frayed ropes
of sunlight, still mottled with dayshine,
grapple it closely: the tawny sun-rusted
tope-cradled slow-lapsing full-flavored
late afternoon.

Waiter, Another Squab

Eat airiness and swallow grace.
Put iridescence where its light
Illuminates the tomb it falls within.

Great paunch, whose utter night
Has thus a star within its arc,
Once more regale us with the sight
Of tallow's greed engulfing wings
While dentures savor loss of flight.

Quarry Scuba: Indiana Dive Partners

I am lost in the milky chocolate silt of the quarry lake
looking for the neon lime stripes of your fins.
At the bottom of this quarry is a school bus.
"Everything underwater is 25 percent larger,
25 percent closer," the dive master assures us every
Wednesday for eight weeks at Greenwood YMCA.

The black lines at the bottom of the pool trained me
to expect clarity with you as my dive partner.
I imagine underwater photos with us holding hands,
floating over brain coral the size of a Volkswagen;
but Indiana water is not like the Caribbean.

With glacial determination, I seek you out in this obscurity.
These things between us, like Indiana, are renowned for lack:
cornhusks, pork carcasses, empty factories, and limestone quarries.
We live in a mid-continental hysterectomy cauterized by summer:
this hollow center where white sheets of snow subdue the fields,
dust the southern Little Smokies hilltops as we wait for spring green.

Driving on the interstates on the obvious flatness, I have lost
you, my dive partner, at the bottom of quarry. Who can see
our place as an ocean of history: dug out and drained. I hover
above a school bus sunken beneath time in Indiana, waiting
as time stops and my air runs out.

Blessing of the Bikes: Bean Blossom, Indiana

The preacher's wife is half bucolic cliché and half dominatrix:
round and ruddy in a gingham check halter top, long and lean
legs in leather chaps, she fries eggs over an open fire, pours
Folger's, flips pancakes, pats ham steaks as hickory ashes fly up,
settle in her hair. "Lord, Bless these bikes," her preacher man
of 27 years intones to his denim and leather-clad congregation.

Last night, we promenaded along the mud motorcycle runway
for the final Bean Blossom Boogie--billed as "The Midwest's Best
Biker Fest." Softails, pan heads, rumbling pipes glide by as artists design
10-point bucks and supine babes on gas tanks. The fat lady
with goggles rides in her old man's sidecar. Two small town
lawyers impeccably coordinate their leather and helmets to their bikes.

Rituals flourish like born again virgins and penitent addicts.
Bikers rub worry stones, coon tails, rabbit feet. Tobacco anoints
lips, sweat baptizes bodies, and the breeze intoxicates and forgives sins.
Some play at ancient pagan rites as the Bikers for Christ try to usurp
the spirituality of the road. "Loud pipes save lives" is our Hail Mary,
gaudy juxtapositions are our grace. Amen. See you next year again.

Distance

Tonight the workmen
with red bandanas are building
a house across the street.
Light spills from the holes
they've left for windows.
They've inched across the roof beams,
buckets of shingles in their arms.
This last man leans after
everyone's gone, his head
on a door that's propped on a tree.
I hear him singing to himself.

We both can't sleep—
his singing, and his hand
that drums a hammer again
and again into the ground.
The cats on the roof disturb him;
he stares and hammers,
hears me typing, or finds me
through the window, bent
to my lamp. I've come to admire

the distance between us,
the noises we make to ourselves
in the night, tired
as the lovers in a Japanese print
who've turned and wiped their genitals
with the blue silk scarves
they had stuffed in their mouths
while coupling.

Red Ochre

Ozone smell: all afternoon
    the rain turned off and on like spray
        slurring out a tap. She's floating along

the fern bar window, and the couples
    scoring paper tablecloths with crayons,
        circles and arrows as they laugh,

cigarette-glow and darting eyes, margaritas
    all around, salt crust on the glass rims.
        Then she's passed their tinted pane,

sidewalk pocked with drizzle, glazing
    while she kills time, waiting to call
        for the test results. She conjures

the lab, the centrifuges' hiss
    and whirl, specimens and samples
        towering in a room her mind makes

long and narrow as the university
    pool she's walking from, and its air
        as thickly humid. Her sari

billows in the wind and spotty rain.
    She's thinking to think
        away: cedar waxwing, goldfinch,

tarpit, a spike of red ochre
    with one side sharpened—
        a writing stick from Pleistocene

Australia, unearthed in this morning's
    section three. And the fifty-two sons
        of Ramses: someone's cleaning rubble

from all the basalt sarcophagi.
    Think away to her thirty-fourth lap,
        her goggles unfogging and then

the good air swallowed,
    great draughts at the poolside,
      great tectonic draughts.

Chlorine sting, the nostrils
    flaring and her own slick palm
      inching her neck to reckon the pulse.

Days of 1994

They wanted rehab—at least a month from her,
not just the writhing days it took for detox.

& anyway by this time it was all a kind of joke:
on the third day she would rise again, transfigured,

to sign herself out. & with the plastic bracelet
still dot-matrixing her name, band inching white

from her black leather jacket, she spat out
curses at the liquor store clerk, who'd told her that

she looked as though she'd already had enough.
Corners where she'd score after teaching

her expensive undergrads to bring
more spondees to their closures. Kitchen floor she'd strafe

& pockmark with her cane, & the bed in the attic room
where I & various others held her nightlong

through the shakes. Heavy the burden
she took upon herself those final days. But calm

& plaintive was her final singing. Track-marked arms
& jet-black sleeves within the coffin silk,

her lips made florid in the mortuary light, kissed
& wept upon by many, who would write their brittle poems

to stylize their grief for her, as if her death
could belong to them as well. O days of 1994,

bring back to me her quickened human form,
even in her fevers & the tremor & exactness

of her curses. Bring back to me the dampened cloth
I wring out in a bowl, cheekbone & clavicle,

as her eyelids flutter & her forehead at last grows cool.
Bring back this broken fever. Let the others have the rest.

Written on the Due Date of a Son Never Born

Echinacea, bee balm, aster. Trumpet vine
I watch your mother bend to prune, water

sluicing silver from the hose—
                                  another morning
you will never see. Summer solstice: dragonflies flare

the unpetaled rose. 6 a.m.
                         & already
she's breaking down, hose flung to the sidewalk

where it snakes & pulses in a steady
keening glitter, both hands to her face. That much

I can give you of these hours.
                             That much only.
Fist & blossom forged by salt, trellising

your wounded helixes against our days,
tell us how to live
                    for we are shades, facing

caged the chastening sun. Our eyes
are scorched & lidless. We cannot bear your light.

Turning to Look Back

> *Grandfather*

I don't even know where we came from.
So many graves stay open too long,
so many girls lie back tonight,
trying to be secret rivers in the limestone.
I want those days when nothing happens.
Not every clocktick needs a martyr.
Let my grave be a filled-in hole.
Stop shoveling me out, in the black suit
I bought for my laying-in,
to mourn your middle age for you.
Look to your own bones, John.

Tobacco-spitting, horse-shoeing, long-johned,
I lead these people out of your invention,
out of a Bible of births and deaths,
school corridors and locker rooms,
out of fumbling back seats,
into the town, trembling to rise.

We touched the first pure water,
thrusting between stones, trailing down shale,
cold and silent. Sometimes, touching water,
we know an early thing.
The women, your mother to be among them,
washed in the old tub, brimming for the cattle,
there, by the salt stone.
Your cousins gathered for the fire.
There we warmed, real as the day you dreamed us,
until the trees widened
into the night before your birth.

As we came down the hill at first light,
the town began from the maple valley
of the river you will call the White.
Sawdust dunes drifted into houses and barns,
where the mill turned on the bright saw
in the first sun of your eyes.
I became your grandfather,
carving a bow you couldn't draw.

I feel your eyes opening
in the dark face of your mother.
When the cord broke in the river
it leaped in a brown ridge through the willows.
Here, on this hill, I see you
letting out the kite like a far eye
over the scatter of smokehouses,
at the field's edge where the town
thins out into corncribs and fishing shacks,
old Fords driving a wood saw,
out past the cannery whistle.
Then, hand over hand, pulling it close,
struggling with the wind in it,
hugging it like the frail ribcage of a young girl;
and on this morning you made us all,
holding it to your face until the trees
stood up red through the tearing tissue.

> Brother
> dead in infancy

Just one step into air,
a step so light
it left a shadowprint
and a name vague as a touch in the throat.

And our mother wept
water as clear
as ice candelabra
and her grief was for the grief she wouldn't have.

And you will see my stone,
salt as the cattle lick
by the algaed tub
where all blood's creatures are drawn from a long graze.

Many roads start out boldly in this country,
six lanes of immaculate concrete:
this way out of the Depression.
But they soon become narrow, dodgy,
snaking around old, caulked trees
and other historical markers,
ending behind a rusting tractor
in a soil bank near Quincy.

John Woods

How many Purdue graduates, tasseled and shorn,
have started West in Jaguars,
kissing the cam covers,
saying a few words over the fuel pump,
and have ended up in a Chevy Six,
with chocolate-bibbed children, spilled goldfish,
parked on the wrong side of a Drive-in,
midnight, lights going brown?

Taking a wrong turn,
you can end up in the Thirties,
on a gravel road past oil-lit farm houses,
then face-to-face with a swivel-jawed cow,
with a look of such staggering ignorance
you feel the presence of the meaning
of time itself. Just one step into air,
but some things come in mother's milk.

Some fill a small hole, some a large.
Much involved language has played back
through your mouth, mostly a complaint
against the one disease. A small stone
or a large, but both salt, salt.

You made me speak for the dead child in you.
I don't know whether you lived my life,
or I lived yours.

The Visits of My Aunt

The visits of my aunt in Martinsville
were invasions. I see the webby arbor
and the tottered shed full of kindling
and games, the willow lacing the pause
of afternoon, and townsmen rocking
under wasp shells and locust husks.
Then my aunt's car would startle dogs
to ragged challenges as she blew her horn
down Grant Street. Puffing out onto the yard
with a moustache and blue-wet dress,
she hugged me breathless. Her car door
slammed down birds from the carved maple.
The keepsakes would jump when she sat:
the plaster horse and carnival cane,
the one ashtray kept for her flourishes.
Our latest uncle tugged the creases
in his pants and face, and tapped his watch.
Summer ventured in her voice.
That rusting crankcase filled with rain,
half-hidden in the weeds, held no
more rainbow than she stroked from air.
The steaming dump up Lincoln Road,
with rats and springs, held no more
oddness than her pocketbook
to trick us with. While she spoke
clouds held their rain, and August
lay like lambs beneath her spell.
The piano repeated, deep in its harps,
her essential hum.
         When she died
under the glass tent, I grew into an answer:
life, as well as death, can last forever.
There is a heaven of things: car doors,
uncles, the ashtray from the Exposition.

But as she withered in the tilted bed
I came with the first frost to another meaning:
something of brown leaves, withered grapes,
the ganged birds exploding from the oak;
that someday the easy wind would knot,
and I'd be helpless in the grip of days.

Barney's Sister

There's something wrong with Barney's sister
under the apple limb. That day
the door blew wide and stood her, white
and washing, in my naked eye,
I knew a sickness had her. I ran,
like from the plague, and laughed it weak
in Barney's cart behind the barn
where horses hang their shoes and collars.
Then I scattered owls with cobs.
The sun laid stalks across the floor.
I pressed my eye against a crack
to see the narrow, sunwide world.
Two roads met in a scramble patch
like what she hid behind her washrag.
Now the world is opener,
since the bathroom door blew wide
and struck me marrow deep. I stood,
white and breathing, in her eyes.
I was nakeder than she.

Once, we were all straight lines
down to the saltlick by the pond.
Barney's sister wrestled me
into the cockleburs. I pinched her
where she wrinkled when she sat,
ruler thin and all wild bone.

But under the bushy sky, the apple
tree, the narrow rises; the paths
that led our hands together twist,
and I am lost in bramble, jay-
swarmed, blood-lashed.

                    Something's wrong
with Barney's sister. I pinch behind
this log and see them bathe in grass.
The moon blows wide. Something tears

in me. O all the world is ill.
Now, in their flinging legs, I see
the dead carts pass, the pyres, the blazing
streets where fever burns its halo.
There she stands in black and smears
the red name Love upon my door.

Today's Horoscope

Indications are for a day of conflict and indecision,
With the emotions held in check by a rather sluggish state of mind.
Watch your step. Travel at your own risk.
Be on your guard against agreements or promises of any kind.

All documents should be sound and clear to the understanding.
Make certain of the detail. Take heed of all particulars.
Direct the mentality always into safe channels.
There are prognostications of disaster in the stars.

Safeguard the possessions against unforeseen loss;
Stocks and bonds and other securities may fall.
Protect the reputation and domestic well-being from treachery.
Beware of whatever is out there in the hall.

Those whose birthday it is may encounter a year
Of contradictory situations. Take no unwarranted chances.
Keep to your side of the street. Look both ways before crossing.
Preserve your balance. Refrain from all extravagances.

A child born on this day may have generous impulses,
With hopes and ambitions beyond his talents or means.
Part of him will never laugh. There is cause for alarm.
Let him look under beds, and behind doors and screens.

Be apprehensive of all relations with man, woman, or child.
Let not the smile spread to the eyes. Surrender that dream.
When you wake the world will be changed.
The conjunction of the planets is inauspicious in the extreme.

Tomorrow's Horoscope

Indications are for a day of promise and fulfillment,
With the cosmic shadows held in check by friendly vibrations.
Events will be exciting. Keep your head in the clouds.
Your achievements will exceed your fondest hopes and expectations.

All matters of business and romance are aspected favorably.
Energize your ambitions. Be aggressive. Be of good cheer.
Propitious influences are at work. Ride the crest of the wave.
There can be no reason to regret. Break the shackles of fear.

Consider that this day begins your cycle of happiness.
Open your mail. Clean out your bureau drawer.
People of affluence and means will be well disposed towards you.
Go bargain hunting. You will find just what you are looking for.

Those whose birthday it is will encounter a year
Of dynamic opportunities. Be on the alert for good news.
The ground will not crumble beneath your feet.
Let down your guard. You can't possibly lose.

A child born on this day will win his heart's desire.
His personality will skyrocket him to fortune and fame.
People will envy him. He will be the life of the party.
For him there can be no hardship, no disappointment, no shame.

You will wake in the morning and remember nothing of the night.
The occult is your ally. Put aside your anxiety.
Ask and it will be yours, whatever you say.
Oh, what will it be? Oh, what will it be, what will it be?

Threshold

After the sagittal and lateral cuts
with the .07 saw into the parietal
and frontal bones, I peel back
the fibrous dura mater. The brain
is glossy, tied in and upon itself
like worms mating. 231
says my friend's brass earring
but, laying my hand across his frontal lobe,
I should know him better. Imagine
touching someone like this,
someone I wouldn't know on the street
even if I held a match to his cigarette,
even if the match didn't seem to light
until a long time after striking.
Under my palm is what the texts call
the region of higher intellect,
which means I could be handling
his life's work on chemical thresholds,
the microscopy of water about
to boil. Next week, I'll cut down
to the hypothalamic nuclei, no bigger
than a thumb, where some neurologists say
there's a spot that could keep us
happy forever.

I'm lucky my lab's this close
to the school of music, the carillon,
and I wish I could make that music
of ice and ice's melting. Yes, I know all about
how it's just a keyboard connected to a computer
and there's no ropes, no harsh November air
unless a window's open. And I know there's no
pulling hard then being lifted
by the low notes that thicken like clouds.
Still, at any moment we can be carried skyward,
there's so little to us.

Catalogues

My slow mailman brings the same
catalogues I get to the door of a friend
of a friend whose husband is
metastasizing in Indianapolis.
She sleeps on a cot beside the respirator,
refusing to leave, go home, wash her hair.
She knows, as we all do, how death
never comes while you wait, only if
you wander off, go home, take a bath
and years later you think, yes, yes, I was
holding a purple washrag when I heard.
She smiles at the night nurse who,
because he knows she teaches, remembers
closing his eyes during tests, trying,
to see the yellow highlighter glow
on his text and the skeletal answers
beneath. Someone probably takes her
her mail every other day. In one of today's
catalogues—pictures of furniture:
chairs, tables, an escritoire for 1200.
Shown actual size the caption says.
Another is all authentic sports clothing
with Pete Rose on the cover. Everything
he has on has a number next to it. Last night
he broke Ty Cobb's record with a looper
into shallow left in the first against
San Diego. I turned the game on
in the second. After it was over he said,
It's hard to know what to feel. I'll be glad
just to play ball again.

The world has too many people.
I remember when I got to the part
about God bless, filling in Mom and Dad
and Sister and . . . then my sister
would nudge me. Quit stalling. Get in bed.
Turn out the light. But I'd go on blessing

friends of friends and mailmen, even
the year's rookies. Blessing tiny men in tuxedos,
tiny women in gowns and emeralds gathered
round a table the size of a popsicle.
What are they saying with their glasses held up?
Here's to us? Here's to the momentum
of our lives that brings us all together
to drink before we shatter
our delicate vessels.

Ode to the Midwest

> *The country I come from*
> *Is called the Midwest*
> *—Bob Dylan*

I want to be doused
in cheese

& fried. I want
to wander

the aisles, my heart's
supermarket stocked high

as cholesterol. I want to die
wearing a sweatsuit—

I want to live
forever in a Christmas sweater,

a teddy bear nursing
off the front. I want to write

a check in the express lane.
I want to scrape

my driveway clean

myself, early, before
anyone's awake—

that'll put em to shame—
I want to see what the sun

sees before it tells
the snow to go. I want to be

the only black person I know.

I want to throw
out my back & not

complain about it.
I wanta drive

two blocks. Why walk—

I want love, n stuff—

I want to cut
my sutures myself.

I want to jog
down to the river

& make it my bed—

I want to walk
its muddy banks

& make me a withdrawal.

I tried jumping in,
found it frozen—

I'll go home, I guess,
to my rooms where the moon

changes & shines
like television.

Blackbottom

Like coffee
I do not care

How bad you miss
me—strong, black, I think

of you, head
aching or is

it heart—each
morning me wishing

you boiling, steamed
with want, then

saying ah, awake, after.

Deep Song

Belief is what
buries us—that

& the belief in belief—
No longer

do I trust liltlessness
—leeward

is the world's
way—Go on

plunge in
—the lungs will

let us float.
Joy is the mile-

high ledge
the leap—a breath

above the lip of the abandoned
quarry—belief

the dark the deep.

The Homecoming

Here the gate creaks heavily. This is our upland pasture
And native heath in the mind's eye reflected.
So the rusted lock gives! We have come with body and soul
Home toward evening, and not once deflected

By the devious way we followed. We have shepherded home
The northern lights, the angels in the storm,
O, by the heart beat guided, by the quickening pulse
And no defect we knew in the golden form.

And the masses, of leaves do fall in the wind amazed.
But we are everywhere the angels lean
And where, in this night, will open the red-hearted flower
Dual with us in the cold, cold summer rain.

For we have come home and brought us here entirely
To this earth meadow and the ticking of fine grass
And the insect winged in the delicate light beam;
We are the finality of journeyers in space.

But I shall be musing forever on this thing,
Whose is the face of the wandering angel there
On Aldebaran in the brightening stream,
Where, in a sourceless light, she binds her hair.

Contributors

Philip Appleman (b. 1926) has published seven volumes of poetry, the latest of which is *New and Selected Poems, 1956–1996* (1996); three novels, including *Apes and Angels* (1989); and half a dozen nonfiction books, including the widely used *Norton Critical Editions of Darwin and Malthus*. He is distinguished professor emeritus at Indiana University.

Donald Baker (1923–2002) published numerous poetry books, among them *Search Patterns, Twelve Hawks, No, Jeopardy*, and *Formal Application: Selected Poems, 1960–1980*. He taught at Brown University from 1947 to 1952 and at Wabash College, where he was the Milligan Professor of English Literature and Poetry in residence. Baker received the McLain-McTurnan Baker Award for Distinguished Teaching.

Willis Barnstone's (b. 1927) publications include *Life Watch, Border of a Dream: Poems of Antonio Machado*, and *The Gnostic Bible*. His book *The New Covenant* was a Book-of-the-Month Club selection. A Guggenheim fellow, he has received awards from the National Endowment for the Arts, the National Endowment for the Humanities, and the Emily Dickinson Award of the Poetry Society of America. His poems have appeared in *Paris Review* and the *New Yorker*. Barnstone is distinguished professor emeritus at Indiana University.

Valerie Berry (b. 1956) is a doctor, writer, and teacher. Her first collection of poems, *difficult news*, was published in 2001 by Sixteen Rivers Press. She lives in California and is medical director of the Primary Care Associate Program, Stanford School of Medicine.

Marianne Boruch (b. 1950) is the author of six poetry collections—the most recent *Grace, Fallen From* (2008) and two books of essays: *Poetry's Old Air* and *In the Blue Pharmacy*. Among her awards are two NEA fellowships, a Guggenheim Fellowship, and two Pushcart Prizes. Her work has appeared in *Best American Poetry* and other anthologies and in such journals as the *New Yorker, New England Review, Poetry London*, the *Yale Review*, and the *Nation*. Boruch teaches in the Master of Fine Arts Program at Purdue University, in the Warren Wilson College Graduate Program for Writers, and has been an exchange professor at the University of Hamburg. In 2005 she served as an artist in residence at Isle Royale National Park in the middle of Lake Superior. The resulting chapbook—*Ghost and Oar*—was published by Red Dragonfly Press in 2007.

Catherine Bowman (b. 1957) is the author of the poetry collections *The Plath Cabinet*, *Notarikon*, *Rock Farm*, and *1-800-Hot-Ribs*—reissued in 2000 by Carnegie-Mellon University Press as part of its Contemporary Classics series. Her writing has been awarded a number of prizes and fellowships. Bowman's poems have appeared in *The Best American Poetry* and many literary magazines, journals, and anthologies. She is the Ruth Lilly Professor of Poetry at IU, teaches at the Fine Arts Work Center in Provincetown, and is the editor of *Word of Mouth: Poems Featured on NPR's "All Things Considered."*

Tony Brewer's (b. 1971) first book of poems, *The Great American Scapegoat*, was published in 2006. He is a 2007 recipient of the Creative Writing Fellowship from the Jason Shephard Greer and Lucy Kim Greer Foundation for the Arts and the Bloomington (IN) Area Arts Council. His work has appeared most recently in *Poetry Midwest*, *decomP*, and *Flying Island*. Brewer is currently working on a new chapbook.

Dan Carpenter (b. 1948) has published poetry in *Illuminations*, *Pearl*, *Poetry East*, *Flying Island*, *Tipton Poetry Journal*, and *Southern Indiana Review*. A columnist for the *Indianapolis Star*, he is the author of *Hard Pieces: Dan Carpenter's Indiana*.

Jared Carter's (b. 1939) books of poetry include *Work, for the Night Is Coming*, *After the Rain*, *Less Barricades Mystérieuses*, and *Cross this Bridge at a Walk*. He lives in Indianapolis.

Richard Cecil (b. 1944) has published four collections of poems, *Einsteins's Brain* (1984), *Alcatraz* (1994), which won the 1991 Verna Emery Poetry Competition, *In Search of the Great Dead* (1991), and *Twenty First Century Blues* (2004). He teaches at IU, Bloomington, and at the Spalding University Brief Residency MFA Program.

Susanna Childress (b. 1978) grew up in Madison, Indiana. She did graduate work in English and creative writing at the University of Texas at Austin and at Florida State University. Her first book of poems, *Jagged with Love*, was selected by Billy Collins for the 2005 Brittingham Prize. Childress has also won a literary competition held every twenty years by the National Society of Arts and Letters. She currently holds a postdoctoral fellowship with the Lilly Fellows Program at Valparaiso University, where she teaches literature and creative writing.

Cristy Cornell (b. 1975) lives in Tippecanoe County, Indiana, where her family has farmed for generations. She graduated from Purdue University and received her MFA from the University of Massachusetts-Amherst. She is a fellowships adviser in the University Honors Program at Purdue University.

Peter Davis (b. 1972) was born in Louisiana, but grew up in Fort Wayne, Indiana. His book of poems is titled *Hitler's Mustache* (2006). Davis edited *Poet's Bookshelf: Contemporary Poets on Books that Shaped Their Art*. His work has been published in *La Petite Zine*, *Court Green*, *the Sonora Review*, and others. He teaches at Ball State University in Muncie, Indiana. Davis's Web site is www.artisnecessary.com/.

Mari Evans's books of poetry are *Continuum* (2007), *A Dark and Splendid Mass* (1992), *Nightstar: 1973–1978* (1981), *I Am a Black Woman* (1970), and *Where Is All the Music?* (1968). She has written a number of books for children and has authored two plays. She is a contributor to and an editor of the volume *Black Women Writers 1950–1980: A Critical Evaluation* (1984). Among her honors are fellowships from the MacDowell Colony, Yaddo, the NEA, and others. Evans has taught at colleges and universities including Spelman College, Purdue University, Cornell University, Northwestern, and IU, Bloomington.

Mary Fell (b. 1947) came to Indiana from Massachusetts in 1981 to teach English at IU East. She has written many poems about Indiana's rural landscape, some of which appeared in her book *The Persistence of Memory* (1984).

Chris J. Foley (b. 1972) grew up in Arkansas and attended the University of Arkansas. He came to Indiana to pursue graduate work and remained in Bloomington after completing his master's degree at IU. His prose and poetry have appeared in *Amaranth*, *Washington Square*, *Fish Stories*, *ACM: Another Chicago Magazine*, and *A Linen Weave of Bloomington Poets*. He coedited *Off the Square: The Waldron Writer's Anthology*. Foley currently serves as the Director of Undergraduate Admissions at Indiana University Purdue University–Indianapolis.

Alice Friman's (b. 1933) ninth collection of poetry, *Vinculum*, is forthcoming from Louisiana State University Press. Previous books are *The Book of the Rotten Daughter* (2006), *Inverted Fire* (1997), and *Zoo* (1999), which won the Ezra Pound Poetry Award and the Sheila Margaret Motton Prize. She has received fellowships from the Indiana Arts Commission, the Arts Council of Indianapolis, and the Bernheim Foundation and won the 2002 James Boatwright Prize from *Shenandoah*. Professor of English at the University of Indianapolis from 1973 to 1993, she now lives in Milledgeville, Georgia, where she is poet in residence at Georgia College and State University.

Jean Garrigue (1914–1972) wrote as an expatriate from Europe in 1953, 1957, and 1962. *The Ego and the Centaur* (1947) was her first full-length publication. She was awarded a Guggenheim fellowship in 1960–61, a National Institute of Arts and Letters grant, and was nominated for a National Book Award for *Country without Maps*. Garrigue authored six additional publications. A professor, she taught at Queens and Smith colleges.

Sonia Gernes (b. 1942) has published a novel, *The Way to St. Ives*, and four books of poetry: *Brief Lives*, *Women at Forty*, *A Breeze Called the Fremantle Doctor*, and *What You Hear in the Dark: New and Selected Poems*. Gernes has held an NEA fellowship, a Fulbright Senior Lectureship, and a Lilly fellowship. She is a professor emerita of English at the University of Notre Dame and is at work on a novel.

Eugene Gloria (b. 1957) is the author of two books of poems, *Hoodlum Birds* and *Drivers at the Short-Time Motel*, which was selected for the 1999 National Poetry Series. He has received grants from the Great Lakes Colleges Association Japan Study program administered by Earlham College and from the IAC. He teaches at DePauw University.

Matthew Graham (b. 1954) is the author of three collections of poetry, *New World Architecture, 1946,* and *A World without End* (2007). He's lived in Indiana for more than twenty years and is a professor of English and director of creative writing at the University of Southern Indiana.

Chris Green (b. 1968) has edited *Coal: A Poetry Anthology*, which shows the deep history of poetry in the Appalachian Mountains. He received his MFA in poetry from IU, worked for the Hoosier Environmental Council, and taught poetry to special education students in Odon. His wife is from Rising Sun—her parents grew up on farms in Russiaville and Wheatland. He currently teaches Appalachian Literature at Marshall University in Huntington, West Virginia.

Sarah Green (b. 1980) spent three years in Tippecanoe County earning her MFA at Purdue University. She misses Cafe Vienna, Von's Bookstore, and the Wabash River pedestrian bridge. She currently lives in her home city of Boston, where she is a visiting professor of creative writing at Emerson and Wheaton Colleges. Her poem "Chances Are, Lafayette, Indiana" is forthcoming in *The Pushcart Prize XXXIII* anthology.

C. E. Greer's (b. 1942) poems have appeared in *Streets Magazine, Flying Island, Wind,* and other publications. His two chapbooks, *Wild Plums* and *No Famous Place,* were published by Pudding House Press (2010). He has been active with the Bloomington Free Verse Poets, and he coedited, with Jenny Kander, *Say This of Horses: A Selection of Poems* published by the University of Iowa Press in 2007. He is retired from the geography department at IU, where his teaching and research focused on the human place in nature. He lived with his family on a farm outside Bloomington from 1978 until 2009, when he returned to his native Colorado.

Jeff Gundy's (b. 1952) fifth book of poems, *Spoken among the Trees* (2007) won the 2007 Society of Midland Authors Poetry Prize. He did masters work in creative writing and a doctorate in American literature at IU, Bloomington. Since 1984, after teaching for four years at Hesston College in Kansas, Gundy has been at Bluffton College, where he is professor of English and former chair of the English/Language Department.

Hannah Haas (b. 1972) earned a BA in English from IU and a MFA in creative writing from the University of Arizona. Her work has appeared in journals such as *ACM* and *Folio*. She is a Greer Foundation Fellowship recipient, and her book manuscript was a finalist for the New Issues Poetry Prize and semifinalist for the Kenyon Review Prize in Poetry. She teaches creative writing and composition at IUPUI.

Anne Haines (b. 1961) is the author of the chapbook *Breach*, published by Finishing Line Press (2008), and the recipient of an Individual Artist Grant from the IAC. Her poems have appeared in numerous journals and anthologies, both online and in print. She has lived for many years in Bloomington, Indiana, where she is a staff member in the IU libraries.

James Hazard (b. 1935) has published eight books of poetry, among them, *A Hive of Souls: Selected Poems 1968–1976* (1977) and *The Shortening of the Days* (2006). He has had fiction and nonfiction published in *Evergreen Review*, *Exquisite Corpse*, the *Mississippi Review*, and the *Richmond Review* (UK), among others. He is a regular contributor to *Milwaukee Magazine*. Having taught at Saint Joseph's College from 1960 to 1962, and Chicago Teacher's College and Wisconsin State University at Oshkosh from 1963 to 1968, Hazard is now an emeritus professor of English, University of Wisconsin-Milwaukee.

Robert Hazel (1921–1993) born in Bloomington, Indiana, was a professor of English and creative writing at New York University from 1963 to 1971. He published three novels and a few stories, but his finest work appears in his five volumes of poetry, among which are *Poems/ 1951–1961* (1961), *Who Touches This: Selected Poems 1951–1979* (1981), and *Clock of Clay: New and Selected Poems* (1992). He taught at the University of Kentucky from 1955 to 1961 and at Oregon State. At Virginia Tech, Hazel served as poetry editor of *The Nation* (1972) and was Virginia Polytechnical Institute's writer in residence (1974–79).

Daniel Hefko's (b. 1972) poems have been published in *Threepenny Review*, *New York Quarterly*, *Seneca Review*, *Poet Lore*, *Tar River Poetry*, and *River Styx*. He has taught creative writing at Purdue University, where he earned an MFA, and the University of Illinois, where he received an Artists Fellowship Award in Poetry from the Illinois Arts Council. As an assistant professor, Hefko taught English at Ball State University from 2003 to 2005. He currently teaches film and college composition at Hanover High School in Mechanicsville, Virginia.

Joseph Heithaus (b. 1962) lives in Greencastle, Indiana, where he is chair of the English Department at DePauw University. He won the 2007 "Discovery"/The Nation prize, and his poems have appeared in a number of journals including the *North American Review*, the *Southern Review*, and *Poetry*. He recently collaborated on the book *Rivers, Rails, and Runways*, a collection of poems by himself and four other poets whose poems are etched in the window murals of the new Indianapolis International Airport. His poem "Sanctuary" was commissioned in 2003 for the Centennial Celebration of the Putnam County Public Library.

Jane Hilberry's (b. 1958) recent collection of poems, *Body Painting* (2005), received the Colorado Book Award for poetry. Her poems have appeared in the *Women's Review of Books*, *Virginia Quarterly Review*, *Hudson Review*, and other magazines. Hilberry, who teaches at Colorado College, has also written a book of art criticism/biography titled *The Erotic Art of Edgar Britton*. She was one of the first editors of the *Indiana Review*.

Karol Hovis (b. 1965) lives in Ellettsville, Indiana. As a special education teacher, she worked with poet Chris Green to develop an intensive poetry project that produced a book of original poetry written, edited, and published by their high school students.

Allison Joseph's (b. 1967) volumes of poetry include *Soul Train*, *Imitation of Life*, and *Worldly Pleasures*. She is a graduate of Kenyon College and IU, currently living in Carbondale, Illinois, where she is part of the creative writing faculty at Southern Illinois University.

George Kalamaras (b. 1956) is the author of four full-length books of poetry and three poetry chapbooks. His latest titles are *The Scathering Sound* (2008) and *Gold Carp Jack Fruit Mirrors* (2008). His poems have appeared in numerous journals and anthologies in the United States, Canada, Greece, India, Japan, Mexico, Thailand, and the United Kingdom. He is the recipient of Creative Writing Fellowships from the NEA (1993) and the IAC (2001) and first prize in the 1998 *Abiko Quarterly* International Poetry Prize (Japan). Kalamaras is professor of English at IUPU, Fort Wayne, where he has taught since 1990.

Jenny Kander's (b. 1933) poetry has appeared in *Flying Island*, *California Quarterly*, *Bathtub Gin*, *Wind*, and the *Southern Indiana Review*. She's the author of two chapbooks, *Taboo* (2004) and *The Altering Air* (2010). She has compiled and edited two volumes of poetry, *The Linen Weave of Bloomington Poets* and *Celebrating Seventy*. With C .E. Greer she coedited *Say This of Horses: A Selection of Poems* and with him is coeditor of this Indiana anthology. Kander produced weekly poetry programs for the Bloomington, Indiana, National Public Radio station, featuring work by local, national, and world poets.

Terry Kirts's (b. 1970) poems have appeared in *Another Chicago Magazine*, *Green Mountains*, and *Gastronomica*, among other journals, and in the anthology *Food Poems*. His creative nonfiction has appeared in *Home Again: Essays and Memoirs from Indiana*. Kirts's restaurant reviews appear regularly in *Indianapolis Monthly*. He teaches creative writing at IUPUI.

Etheridge Knight (1931–1991) began writing poetry during his eight years in the Indiana State Prison and published his first book of poems, *Poems from Prison* (1968) while incarcerated. After his release in 1969, he became involved in the Black Arts Movement and a year later edited a collection titled *Black Voices from Prison*. Knight's books and oral performances drew popular and critical acclaim, and he was awarded honors from the Guggenheim Foundation, the Poetry Society of America, and the NEA. In 1990, one year before his death, he earned a bachelor's degree in American poetry and criminal justice from Martin Center University in Indianapolis.

Yusef Komunyakaa (b. 1947) has published numerous books of poems and won a variety of awards, prizes, and fellowships, including a Pulitzer Prize for *New and Selected Poems 1977–1989*. His critical acclaim has garnered him biographical and critical inclusion in such collections as the *Norton Anthology of Southern Literature*, the *Oxford Companion to African American Literature*, and the *Norton Anthology of African American Literature*. In 1985 he became an associate professor at IU, Bloomington, where he held the Ruth Lilly Professorship from 1989 to 1990. In 1999 he was elected a Chancellor of The Academy of American Poets. Komunyakaa was a professor in the Council of Humanities and Creative Writing Program at Princeton University. He is currently Distinguished Senior Poet and Professor in the Graduate Creative Writing Program at New York University.

Barbara Koons's (b. 1930s) first book of poetry, *Night Highway* (2005) was a finalist in the Rhea and Seymour Gorsline First Book Competition. In 2006 *Night Highway* was named one of the best books of Indiana by the Indiana State Library. Koons's poems have appeared in *Crazyhorse*, *Earth's Daughters*, *Flying Island*, the *Hopewell Review*, and elsewhere. She has received awards for her poetry, including semifinalist status in the "Discovery"/The Nation Competition in 2003. Actively involved with the Writers' Center of Indiana, Koons served as events coordinator and as director of the Poetry in the Gallery reading series cosponsored with the Indianapolis Museum of Art.

Tom Koontz (b. 1939) is the editor of the Barnwood Press and *Barnwood Magazine* (poetry). Recent chapbooks of his poems are *In Such a Light* and *A Sudden Gust*. Retired from Ball State University, where he directed the program in creative writing, he moved from the remnant of a farm near Selma, Indiana, to Seattle, Washington.

Karen Kovacik's (b. 1939) most recent poetry collections are *Metropolis Burning* (2005), winner of the Best Book of Indiana (poetry division) in 2006, and *Return of the Prodigal* (1999). Her awards include the Charity Randall Citation from the International Poetry Forum (2007), a Fulbright Translation Fellowship (2004–5), and a Creative Renewal Fellowship from the Arts Council of Indianapolis (2003–4). She directs the creative writing program at IUPUI.

Elizabeth A. Krajeck (b. 1948) is the author of two chapbooks, including *Trigger*, winner of the third Indiana chapbook competition. A recipient of a Creative Renewal Fellowship from the Arts Council of Indianapolis, Krajeck collaborates with visual artists Angela Edwards and the late Jack Hartigan. A founding member of the Writers' Center of Indiana, Krajeck's prose poem projects, with Partners in Housing Development Corporation and the G. C. Lucas Gallery, document day-to-day activities of the people of Indiana.

Norbert Krapf (b. 1943), former Indiana Poet Laureate from Jasper, moved to Indianapolis from the East Coast with his family in 2004. His recent work includes *Invisible Presence* (2006), a collaboration with photographer Darryl Jones; the CD with jazz pianist-composer Monika Herzig, *Imagine—Indiana in Music and Words* (2007); *The Ripest Moments: A Southern Indiana Childhood* (2008); and *Bloodroot: Indiana Poems* (2008).

David Landrum (b. 1951) began writing poetry in high school and has written and published since that time. His poems have appeared in *Riverrun*, the *Formalist*, *Hellas*, *The Blind Man's Rainbow*, *Classical Outlook*, *Driftwood Review*, and many other journals and magazines. He is currently an instructor at Grand Valley State University, Allegan, Michigan. He edits the online poetry journal, *Lucid Rhythms*, www.lucidrhythms.com/.

Mary Leader (b. 1948), author of the award-winning collections *Red Signature* and *The Penultimate Suitor*, practiced law for many years and is the former assistant state attorney general of Oklahoma. She has also served as referee for the Supreme Court of Oklahoma. She earned a MFA from the Program for Writers at Warren Wilson College and a PhD in literature at Brandeis University. Leader, an associate professor at Purdue University, teaches writing and poetry to both undergraduate and graduate students.

Michael List (1947–2005) was a sporadic late-night poet and small-animal and former equine veterinarian. He read his poems on local radio and at gatherings in Bloomington, Indiana. His work appears in the collection, *Celebrating Seventy*, edited by Jenny Kander, and in *Say This of Horses: A Selection of Poems*, coedited by Greer and Kander.

Amy Locklin (1965) completed her MFA in poetry at IU, where she directed the IU Writers' Conference for four years. Her poetry, fiction, and nonfiction have most recently appeared in *Maize* and *Quarter After Eight*. She received an IAC grant to complete a collection of related stories. Locklin currently teaches at Butler University in Indianapolis.

A. Loudermilk's (b. 1970) first book of poetry, *Strange Valentine*, won the Crab Orchard Series in Poetry First Book Award and was published in 2005. Individual poems have appeared in *Pool*, *Margie*, *Tin House*, and *Cream City Review*, with fiction in *Carolina Quarterly* and essays in a number of journals. Originally from southern Illinois, Loudermilk lived in Bloomington from 1997 to 2004, where he taught creative writing and composition at IU. He now lives in Baltimore, where he has finished a memoir called *Bad Teeth* and teaches at the Maryland Institute College of Art.

Doris Lynch's (b. 1949) chapbook *Praising Invisible Birds* was published by Finishing Line Press in fall 2008. She has work forthcoming in *Commonweal* and has published poems in *Quercus Review*, *Shenandoah*, *Calyx*, the *Berkeley Poetry Review*, and in many anthologies including *A Linen Weave of Bloomington Poets*, *Celebrating Seventy*, and *Poems for the Wild Earth*. She has won three individual artist's grants from the IAC. Lynch is a reference librarian at the Monroe County Public Library, Bloomington, Indiana.

Jessica Maich (b. 1949) is a native of Indiana, residing currently with her family in South Bend. She is the author of two chapbook collections, *The West End* and *Twenty-Four Questions for Billy*. Her poem titled "The Robakowski Sisters" was nominated for a Pushcart Prize. She received her MFA in creative writing from the University of Notre Dame in 1997 and has taught at Saint Mary's College for the past four years.

Maurice Manning (b. 1966) lives in Kentucky and Bloomington, Indiana. He has published three books of poetry and was the recipient of the 2000 Yale Series of Younger Poets Award. His poems have appeared in the *New Yorker*, *Shenandoah*, the *Southern Review*, *Virginia Quarterly Review*, and elsewhere. He has held a fellowship to the Fine Arts Works Center in Provincetown. Manning teaches in IU's MFA program.

Jayne Marek (b. 1954) earned the MFA from the University of Notre Dame and her PhD from the University of Wisconsin. Her poetry has appeared in small publications such as *Isthmus*, *The Occasional Reader*, *Wisconsin Academy Review*, and *Windless Orchard*. She compiled the complete index to *Poetry Magazine* and publishes scholarly articles about literary history. Marek is associate professor of English at Franklin College, teaching literature, film studies, creative writing, and composition.

Adrian Matejka (b. 1971) was raised on the northwest side of Indianapolis. He received his BA in English from IU, Bloomington, and an MFA from Southern Illinois University Carbondale. He is a Cave Canem fellow, and his work has appeared in the *American Poetry Review*, *Crab Orchard Review*, *Gulf Coast*, and *Prairie Schooner*. Matejka is the author of *The Devil's Garden*.

Khaled Mattawa (b. 1964) was born in Benghazi, Libya, and in 1979 immigrated to the United States. He earned an MA in English and an MFA in creative writing from IU, where he taught creative writing and won an Academy of American Poets Award. Mattawa has published three volumes of poetry, *Ismailia Eclipse*, *Zodiac of Echoes*, and *Amorisco* and has poems in numerous magazines and *The Pushcart Prize Anthology*. He was awarded the Alfred Hodder Fellowship at Princeton University, a Guggenheim fellowship, and an NEA translation grant. A professor of English and creative writing at the University of Michigan in Ann Arbor, Mattawa is renowned as perhaps the leading translator of Arab poetry into English.

Antonia Matthew (b. 1938) is a member of the Bloomington writing group, Five Women Poets. She has attended the Indiana Writers' Conference several times, most recently studying with Maureen Seaton. She has been published in *Nimrod*, *California Quarterly*, *Indiana Writes*, *Passenger*, *Wind* and the anthologies *A Linen Weave of Bloomington Poets* and *Celebrating Seventy*.

John Matthias (b. 1941) has published some twenty books of poetry, translation, criticism, and scholarship. His most recent books of poems are *New Selected Poems*

(2004) and *Kedging* (2007). In 1998 Robert Archambeau edited *Word Play Place: Essays on the Poetry of John Matthias*. Matthias is poetry editor of *Notre Dame Review* and lives in South Bend.

Bonnie Maurer (b. 1949), MFA in poetry from IU, is the author of *Ms Lily Jane Babbitt before the Ten O'clock Bus from Memphis Ran over Her, Old 37: The Mason Cows*, and *Bloodletting: A Ritual Poem for Women's Voices*. Awarded a Creative Renewal Arts Fellowship by the Arts Council of Indianapolis in 2000, Maurer wrote *The Reconfigured Goddess: Poems of a Breast Cancer Survivor*. Currently she works as a poet in the schools and community for Young Audiences of Indiana, as a copy editor for the *Indianapolis Business Journal,* and as an Ai Chi (aquatic flowing energy) instructor.

Jim McGarrah's (b. 1948) award-winning collection of poems, *Running the Voodoo Down*, was published in 2003. He has been nominated for a Pushcart Prize, and new poems have appeared most recently in *Connecticut Review*, *North American Review*, *Cafe Review*, and *Elixir Magazine*. McGarrah's newest book of poems, *When the Stars Go Dark*, will soon be available from Main Street Rag Publishing House.

Marc McKee (b. 1976) holds a BA from IU, a MFA from the University of Houston, and is currently pursuing a PhD at the University of Missouri at Columbia, where he lives with his wife, Camellia Cosgray. His work has appeared in various journals, such as *Boston Review*, *Cimarron Review*, *Conduit*, *Crazyhorse*, *diagram*, *Forklift*, *Ohio*, *LIT*, *Pleiades*, the *Journal*, *Salt Hill*, and *Subtropics*, among others. His chapbook, *What Apocalypse?*, won the New Michigan Press/*Diagram* 2008 Chapbook Contest.

Todd McKinney (b. 1972) teaches in the English Department at Ball State University in Muncie, Indiana. His work has appeared in *Puerto del Sol*, the *Greensboro Review*, *Smartish Pace*, *BorderSenses*, *storySouth*, and the *Cimarron Review*, among others. In 2007 Mississinewa Press handmade and published his chapbook, *A MATTER OF PUBLIC RECORD.*

Joyelle McSweeney (b. 1976) is the author of two books of poetry, *The Red Bird* and *The Commandrine and Other Poems*, and two novels, *Nylund, the Sarcographer* and *Flet*. She is a cofounder of Action Books. McSweeney lives in Mishawaka and has taught in Notre Dame's MFA program since 2006.

Norman Minnick's (b. 1970) collection, *To Taste the Water*, won the First Series Award in Poetry and was published by Mid-List Press. He is the editor of an anthology, *Between Water and Song*, forthcoming from White Pine Press. Minnick lives in Brownsburg, Indiana.

Mark Minster (b. 1969) was a finalist for the 2007 James Hearst Poetry Prize from *North American Review*. He teaches English and Comparative Literature at Rose-Hulman Institute of Technology in Terre Haute and has lived in Indiana since 1997.

Roger Mitchell (b. 1935) is the author of eleven books of poetry and a work of nonfiction. His most recent book is *Lemon Peeled the Moment Before: New & Selected Poems* (2008). *Delicate Bait* (2003) won the 2002 Akron Prize. Further recognition for Mitchell's writing includes the Midland Poetry Award for his first book *Letters from Siberia and Other Poems* (1971; reprinted 1974), The John Ben Snow Award for his work of nonfiction *Clear Pond*, two fellowships each from the IAC and the NEA, and the River Styx International Poetry Award. Mitchell is a 2005 Fellow in Poetry from the New York Foundation for the Arts. He directed the Creative Writing Program at IU and held the Ruth Lilly Chair of Poetry.

William Vaughn Moody (1869–1910) was born in Spencer, Indiana, and published an untitled volume and two poetic dramas but is mostly noted for his 1906 play *The Great Divide*, hailed at the time as the "Great American Drama." In 1908 he was inducted into the American Academy of Arts and Letters. Moody was coeditor of *Harvard Monthly*. From 1894 to 1895 he held the position of assistant to Louis E. Gates in the Harvard English Department. He was an instructor at the University of Chicago from 1895 to 1903, when he was promoted to an assistant professorship. In 1907 Moody left the university to concentrate on his poetry.

Cheryl Soden Moreland (b. 1956), Hoosier born and bred, has had poetry published in the *Tipton Poetry Journal* and in two anthologies—*Sunrise and Soft Mist* and *Poetic Voices of America*—and was honored by the International Library of Poetry as the Editor's Choice Award recipient for her poem, "A Mother's Love." She has had several essays published in the *Indianapolis Star*, *NUVO*, and *Urban Tapestry: Indianapolis Stories*.

Lisel Mueller (b. 1924) is the author of six books of poetry and two volumes of translations. Her latest publication is *Alive Together: New and Selected Poems* (1996). She is a recipient of the Pulitzer Prize and the National Book Award. Though Mueller currently resides in Chicago, she has lived in both Evansville and Bloomington, Indiana.

Neil Nakadate (b. 1943) was born in East Chicago, Indiana. His publications have appeared in *Aethlon*, *Cottonwood*, *Mississippi Quarterly*, *Western Humanities Review*, *Tennessee Studies in Literature*, *Annals of Internal Medicine*, and elsewhere. He has edited two books on Robert Penn Warren and in 1999 published a critical study of Jane Smiley's fiction. He teaches in the Department of English at Iowa State University.

Mark Neely (1971) grew up in Champaign, Illinois. His poems have appeared in *Boulevard*, *Indiana Review*, *Salt Hill*, *Meridian*, *North American Review*, and elsewhere. He teaches at Ball State University in Muncie, where he lives with his wife, writer Jill Christman, and their two children.

Tam Lin Neville's (b. 1944) poems have been published in numerous magazines, among them, *Harvard Review*, *American Poetry Review*, *Crazyhorse*, the *Massachusetts Review*, and in a number of anthologies. Her essays and reviews have appeared in *American Poetry Review*, *Threepenny Review*, and *Hungry Mind Review*, among others. Her book of poems, *Journey Cake*, was published in 1998. She lives in Boston and with her poet husband, Bert Stern, is an editor for Off the Grid Press, which publishes poetry books by people over sixty. She works for Changing Lives through Literature, an organization that teaches people on probation.

Richard Newman (b. 1966) was born in Illinois, raised in southern Indiana, and now lives in Saint Louis. He is the author of the poetry collection *Borrowed Towns* and several chapbooks. His poems, stories, and essays have appeared in *Best American Poetry*, *Boulevard*, *Crab Orchard Review*, *Pleiades*, *Poetry East*, the *Sun*, and many other periodicals and anthologies. Newman teaches at Washington University and Saint Louis Community College, reviews books for the *Saint Louis Post-Dispatch*, and for the last thirteen years has served as editor of *River Styx*.

Brian O'Neill (b. 1949) was born in South Bend, Indiana, and was educated at the University of Notre Dame and IU, Bloomington. His poems have appeared in many periodicals, and he has served as a poetry editor for *Indiana Writes*—now the *Indiana Review*— and *College English*. O'Neill is presently Senior Project manager at Strategic Development Group and lives in Bloomington with his wife, Ann.

Matt O'Neill (b. 1950) is a native of Dublin, Ireland. He has poems in *Celebrating Seventy* and is the author of a cookbook, *The Seasons at Walden Inn*. He lives in Bloomington, where he is a restaurateur and chef.

William Orem (b. 1966) has won multiple awards for his writing, including two Pushcart nominations, the GLCA New Writer's Award, and a grant from the Christopher Isherwood Foundation. His poetry, fiction, and essays have appeared in more than one hundred publications, and his plays have been produced in Miami, Buffalo,

Kentucky, and Boston. Orem lived in Bloomington, Indiana, from 1991 to 2001. He is currently a writer in residence at Emerson College in Boston.

Bryan Penberthy's (b. 1976) first collection of poetry, *Lucktown*, won the National Poetry Review Book Prize and was published in 2007. His poetry has appeared in many venues, including *Crazyhorse*, *New Orleans Review*, *Poetry International*, and the *Midwest Quarterly*, as well as online via *Poetry Daily*, *Verse Daily*, and *Blackbird*. He holds an MFA from Purdue University, where he received the Leonard Neufeldt Award for his work and served as poetry editor for *Sycamore Review*.

Roger Pfingston (b. 1940), born in Evansville, Indiana, published some of his first poems in the *New York Times* while still in the navy in the early 1960s. Since that time his work has appeared widely in magazines and anthologies. Two chapbooks, *Earthbound* and *Singing to the Garden*, were released in 2003. He is a retired Bloomington high school teacher of English and photography.

Dick Pflum (b. 1932) has published five books of poetry, *Moving Into the Light* (1975), *A Dream of Salt* (1980), *A Strange Juxtaposition of Parts* (1995), *Listening with Others* (2007), and *The Haunted Refrigerator and Other Poems* (2007). Pflum's poems also appear in regional and national anthologies: *Glassworks*, *A New Geography of Poets*, *The Indiana Experience*, and *Bear Crossings*. He was Poet of the Month in the archive of *PoetryNet* in October 2003. Pflum taught in the poetry-in-the-schools program, was part-time instructor of Advanced Poetry Writing at IUPUI during the late 1980s, and ran a Poetry Salon for The Writers' Center of Indiana in Indianapolis.

Michael J. Phillips (1937–2005) authored twenty-three brief poetry manuscripts. He was a lecturer in English at the University of Wisconsin-Milwaukee (1970–71, 1973–79) and an instructor in English at numerous Indiana universities. From 1977 to 1979 Phillips was Visiting Fellow at Harvard University. He lived most of his adult life in Bloomington, Indiana.

Donald Platt (b. 1957) is the author of four volumes of poetry, *Fresh Peaches, Fireworks, and Guns* (1994), *Cloud Atlas* (2002), *My Father Says Grace* (2007), and *Dirt Angels* (2009). His fine-press, limited-edition chapbook *Leap Second at the Turn of the Millennium* was published in 1999. Platt's poems have appeared in many journals and anthologies, including the *New Republic*, *Nation*, *Best American Poetry 2000* and *2006*, and *Pushcart Prize XXVII* and *XXIX*, 2003 and 2005 editions, among others. A recipient of a fellowship from the NEA, the Paumanok Poetry Prize, the "Discovery"/The Nation Prize, and others, Platt is professor of English at Purdue University. He lives in West Lafayette.

Jim Powell (b. 1950) served as founding executive director of the Writers' Center of Indianapolis (now Indiana) for twenty years. He teaches argumentative and creative writing as well as Indiana literature as a senior lecturer at IUPUI, where he is also Associate Chair for Students (lead adviser) in the English Department. A native of Elwood, Indiana, Powell holds a MFA in fiction writing from Bowling Green State University.

Nancy Pulley's (b. 1948) poems have appeared in *Indiannual*, *Flying Island*, *Arts Indiana Literary Supplement*, the *Sycamore Review*, *The Humpback Barn Festival Collection*, and *A Linen Weave of Themes*—a collection of poetry on tape. She has a poem in *Literature and Integrated Studies*, a middle-school textbook published by Scott Foresman. *Tremolo of Light* won the Writers' Center Poetry Chapbook Contest in 1991. She lives in Ogilville, Indiana.

Fran Quinn (b. 1942) was born in Easthampton, Massachusetts, and moved to Indiana in 1988. His four publications are *Milk of the Lioness*, *At the Edges of the World*, *The Goblet Crying for Wine*, and *A Horse of Blue Ink*. A special issue of the *Worcester Review* was dedicated to him. Quinn was nominated for two Pushcart Awards and has won the Hopewell Award. He presently runs independent monthly workshops in New York, Boston, and Indianapolis.

Linda Neal Reising (b. 1955) is a poet and fiction writer. Her poems have been published in the *Southern Indiana Review*, *Open Twenty-Four Hours*, and the *Comstock Review*. Reising's work was also included in *Fruitflesh: Seeds of Inspiration for Women Who Write*, a book published by HarperCollins in 2002. In her real life, she teaches eighth grade English at North Posey Junior High.

Eric Rensberger (b. 1950), a native Hoosier who grew up in Elkhart County, has lived in Bloomington since 1979. He is the author of *Letters*, *Standing Where Something Did*, *Blank of Blanks*, and *The Sad Mailbox*. His poems have appeared in various journals and magazines, as well as in the anthologies *A Linen Weave of Bloomington Poets* and *Celebrating Seventy*. Rensberger's collected poems, including the chronological sequence Account of My Days, may be found at www.ericrensbergerpoetry .net/.

Kenneth Rexroth (1905–1982) was born in South Bend, Indiana, and was a poet, translator, and critical essayist. He was among the first poets in the United States to explore traditional Japanese poetic forms such as haiku. He is regarded as a chief figure in the San Francisco Renaissance. Rexroth wrote a large body of literary and cultural criticism, much of which has been compiled in anthologies. A professor at the University of California, Santa Barbara, from 1968 to 1973, he spent his final years translating Japanese and Chinese women poets and promoting the work of women poets in America and overseas.

James Whitcomb Riley (1847–1916), writer and poet called the "Hoosier poet" and America's "Children's Poet," made a start writing newspaper verse in Hoosier dialect for the *Indianapolis Journal* in 1875. Known for his dialect recitations and pithy pragmatic remarks, his popular verse was humorous or sentimental. As the "People's Laureate," Riley's poems were considered so inspiring that in 1915 the secretary of the interior suggested one be read in each schoolhouse in the land. His last collection was *Knee Deep in June* (1912).

Shana Ritter (b. 1953) has had poems published in *Georgetown Review*, *A Linen Weave of Bloomington Poets*, and *Common Ground*. She also writes fiction, essays, and articles. Recipient of two Indiana Individual Artist's Grants, Ritter is currently working on a series of prose poems. She is a diversity educator and works with schools on creating equitable change. She lives out in the country, south of Bloomington, Indiana.

Dana Roeser (b. 1953) won the Samuel French Morse Prize for both her second book, *In the Truth Room* (2008), and her first, *Beautiful Motion* (2004). Other awards include a 2007 NEA Literature Fellowship, the Great Lakes Colleges Association New Writers Award, and the Jenny McKean Moore Writer-in-Washington Fellowship. She has received fellowships to Yaddo, Ragdale, the Virginia Center for the Creative Arts, and Mary Anderson Center for the Arts. Her poems have appeared in such journals as the the *Iowa Review*, *Antioch Review*, *Southern Review*, *Harvard Review*, *Northwest Review*, *Sou'wester*, and on Poetry Daily. Roeser lives in West Lafayette, Indiana, where she teaches poetry writing at Purdue University.

Ernest Sandeen's (1908–1997) *Collected Poems* (1977) were followed by *A Later Day, Another Year* (1988), and *Can These Bones Live?* (1994). He published regularly in magazines such as the *New Yorker*, *Poetry*, and the *Hudson Review*, among others. Sandeen was professor of English at the University of Notre Dame from 1946 until his retirement in 1978 and served as emeritus professor of English at the university until his death in 1997.

John Sherman (b. 1944) has published three volumes of poetry. The manuscript for his book, *Marjorie Main: Rural Documentary Poetry*, earned him a finalist position in the Walt Whitman Award competition sponsored by the Academy of American Poets. His poems have been published in many literary magazines. A resident of Indianapolis, he gives frequent readings throughout the state. Sherman is also the author of several nonfiction books, the latest of which is *New Faces at the Crossroads: The World in Central Indiana* (2007).

Dennis Sipe (b. 1959), born in Seymour, Indiana, has left Indiana a few times: for Fairbanks, Alaska, and Great Cranberry Island, Maine. He has had poems in various magazines, published a chapbook: *My Days Are Stray Dogs That Won't Come When I Call,* and written a screenplay called "Releasing Herschel." He is working on stories and two novels and received an IAC grant in 1992. Sipe has had more than fifty crazy writer jobs and given readings in eight states.

Laurel Smith's (b. 1955) poetry has appeared in *Natural Bridge, New Millennium Writings,* and *JAMA.* She is coauthor of *Early Works by Modern Women Writers: Woolf, Bowen, Mansfield, Cather and Stein* (2006). Her poems have been featured with visual art exhibits, including the Indianapolis Museum of Art Poetry project. Other collaborations include writing musical lyrics and creating an imagistic history of New Harmony, Indiana. Smith is professor of English at Vincennes University.

Bruce Snider (b. 1971) is the author of *The Year We Studied Women* and winner of the 2003 Felix Pollak Prize in Poetry from the University of Wisconsin Press. Born and reared in Columbia City, Indiana, he has spent the last few years as a Wallace Stegner Fellow and Jones Lecturer in Poetry at Stanford University.

Mary Ellen Solt's (1920–2007) concrete poems have been included in several multimedia presentations, exhibitions, and publications. She has authored three books of poetry and a chapbook and coedited *Concrete Poetry: A World View,* received grants, and won a number of awards, including design. From 1980 to 1991 Solt was professor emerita of comparative literature and director of the Polish Studies Center at IU, Bloomington.

Maura Stanton's (b. 1946) first book of poetry, *Snow on Snow,* won the Yale Series of Younger Poets Award in 1975. *Cries of Swimmers* followed; both were reprinted in the Carnegie Mellon Classic Contemporary Series. Subsequent poetry titles are *Tales of the Supernatural* (1988), *Life among the Trolls* (1998), and *Glacier Wine* (2001). Stanton's poems, award-winning stories, and essays have appeared in numerous magazines, and she has published short stories and a novel. Stanton is professor of English at IU, teaching in the Master of Fine Arts Program in Creative Writing.

Felix Stefanile (b. 1920), the first-generation son of Italian immigrants, has published eleven books of verse (three of them translations of Italian poets) and won numerous prizes, including awards from the NEA and the *Virginia Quarterly Review.* Invited by Purdue to teach for one year as a visiting professor, he was appointed full professor in 1970. In 1973 he received a Best Teacher award from Standard Oil of

Indiana (now the Amoco prize). Stefanile chaired the editorial board of the Purdue publishing program for five years and remained at Purdue until his retirement in 1987.

Kevin Stein (b. 1954) was born and raised in Anderson, Indiana. The author of nine books of poetry and literary criticism, Stein's most recent collection is *Sufficiency of the Actual* (2008). He has earned fellowships from the NEA and the Illinois Arts Council and has received the *Indiana Review* Poetry Prize. Stein is the current Poet Laureate of Illinois. He teaches at Bradley University.

Bert Stern's (b. 1930) poems and essays have appeared in journals including the *Beloit Poetry Journal*, *Hunger Mountain*, *Sewanee Review*, the *China Review*, the *American Poetry Review*, and in more than a half dozen anthologies. He is the recipient of an artist's grant from the Somerville, Massachusetts, Arts Council. Stern is Milligan professor emeritus of English at Wabash College, Crawfordsville, Indiana, and retired chief editor of Hilton Publishing. With his wife, Tam Lin Neville, he edits for Off the Grid Press, which publishes poets over age sixty. His new book, *Steerage*, will be published in February 2009.

Ruth Stone (b. 1915) moved from Roanoke, Virginia, to her grandparents' home in Indianapolis, where poetry was an essential ingredient of life. She is the author of nine books of poetry and has received the National Book Award, the Wallace Stevens Award, a National Book Critics Circle Award, and the Shelley Memorial Award. Her recent books of poetry include *In the Next Galaxy* (2002), *Ordinary Words* (1999), and *Simplicity* (1997). Stone has published poems in numerous anthologies and literary journals. She taught creative writing at many universities, finally settling at SUNY Binghamton. She has lived in Vermont since 1957.

F. Richard "Dick" Thomas (b. 1940) has published eight collections of poetry, including his most recent, *Extravagant Kiss* (2007). In 2004 he was awarded the Mark Twain Award from the Society for the Study of Midwestern Literature for his poetry and prose. Born and raised in Evansville, Indiana, Thomas attended Purdue and Indiana universities. He is professor emeritus of Michigan State University.

Thomas Tokarski (b. 1939) is a longtime resident of Indiana and a member of the Bloomington Free Verse Poets. His poems have appeared in various journals, and in 1993 he won first prize for poetry in a contest sponsored by the Ohio Valley Writers Guild. In the spring of 2008 he won first place, adult category, in the Spring Mill State Park Nature Poetry Contest. He currently resides in a rural area near Bloomington, Indiana.

Jon Tribble (b. 1962) lives, writes, and works in Carbondale, Illinois, where he is managing editor for the national literary journal *Crab Orchard Review* and series editor for the Crab Orchard Series in Poetry annual competitions. His poems have been awarded recognition from the Sewanee Writers Conference and the Illinois Arts Council. A native of Little Rock, Arkansas, Tribble is a double-degree graduate of IU, Bloomington, where he served as both editor and business manager for *Indiana Review*.

Robin Vogelzang (b. 1978) is a PhD candidate in American literature, having received an MFA in creative writing from IU, Bloomington. She currently resides in Brussels, Belgium.

Charles Wagner (b. 1954) received an MA in English from the University of Kansas and an MFA in creative writing from IU, Bloomington. His poems have appeared in *Poetry Now, Cottonwood Review, Vanderbilt Review, Kansas Quarterly*, and *Flying Island*. In 2003 he received a Creative Renewal Fellowship from the Arts Council of Indianapolis. For the last fourteen years he has taught English and creative writing at Brebeuf Jesuit Preparatory School in Indianapolis.

Shari Wagner (b. 1958) is from Goshen, Indiana. Her first book of poems, *Evening Chore*, was published in 2005 by Cascadia Publishing House. She teaches for the Writers' Center of Indiana and has had work appear in *North American Review, Black Warrior Review, Christian Century*, and *A Cappella: Mennonite Voices in Poetry*. Since 2001, when she received a Creative Renewal Fellowship from the Arts Council of Indianapolis, she has been writing a collection of poems about sacred places in Indiana.

David Wagoner (b. 1926), an Ohio native who grew up in Whiting, Indiana, has published seventeen books of poems, most recently *Good Morning and Good Night* (2005), and ten novels, one of which, *The Escape Artist*, was made into a movie by Francis Ford Coppola. He won the Lilly Prize in 1991 and edited *Poetry Northwest* until its end in 2002. In 2011 he was awarded the American Academy of Arts and Letters Arthur Rense Poetry Prize for consistent excellence over a long career. Wagoner is a professor emeritus at the University of Washington.

Jim Walker (b. 1968) has authored the writing guide *Poetry Report* and three chapbooks. His poetry and prose have been published in *Painted Bride Quarterly, Hanging Loose, pLopLop*, and other journals. A graduate of the Warren Wilson College MFA program for writers, Walker lives in Indianapolis with his wife and two children. He is the director of a nonprofit writing center for kids called the Second Story and teaches at Butler University.

Jessamyn West (1903–1984) was born in Jennings County, Indiana, and wrote memoirs, novels, short stories, poetry, essays, articles, plays, songs, and lyrics for an opera. Among other awards, West received the Indiana Authors' Day Award, 1956, for *Love, Death, and the Ladies' Drill Team*. She taught at many writers' conferences and was a visiting professor and lecturer at several colleges. Napa Valley College awards the Jessamyn West Poetry and Fiction Award for literary merit to a student of that college.

Katerina Tsiopos Wills (b. 1957) likes to read her poems around the world: Café Trieste (San Francisco), the Indianapolis Museum of Art, at the StoneSong Arts Festival (Bloomington, Indiana), in the Skokie Public Library (Illinois), Thessalonica (Greece), and many other venues. Her poems appear in *Poetry Motel*, *ART/LIFE*, *River Styx*, *Y-Bird*, and *The Otherwise Room Anthology of Poetry* and are featured on two audiotapes from the *Linen Weave Poetry Anthology* series. She lives with her husband, Howard, and their animal menagerie in Brown County, Indiana.

David Wojahn (b. 1953) has authored six books of poetry, among them *Icehouse Lights* (1982), winner of the Yale Younger Poets Award, *Glassworks* (1987), *Late Empire* (1994), and *Spirit Cabinet* (2002). Essayist and editor (he coedited *A Profile of Twentieth Century American Poetry* [1987]), he has received fellowships, numerous awards, honors, and writing residencies. His poetry, essays, and reviews have appeared in many journals and anthologies. Wojahn was Lilly Professor of Poetry at IU, Bloomington, from 1985 to 2003. He currently teaches at Virginia Commonwealth University and in the low-residency MFA Program at Vermont College. He lives in Richmond, Virginia.

John Woods (1926–1995) was born in Indiana. His first collection of poems, *The Deaths at Paragon, Indiana*, was published in 1955, when he was twenty-nine. His final volume was *Black Marigolds* (1994). From 1956 to 1992 he was an English professor at Western Michigan University.

Samuel Yellen (1906–1983), author of seven books of poetry and social criticism, won the Indiana Author's Award in 1958. He taught creative writing and literature at IU, Bloomington, from 1929 to 1973 and became professor of English in 1963. He founded and subsequently edited the IU Press Poetry Series. Yellen was a Guggenheim fellow from 1964 to 1965.

Dean Young (b. 1955) is a graduate of IU's creative writing program. He has published eight books of poetry that include *Strike Anywhere* (1995), which won the Colorado Prize for Poetry, *Skid* (2002), finalist for the Lenore Marshall prize, *Elegy on Toy Piano* (2006), finalist for a Pulitzer Prize, and most recently, *embryoyo* (2007). He has received a Stegner fellowship from Stanford University, twice been awarded fellowships by the John Simon Guggenheim Memorial Foundation and from the NEA. Young currently divides his time between Berkeley, California, and Iowa City, Iowa, where he is a member of the permanent faculty of the Iowa Writers' Workshop. He also teaches in the low-residency Master of Fine Arts Program at Warren Wilson College.

Kevin Young (b. 1970s) is the author of six books of poetry, most recently *For the Confederate Dead*, winner of the Quill Award in Poetry and the Paterson Poetry Prize for Sustained Literary Achievement, and *Dear Darkness*, a book of odes and elegies published in fall 2008. He is also the editor of four books, including *Everyman's Pocket Poets Blues Poems* and *Jazz Poems* and the Library of America's *John Berryman: Selected Poems*. Young is currently Atticus Haygood Professor of English and Creative Writing and curator of the Danowski Poetry Library at Emory University.

Marguerite Young (1902–1984) was born in Indianapolis and studied at Butler University and the University of Chicago. A teacher, writer, and poet, she authored two books of poetry, *Prismatic Ground* (1937) and *Moderate Fable* (1944), and a history located in New Harmony, Indiana: *Angel in the Forest: A Fairy Tale of Two Utopias* (1945), comprising short stories, essays, and a biography of Eugene Victor Debs. *Country without Maps* is a compilation of her essays.

● Mentions in Poems

1. Whiting
2. Calumet City
3. Gary
4. Crown Point
5. Indiana Dunes
6. Portage
7. Notre Dame
8. Goshen
9. Topeka
10. Demotte
11. Plymouth
12. Warsaw
13. Columbia City
14. Auburn
15. Fort Wayne
16. Monon
17. Judyville
18. Lafayette
19. Delphi
20. New London
21. Marion
22. Peru
23. Crown Point
24. Tipton
25. Gessie
26. Lebanon
27. Arcadia
28. Westfield
29. Noblesville
30. Elwood
31. Muncie
32. Greencastle
33. Brownsburg
34. Greenfield
35. Carthage
36. Cottage Grove
37. Terre Haute
38. Quincy
39. Mooresville
40. Monrovia
41. Brooklyn
42. Paragon
43. Martinsville
44. Greenwood
45. Hindustan
46. Bean Blossom
47. Stoney Lonesome
48. Gnaw Bone
49. Nashville
50. Harrodsburg
51. Oolitic
52. Bedford
53. Brownstown
54. Medora
55. Vernon
56. Milan
57. Princeton
58. Lyles
59. Petersburg
60. Claysville
61. Paoli
62. French Lick
63. Salem
64. Vienna
65. Madison
66. Hanover
67. Rising Sun
68. New Harmony
69. Mount Vernon
70. Mount St. Francis
71. Floyds Knobs
72. Ferdinand

■ Birthplace for Poets

1. East Chicago
2. Hammond
3. Winfield
4. Mishawaka
5. South Bend
6. Elkhart
7. Jasper
8. Kendallville
9. North Manchester
10. West Lafayette
11. Kokomo
12. Portland
13. Crawfordsville
14. Carmel
15. Anderson
16. Yorktown
17. Selma
18. Winchester
19. Indianapolis
20. Richmond
21. Franklin
22. Spencer
23. Unionville
24. Bloomington
25. Columbus
26. Ogilville
27. Vincennes
28. Shoals
29. Seymour
30. Crothersville
31. Poseyville
32. Evansville
33. Jasper
34. Goshen

⬠ Natural Areas Mentioned

1. Jasper–Pulaski Wildlife Area
2. Asa Bales Park
3. Lieber State Park
4. Lake Griffy
5. Lake Monroe
6. Yellowood State Forest
7. Muskatatuck Natural Wildlife Refuge

Counties listed on map are mentioned by name in poems or biographies.

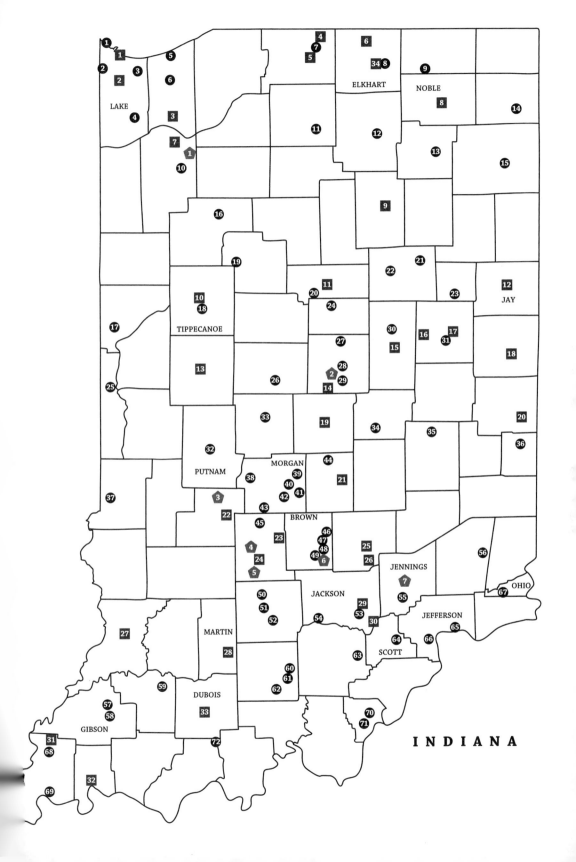

INDIANA

Permissions

Philip Appleman: "Train Whistles," "Memo to the 21st Century," "How Evolution Came to Indiana," and "To the Garbage Collectors in Bloomington, Indiana, the First Pickup of the New Year" from *New and Selected Poems, 1956–1996*. Copyright © 1996 by Philip Appleman. Reprinted with the permission of the University of Arkansas Press, www.uapress.com/.

Donald Baker: "Twelve Hawks" and "Advising" from *Formal Application Selected Poems 1960–1980* (Barnwood Press, 1982). Copyright © Estate of Donald Baker. Reprinted by permission of Barnwood Press. "Jeopardy" and "No" from *Search Patterns* (Sugar Creek/Steppingstone, 1996). Copyright © Donald Baker Estate.

Willis Barnstone: "With My Redneck Sons in Southern Indiana," "This evening after I was asked to leave," "I Knew a Woman with One Breast," and "Aliki in the Woods" from *Algebra of Night: New and Selected Poems 1948–1998* (Sheep Meadow Press). Copyright © 1999 Willis Barnstone. Reprinted by permission of the author.

Valerie Berry: "Corn/Sorghum/Sumac." Copyright © Valerie Berry. Reprinted by permission of the author.

Marianne Boruch: "Car Covered with Snow," "The Going-Out-of-Business Greenhouse," "Wind Storm, Late March," and "At Horticulture Park" from *Poems New and Selected*. Copyright © 2004 by Marianne Boruch. Reprinted with the permission of Oberlin College Press, www.oberlin.edu/ocpress/.

Catherine Bowman: "Broke Song," "Broke Song (Later)," and an excerpt from "From 1000 Lines" from *Notarikon*. Copyright (c) 2006 by Catherine Bowman. Reprinted by permission of Four Way Books. All rights reserved. "No Sorry" from *Rock Farm*, Gibbs-Smith. Copyright © Catherine Bowman. Reprinted by permission of the author.

Tony Brewer: "The Colonists" from *The Great American Scapegoat* (Author House, 2006). Copyright © Tony Brewer. Reprinted by permission of the author.

Dan Carpenter: "At the Indiana Transportation Museum." Copyright © Dan Carpenter. Reprinted by permission of the author.

published in *Country without Maps: New Poems* (Macmillan Co. NY). Copyright © Jean Garrigue 1959–1964. Reprinted by permission of Aileen Ward, executor, Jean Garrigue's estate.

Sonia Gernes: "Auction" and "Plainsong for an Ordinary Night" from *Brief Lives: Poems by Sonia Gernes* (University of Notre Dame Press, 1981). "Dust," "Keeping the Hedge," and "Geese Crossing the Road" from *Women at Forty: Poems by Sonia Gernes* (University of Notre Dame Press, 1988). Copyright © Sonia Gernes. Reprinted by permission of the author.

Eugene Gloria: "Here, on Earth" and "Lullaby for Rabbit." Copyright © Eugene Gloria. Reprinted by permission of the author.

Matthew Graham: "New Harmony" first appeared in *1946* (Galileo Books, 1991). Copyright © Matthew Graham. Reprinted by permission of the Galileo Press Ltd. "Postcards from Southern Indiana." Copyright © Matthew Graham. Reprinted by permission of the author.

Chris Green: "Limit 55" and "Chime." Copyright © Chris Green. Reprinted by permission of the author.

Sarah Green: "*Chances Are*, Lafayette, Indiana," *Gettysburg Review* (Summer 2007) and *Pushcart Anthology* 2009. Copyright © Sarah Green. "Cause and Effect." Copyright © Sarah Green. Reprinted by permission of the author.

C.E. Greer: "Crux" (under different title) *Flying Island* 8 no. 2 (Summer/Fall, 2000). Copyright © C.E. Greer. Reprinted by permission of the author.

Jeff Gundy: "And So Heavy with Life the Crust of the World is Still" from *Flatlands* (Cleveland State University Poetry Center 1995). Copyright © Jeff Gundy. Reprinted by permission of the Cleveland State University Poetry Center.

Hannah Haas: "Hedge Apples" and "Frequency." Copyright © Hannah Haas. Reprinted by permission of the author.

Anne Haines: "8-Bar Solo" from *The Linen Weave of Bloomington Poets* (Wind, 2002). Copyright © Anne Haines. "Brood X." Copyright © Anne Haines. Reprinted by permission of the author.

James Hazard: "New Year's Eve in Whiting, Indiana," "Fire in Whiting, Indiana," "Gypsies in Whiting, Indiana," and "A True Biography of Stan Getz" from *The Fire in Whiting, Indiana* (Juniper Press, 1983). Copyright © James Hazard. Courtesy Lilly Library, Indiana University, Bloomington, Indiana. Reprinted by permission of the author.

Todd McKinney: "Surrender" and "Some Very Important Business," *storySouth* (Spring/Summer 2007). Copyright © Todd McKinney. Reprinted by permission of the author.

Joyelle McSweeney: "WNDU." Copyright © Joyelle McSweeney. Reprinted by permission of the author.

Norman Minnick: "Pissarro's the House of the Deaf Woman and the Belfry at Eragny" from *To Taste the Water: Poems*. Copyright © 2007 by Norman Minnick. Published by Mid-List Press, Minneapolis, Minnesota. Used by permission.

Mark Minster: "Where You Are" and *"poem she sent."* Copyright © Mark Minster. Reprinted by permission of the author.

Roger Mitchell: "The Quickest Way to Get There" from *Celebrating Seventy*," (*WIND*, 2003). "Why We're Here" from *A Linen Weave of Bloomington Poets* (2002) and *Delicate Bait* (University of Akron Press, 2003). Copyright © Roger Mitchell, "City of Backyards," "Clang," and "Four-Hundredth Mile" from *The Word for Everything* (BkMk Press, University of Missouri-Kansas City, 1996). Copyright © Roger Mitchell. Reprinted by permission.

William Vaughn Moody: "The Daguerrotype" *The Poems and Plays of William Vaughn Moody,* vol. 1 (Houghton Mifflin Company 1912). Copyright ©1912 by Harriet C. Moody.

Cheryl Soden Moreland: "Fountain Square Mama . . . in Heat." Copyright © Cheryl Soden Moreland. Reprinted by permission of the author.

Lisel Mueller: "Illinois, Indiana, Iowa," (excerpt from "Highway Poems") "Scenic Route," "Pigeons," and "Letter to California" from *Alive Together: New and Selected Poems* (Louisiana State University). Copyright © 1996 Lisel Mueller. Reprinted by permission of Louisiana State University Press. "A Grackle Observed" from *Dependencies* by Lisel Mueller. Copyright © 1965 by Lisel Mueller. Published by the University of North Carolina Press. Used by permission of the publisher. www.uncpress .unc.edu/.

Neil Nakadate: "Hoosiers (2)" and "Crossing the Line." Copyright © Neil Nakadate. Reprinted by permission of the author.

Mark Neely: "The Bowling Alley," *North American Review* 291, nos. 3–4 (May–August 2006); "A Promise," *Maize* 3 (March 2004). Copyright © Mark Neely. Reprinted by permission of the author.

Tam Lin Neville: "An Afternoon to be Filled with Kicked Snow" and "Small Town Ceremony." Copyright © Tam Lin Neville. Reprinted by permission of the author.

Robin Vogelzang: "Cicada Sonnet." Copyright © Robin Vogelzang. Reprinted by permission of the author.

Chuck Wagner: "The Lucky Bamboo" and "The Topeka Auction Restaurant." Copyright © Chuck Wagner. Reprinted by permission of the author.

Shari Wagner: "Washington Street, Indianapolis, at Dusk." First Place in the *Writing What You See* contest sponsored by the Writers' Center of Indianapolis, judged by Mari Evans and sponsored by Writers' Center of Indianapolis and the Indianapolis Museum of Art. "Anti-Slavery Cemetery." Copyright © Shari Wagner. Reprinted by permission of the author.

David Wagoner: "The Junior High School Band Concert," "A Valedictory to Standard Oil of Indiana," "Looking for Nellie Washington," and "The Shooting of John Dillinger Outside the Biograph Theater, July 22, 1934," from *Travelling Light* (University of Illinois Press, 1999). Copyright © David Wagoner. "Their Bodies" from *Through the Forest: New and Selected Poems 1977–1987* (Atlantic Monthly Press 1987). Copyright © David Wagoner. All reprinted by permission of the author.

Jim Walker: "Brooklyn, Indiana" and "City." Copyright © Jim Walker. Reprinted by permission of the author.

Jessamyn West: "Late Afternoon" and "Waiter, Another Squab" from *The Secret Look* (Harcourt Brace). Reprinted by the permission of Russell and Volkening as agents for the author. Copyright © 1974 by Jessamyn West.

Katerina Tsiopos Wills: "Quarry Scuba: Indiana Dive Partners" and "Blessing of the Bikes: Bean Blossom, Indiana." Copyright © Katerina Tsiopos Wills. Reprinted by permission of the author.

David Wojahn: "Days of 1994" and "Written on the Due Date of a Son Never Born" from *Interrogation Palace: New and Selected Poems 1982–2004* by David Wojahn, © 2006. Reprinted by permission of the University of Pittsburgh Press. "Red Ochre" from *Spirit Cabinet* by David Wojahn © 2002. Reprinted by permission of the University of Pittsburgh Press. "Distance" from *Icehouse Lights* by David Wojahn, Yale University Press 1982. Copyright © by Yale University Press. Reprinted by permission.

John Woods: "Turning to Look Back" from *Keeping Out of Trouble* (Indiana University Press, 1968); "The Visits of My Aunt" and "Barney's Sister" from *Deaths at Paragon, Indiana* (Indiana University Press, 1955). Copyright © John Woods.

Samuel Yellen: "Today's Horoscope" and "Tomorrow's Horoscope" from *In the House and Out and Other Poems* (Indiana University Press, 1952). Copyright © Samuel Yellen.

Index of Poets and Titles